Memories of
Underdevelopment

Para Travis
con un Saludo
cordial

Stanford
Mayo 94

Rutgers Films in Print

Charles Affron, Mirella Jona Affron, and Robert Lyons, editors

My Darling Clementine, John Ford, director
edited by Robert Lyons

The Last Metro, François Truffaut, director
edited by Mirella Jona Affron and E. Rubinstein

Touch of Evil, Orson Welles, director
edited by Terry Comito

The Marriage of Maria Braun, Rainer Werner Fassbinder, director
edited by Joyce Rheuban

Letter from an Unknown Woman, Max Ophuls, director
edited by Virginia Wright Wexman with Karen Hollinger

Rashomon, Akira Kurosawa, director
edited by Donald Richie

8½, Federico Fellini, director
edited by Charles Affron

La Strada, Federico Fellini, director
edited by Peter Bondanella and Manuela Gieri

Breathless, Jean-Luc Godard, director
edited by Dudley Andrew

Bringing Up Baby, Howard Hawks, director
edited by Gerald Mast

Chimes at Midnight, Orson Welles, director
edited by Bridget Gellert Lyons

L'avventura, Michelangelo Antonioni, director
edited by Seymour Chatman and Guido Fink

Meet John Doe, Frank Capra, director
edited by Charles Wolfe

Invasion of the Body Snatchers, Don Siegel, director
edited by Al LaValley

Memories of Underdevelopment, Tomás Gutiérrez Alea, director
introduction by Michael Chanan

Memories of Underdevelopment

Tomás Gutiérrez Alea, Director

and

Inconsolable Memories

Edmundo Desnoes, Author

Introduction by
Michael Chanan

CASTRO

Rutgers University Press

New Brunswick and London

Memories of Underdevelopment is volume 15 in the Rutgers Films in Print series
Copyright © 1990 by Rutgers, The State University
All Rights Reserved
Manufactured in the United States of America

Library of Congress Cataloging-in-Publication Data

Memorias del subdesarrollo. English.
    Memories of underdevelopment / Tomás Gutiérrez Alea, director. Inconsolable memories / Edmundo Desnoes, author; introduction [to both] by Michael Chanan.
        p. cm. — (Rutgers films in print; v. 15)
    Contains the complete continuity script of Memories of underdevelopment (original title: Memorias del subdesarrollo); the complete novel, Inconsolable memories, on which the film was based (original title: Memorias del subdesarrollo); and critical apparatus.
    "Alea filmography. 1955–1984"; p.
    Includes bibliographical references (p.   ).
    ISBN 0-8135-1536-X (cloth)
    ISBN 0-8135-1537-8 (pbk.)
    1. Cuba—Politics and government—1959–
—Drama. 2. Cuba—Economic conditions—
1959– —Drama 3. Memorias del subdesarrollo (Motion picture) 4. Desnoes, Edmundo, 1930– —Film and video adaptations.
5. Cuba in motion pictures. I. Gutiérrez Alea, Tomás, 1928–   .
II. Desnos, Edmundo, 1930– Memorias del subdesarrollo. English. 1990.
III. Title. IV. Title: Inconsolable memories. V. Series.
PN1997.M434513   1990
791.43'72—dc20   89-70225
                                                                                    CIP
British Cataloging-in-Publication information available

Continuity script and all illustrations published by permission of Tomás Gutiérrez Alea and Edmundo Desnoes.
    Inconsolable Memories copyright © 1967 by Edmundo Desnoes.
    Henry Raymont, "Federal Agents Seize Cuban Festival Films Here," *New York Times,* 26 March 1972, copyright © 1972 by The New York Times Company, reprinted by permission. David Binder, "U.S. Refuses Visa to Cuban Director to Get Film Award," *New York Times,* 17 January 1974, copyright © 1974 by The New York Times Company, reprinted by permission. Editorial, "Celluloid Menace," *New York Times,* 19 January 1974, copyright © 1974 by The New York Times Company, reprinted by permission.
    Julianne Burton, "Individual Fulfillment and Collective Achievement: An Interview with Tomás Gutiérrez Alea," *Cinéaste* 8, no. 1 (Summer 1977): 8–15, 59, reprinted by permission of *Cinéaste* and Julianne Burton.
    Review by Vincent Canby, *New York Times,* 2 April 1972, copyright © 1972 by The New York Times Company, reprinted by permission. Review by Stanley Kauffmann in *The New Republic* was reprinted in his collection *Living Images* (New York: Harper & Row, 1975), used by permission. "Thought's Empire" by Penelope Gilliatt, from *The New Yorker,* 26 May 1973, copyright © 1973 by The New Yorker Magazine, Inc., reprinted by permission. Review by Don Allen, *Sight and Sound* 38, no. 4 (Autumn 1969): 212–213, reprinted by permission. Review by Mireille Amiel, *Cinema 74* [Paris] (October 1974), reprinted by permission of *Cinema* and Editions de Témoignage Chrétien. Review by Piero Spila, *Cinema & Film* [Rome], no. 5–6 (Summer 1968): 52, reprinted by permission.
    Fernando Pérez, "A Dialectical and Partisan Film," *Pensamiento Crítico* [Havana] 42 (1970), reprinted by permission. Julianne Burton, *"Memories of Underdevelopment* in the Land of Overdevelopment," *Cinéaste* 8, no. 1 (Summer 1977): 16–20, reprinted by permission of *Cinéaste* and Julianne Burton. Enrique Fernández, "'Witnesses Always Everywhere': The Rhetorical Strategies of *Memories of Underdevelopment,"* *Wide Angle* 4, no. 2 (Winter 1980): 52–55, reprinted by permission.

Acknowledgments

This volume could not have been attempted, much less completed, without the cooperation and assistance of the Center for Cuban Studies in New York City. We are especially grateful to Sandra Levinson, the executive director of the Center, for her commitment to the project and for her help in many aspects of this volume's preparation. We are also indebted to Alexander Coleman of New York University, who offered guidance in the translation of the continuity script.

The General Editors

Contents

Introduction

Lessons of Experience / 3
Michael Chanan

Tomás Gutiérrez Alea: A
Biographical Sketch / 15

Chronology / 23

Memories of Underdevelopment

Credits and Cast / 28

The Continuity Script / 31

Notes on the Continuity
Script / 99

Contexts

Source

Inconsolable Memories / 115
Edmundo Desnoes

Aftermath: Politics and Cinema

Federal Agents Seize Cuban
Festival Films Here / 179
Henry Raymont

Film Critics' Letter / 180

U.S. Refuses Visa to Cuban
Director to Get Film Award / 181
David Binder

Editorial: Celluloid Menace / 182

Telegram from Tomás Gutiérrez
Alea / 183

Personal Recollections of T. G. Alea

Individual Fulfillment and
Collective Achievement: An
Interview with Tomás Gutiérrez
Alea / 187
Julianne Burton

Memories of *Memories* / 199
T. G. Alea

Reviews and Commentaries

Reviews

New York Times / 217
Vincent Canby

The New Republic / 219
Stanley Kauffmann

The New Yorker / 220
Penelope Gilliatt

Sight and Sound [London] / 222
Don Allen

Cinema 74 [Paris] / 224
Mireille Amiel

Cinema & Film [Rome] / 226
Piero Spila

Commentaries

A Dialectical and Partisan
Film / 227
Fernando Pérez

Memories of Underdevelopment
in the Land of
Overdevelopment / 232
Julianne Burton

"Witnesses Always Everywhere":
The Rhetorical Strategies of
*Memories of
Underdevelopment* / 248
Enrique Fernández

Filmography and Bibliography

Alea Filmography, 1950–
1988 / 255

Selected Bibliography / 257

Memories of
Underdevelopment

Introduction

Lessons of Experience

Michael Chanan

The first English edition of the novella by Edmundo Desnoes was called *Inconsolable Memories;* Tomás Gutiérrez Alea called the film *Memories of Underdevelopment*. First of all, therefore, we could do worse than ask what the change in the name signifies. The film title is not only far more evocative but also (to follow the terminology of the semiotician Roman Jakobson) metaphoric rather then metonymic: a displacement of meaning, not just an association of meaning. It remains reflexive, but changes the emphasis from the personal to the public, and shifts the sense from the subjective to the historical. Underdevelopment is an economic concept, referring to the relationship between a country with the status of an economic colony and the metropolis that colonizes it. The title therefore claims that now colonization is over. Underdevelopment has been replaced by the Revolution. But it turns out that the new title is somewhat ironic, for what the film shows is the way that people continue to carry the mentality of underdevelopment within them, how it weighs them down, and how it becomes a problem. This sense of irony runs throughout the film; it is partly responsible, even today, for a feeling among certain viewers that the film's intentions are divided. But then it is also ironic that these doubts arise not in the ex-colony where *Memories* was made but in the countries that had been its exploiters. Indeed, in this respect, this one film may exemplify the misunderstanding liable to affect almost any third world cultural product that manages to reach the metropolis.

The protagonist, Sergio, belongs to the rentier class. Before the Revolution he owned a furniture store given him by his father. Now he lives off the payments made to him by the state in compensation for the confiscation of his property as a landlord, for he also owned the apartment block in the Vedado district of Havana where he now lives. He lives alone, since his wife left with his parents for the United States during 1961 in the mass exodus of the bourgeoisie. This is the point in Sergio's tale of woe at which the film opens.

Sergio is suspended between the old and the new. He never wanted to be a businessman, but a writer. The novella personifies his situation. It is written in the first person by a character with the ambition to be a writer and an ambiguous relationship to the author of the pages we are reading, Edmundo Desnoes, who himself becomes a character in the novella. This is a conceit repeated in the film in the shared first name of the character and the actor who plays him, Sergio Corrieri, as well as the appearance in the film of Edmundo Desnoes, playing himself. In part this is a familiar kind of play upon the identity of the author that is a typical trait of modernist narrative, and not only in Europe and North America. In the work of Jorge Luis Borges, for example, such conceits are used to set up metaphysical conundrums about the human condition. In the novella by Desnoes, however, the purpose is to capture, in the labyrinths of language, certain elusive aspects of the identity crisis of the artist within the revolutionary process, the problem that Latin American intellectuals have called the *desgarramiento*, the ideological rupture with the past. In the words of the Salvadorean poet Roque Dalton, "In every rupture we intellectuals are accustomed to see first an ideological problem and then, always as a result of this, moral and sentimental problems. These resulting problems can only be resolved through the solution of the fundamental ideological conflict." In this sense, says the poet, revolution is a constant challenge: its advance makes it insufficient simply to accept its overall principles and latest positions in a general way, "but requires permanent incorporation of its totalizing practice."[1] The process brings on a crisis of individualism, which the whole weight of bourgeois ideology pushes the artist to defend—after all, the bourgeois myth of the artist was created around the ideology of individualism. But if the film is devoted to a questioning of this myth and this ideology, it does so from the only point of view from which such questioning can be carried out with empathy—that of the artist whose condition is under challenge.

How can you translate the first person of the narrator to the screen as more than a conceit? The convention of a voice on the soundtrack is logically not the same; in film, there is no true equivalent of the first-person narrator in literature, for the camera as an analogue of the writer's pen is impersonal: it cannot say "I"; it always says "there is," "here is."

Alea's answer is not to alleviate but to intensify this difference by incorporating documentary footage in which this evidential quality is foregrounded. Moreover, he does this in several ways, not only by including archive footage, for example, but also by filming certain scenes in actuality settings. The latter are of several types. First, they include street scenes where events take place of their own volition. Second, Sergio and the camera become participant observers in public events, notably the round table he attends on Literature and Underdevelopment. Third, there is the use of Ernest Hemingway's house, which became a museum dedicated to the writer after his death, as a setting for fictive action. In

1. *El intelectual y la sociedad* (Mexico City: Siglo Veintiuno, 1969), p. 92.

these last two examples, another veridical dimension insinuates itself, in the presence of real people not as extras, but as named participants appearing as themselves. They include, in the round table discussion, the author of the novella, Edmundo Desnoes, and, among the audience, the author of the Foreword to the English edition, Jack Gelber. On top of this, Alea does not disdain to use the convention of the narrator's voice-over. He deliberately confuses things, however, by using it not only subjectively, but also for commentary over documentary footage of the prisoners who were captured at the invasion of Playa Girón (Bay of Pigs). This seeming hodgepodge is held together by intertitles functioning like chapter headings ("Pablo," "Noemí," "A Tropical Adventure," etc.) for the episodes that comprise the loose-knit narrative.

In the middle, almost incidentally, there is a sequence with another, but hidden, conceit; the scene in a screening room at the Cuban Film Institute (ICAIC) where the participants include, this time unnamed, the director of the film we are watching, Tomás Gutiérrez Alea. If this is partly an in-joke, the way the sequence is designed makes it immaterial whether the viewer recognizes Alea or not. We have been watching a series of semi-pornographic film clips, which repeat themselves in bizarre fashion. The images stop and the lights go up. "Where did you get the clips?" asks Sergio. His friend the director (Alea) replies, "They showed up one day. These are the cuts the commission [Batista's censors] made. They said they were offensive to morals, good breeding, all that." "What are you going to do with them?" Sergio asks. The director explains that he's going to put them into a film. "It'll be a 'collage' that'll have a little bit of everything." Obviously it is the film we're watching. "Will they approve it?" asks Sergio. This scene is much more than a clever way of suggesting (as certain metropolitan critics thought) that the new regime was not as mindless as its predecessors. Its ironic self-reference places it at the very heart of the film, the metaphorical equivalent of the reflexivity of the novella.

The film thus becomes an exemplary exercise in the fragmentation and displacement of imagery and representation, not only in the modernist manner, that of the cubist prism, but apparently also in the dissociative form that is now called postmodernism, a mirror of multiple reflection. If this technique is to be read as a kind of pathetic fallacy for Sergio's problems, it is far from being the only Cuban film of its day which employs such a language. The first problem confronting foreign critics at the time was simply that they had seen hardly any of the others.

The late sixties in Cuba produced a series of exuberant experimental films that launched a broadside attack on the stable and established filmic perception of mainstream cinema through exploration of the techniques of decentered narrative, directed against not only Hollywood commercialism but also the individualistic artistic license of European cinema. Alea's *Memories* is one of them. Others include Julio García Espinosa's *Las aventuras de Juan Quin Quin, La primera carga al machete* by the late Manuel Octavio Gómez, and *Lucia* by

Humberto Solás. Also, on another front, and from as early as 1964, the influence
of the documentarist and newsreel producer Santiago Alvarez was felt throughout ICAIC. Typically, the means adopted in these films included a radical hand-
held camera style and pyrotechnic editing techniques, with a high degree of
tolerance for visual discontinuity and disorder that is as far removed from Hollywood as from Moscow and the orthodoxy of socialist realism.

Alvarez played a key but curious role in the development of this cinema. In his
brilliant but highly personal experimentation, he justified the vociferous arguments in favor of the greatest aesthetic freedom, which Alfredo Guevara, the
president of ICAIC, clearly and consistently put forward at every opportunity.
Neither of them could possibly be suspected of anything but the purest motives
and the greatest revolutionary zeal. Indeed it is not an accident that when the
visual metaphors of Alvarez's style are turned back into words, the results are
frequently perfectly orthodox political slogans, which correspond to the peculiarly Cuban mix of Marxist-Leninism and José Martí which is called Fidelismo.
But if what Alvarez achieved aesthetically lent legitimacy and provided encour-
agement for more and more experimentalism, his work also demonstrated un-
suspected links with the roots of Soviet cinema in the twenties, in particular the
work of Dziga Vertov—although Alvarez knew nothing of Vertov's work until
later. This is one of those coincidences of history which is not such a coincidence.

It was not only the exuberance of the young revolution that promoted this
experimentalism, but also the example of Cuban modernism, a movement in-
volving writers, painters, and composers that dates back to the 1920s and '30s.
Cuban modernism combined the tendencies of European modernism with the
influence of Afrocubanism. Both trends have an unsettling effect on previous
aesthetic categories. According to Gestalt psychology, art is traditionally concerned with organizing perception into stable forms according to the laws of
unity, segregation, and balance, which reveal harmony and order and stigmatize
discord and disorder. Modernism, however, is more interested in the complex
relationships that refuse to be caught in such a stable and neat grid, and prefers
incompatible outlines and surfaces which permeate each other, and try to crowd
themselves into the same time and space. In cinema, this kind of avant-gardism
found itself restricted not only by the aesthetic conservativism of big money but
also by the doctrines of socialist realism in the Soviet Union. The fear which in
both cases motivated this refusal was dread of the inevitable disruption of the
naturalistic illusion and the "realism effect," and the destruction of the exemplary nature of the narrative. Cuban cultural sensibility remains happily free of
this dread (except, as the literary critic Ambrosio Fornet once put it, for a small
number of "night-prowling tom-cats who still confused jazz with imperialism
and abstract art with the devil"[2]). This is largely because of the syncretistic

2. Ibid., p. 48.

qualities of the Afro-Caribbean heritage, already cultivated by Cuban modernism, which lead entirely in the opposite direction.

Syncretism is not a term familiar in Anglo-Saxon intellectual culture. The concept is taken from anthropology, where it refers to the fusion of elements of the symbolic languages of clashing cultures. In religion, for example, Catholic and pagan symbols are conjoined. In Cuba, where the indigenous population was replaced with slaves from Africa, the Christian Lazarus acquires an alter ego in Babalú, the African god with whom he shares a number of characteristics, most importantly his healing powers. The result is that Lazarus and Babalú are no longer separate figures, the one identified with the other merely for convenience and an easy life—they are one and the same, Christian and African at the same time, or rather, Afrocuban. The same process has produced Afrocuban music, principally out of the fusion of African rhythm and European melody. These European and African dimensions find stylistic analogies in cinema, the one on the level of imagery, the other in the syncopation of its rhythms. It was an organic result of the revolutionary process that filmmakers began to explore these qualities at the same time that they came to celebrate their own self-discovery as filmmakers. The result is a discourse which sometimes seems to foreign eyes to be involved in a secret dialogue with itself, or else to call up what seem to be haphazard associations that are difficult to connect, or even to be curiously nonchalant about narrative integrity, *découpage,* and other aspects of film language itself. All of these characteristics are present at one moment or another in *Memories of Underdevelopment,* although at the same time it possesses a lucidity that prevents its ever becoming hermetic and inaccessible.

While *Memories of Underdevelopment* is not a direct expression of Afrocuban themes or imagery, the world according to Santiago Alvarez, a place of unorthodox orthodoxy, is implicit in the world inhabited by its protagonist Sergio. With his inconsolable memories of underdevelopment, it is a world he understands well enough, but cannot commit himself to. This presented inescapable problems to the metropolitan critics, especially because the film's syncretic idiom, halfway between modernism and postmodernism, threw their own image straight back at them. They perceived in Sergio a kind of intellectual antihero like the young Mastroianni in a film by Antonioni or Fellini. However, as Michael Myerson observed in the introduction to a previously published version of the film script, there is no European nihilism here: "revolutionary Cuba is not capitalist Italy, and the milieu in which Corrieri's Sergio operates (or rather, cannot operate) is far different."[3]

Indeed, such are the differences that postmodern tendencies in a director like

3. Michael Myerson, ed., *Memories of Underdevelopment: The Revolutionary Films of Cuba* (New York: Grossman, 1973), p. 118.

Alea filming the round table sequence of *Memories*

Alea hardly lead to the apolitical and ethically indifferent stance which, to follow Frederic Jameson, is liable to develop in the metropolis.[4] *Memories* is rather the result of an artistic and intellectual community discovering itself in the act of breaking down the vocabulary of its own existence, in other words, of swapping the pride which the Cuban intelligentsia once took in its worldly sophistication for the challenge of the *desgarramiento*. If this does not appear altogether dissimilar to the nihilistic postmodernism of the metropolis, all that this shows is that aesthetics are overdetermined, and the cultural implosion induced by the new information order, which is one of the determinants of postmodernism, is indeed universal. However, it is one of the symptoms of the rift between the metropolis and the world of underdevelopment that the flow of information is not free, but unequal, for the channels of communication are owned and controlled by the North and its local agents. And as far as the Cubans are concerned, as Ambrosio Fornet put it in a recent filmed interview, "We do not agree that the medium is the message. The message can be different depending on who the sender is."[5]

To grasp the difference one must understand how completely opposed were the lived experiences of Cuba and, let us say, New York, over the course of the sixties. It is not such an arbitrary comparison. Fidel Castro himself was one of the great celebrities of the day in New York, which he visited more than once. (Che Guevara was also there, but more mysterious because less flamboyant.) New York was where Castro and Khrushchev met for the first time in 1960, in the full glare of the media, when they stole the limelight at the opening of the Twenty-Fifth Session of the United Nations. There was also a famous incident when Castro, insulted at being asked to pay his hotel bill in advance in cash, took his whole retinue off to a hotel in Harlem, where the Soviet leader came to visit him. The conscience of New York liberalism was alive in the Fair Play for Cuba movement, which met with Fidel at a dinner on the eve of his address to the United Nations in 1960, an event most beautifully recorded in the photographs of Henri Cartier-Bresson.

But the way that North America, guided by New York's eyes, saw Castro and hence Cuba was its own. One of the traits of postmodernism is to see reality as the imitation of the image instead of vice versa. A recent biographer of Castro, Peter Bourne, wrote: "It was as though Americans saw Fidel as a kind of romantic Hollywood hero," and they therefore became disillusioned with him when things began to happen that Hollywood heroes aren't supposed to get involved in, like the trials of political opponents.[6] For the Cubans themselves, however, according to Jean-Paul Sartre, the most perceptive foreign observer of the

4. See Fredric Jameson, "The Cultural Logic of Capital," *New Left Review,* no. 146 (July–August, 1984), pp. 80–85.
5. Ambrosio Fornet, interviewed in "Havana Report," directed by Holly Aylett and the present writer, transmitted Channel Four Television, 30 June 1986.
6. Peter Bourne, *Castro* (London: Macmillan, 1986), p. 168.

Revolutionary process in its early years, Castro was a real-life hero, and what he did disillusioned only those with reason to doubt the Revolution itself.[7]

This too may seem like a stereotype, except that behind Sartre's insight is his recognition of a process that powerfully evokes the experience of the French Revolution. Castro, for example, did not 'invent' a fancy theory of 'direct democracy' to justify not holding elections, as another recent biographer, Tad Szulc (and many like him), seems to believe, for the theory of direct democracy originated with Jean-Jacques Rousseau and became part of the ideological armory of the Jacobins.[8] This kind of ignorance on the part of the pundits of the mass media is also symptomatic of the postmodern condition. But there are many parallels to be found, not least between the ideas of Rousseau and Che Guevara's concept of *el hombre nuevo*, the 'new man.' Recognition of these parallels to French revolutionary history would help to explain many of the attitudes of the Cuban Revolution portrayed in the film. For example, the attitude toward the émigrés was in both cases basically the same—they were seen as traitors to their country. Here Sergio, even if his reasons are ambiguous, derides them for their departure and remains the patriot.[9]

Let us therefore make a leap of imagination and follow Sartre. What emerges is that by choosing for its protagonist the rentier and would-be writer Sergio, the film becomes, for anyone like him, a trap. This, at least, is how it appears to be designed. Time and again there are symbols of Sergio's point of view—the telescope on his balcony, the mirror in the bedroom—which distance the viewer from both the vivid and pulsating exterior world of the Revolution and from Sergio himself. It is as if, with ironic intent, the film is testing out the question, how far it is possible to doubt and remain unconvinced, and yet not become a counter-revolutionary (for Sergio is not that, he perceives too clearly what motivates those who are). But this the metropolitan critics were in no position to register, for as they watched, it was they who looked through the telescope and in the mirror.

If the imagery of the point of view and interrupted vision is entirely fitting, the effect of distanciation it produces is intensified by the tape recorder on which Sergio plays back to himself the argument with his wife that he recorded on the eve of her departure. The way the film deals with Sergio's relations with women is described in my own account of the film, where I also consider another central theme—the questions that are raised about the status of the artist and intellectual

7. See Jean-Paul Sartre, *On Cuba* (New York: Ballantine Books, 1961).

8. Tad Szulc, *Fidel: A Critical Portrait* (New York: Morrow, 1986).

9. Readers who wish to pursue these themes should consult J. S. Talmon's classic work of liberal scholarship, *The Origins of Totalitarian Democracy* (New York: Praeger, 1960). One need not be committed to his terminology—or to a cyclical interpretation of history—to see that there are indeed characteristic processes which revolutions continue to experience and which may well continue to worry them for years; the Cuban émigré problem is one of them.

in the two sequences of the round table and the visit to Hemingway's house.[10] The latter is like an interpolated essay on the social and historical relations of the writer and is in many ways the philosophical pivot of the entire film: the confluence of Sergio's most objective reflections on the subject and the film's own analysis, which at one and the same time pays not uncritical homage to the tradition of the writer as the embodiment of social conscience and reflects upon the transformation which this conscience must now undergo. It does not appear that the metropolitan critics grasped the irony of this sequence, the unspoken question mark of Hemingway's suicide, which becomes, in the context, symbolic of the inevitable death, the spiritual suicide, of the old kind of artist in the face of the new society. The same provocative irony occurs again at the unscripted round table, when it is Jack Gelber, the North American in the audience, who asks (in English), "Why is it that if the Cuban Revolution is a total revolution, they have to resort to an archaic form of discussion such as a round table, and treat us to an impotent discussion of issues that I'm well informed about and most of the public here is well informed about, when there could be another more revolutionary way to reach a whole audience like this?"

The closing section of the film shows Sergio's ultimate self-paralysis as the city around him engages in defense preparations during the unfolding of the so-called Cuban Missile Crisis. If the confrontation between the United States and the Soviet Union in October 1962 over the placing of missiles in Cuba was experienced throughout the world as a moment of reckoning, the place it occupies within collective and individual memory in Cuba itself is saturated with peculiar significance. It was another of the experiences of the Revolution's early years that played a definitive role in forging social cohesion and bonding the island's unity, like the experiences of the Literacy Campaign and the invasion of the Bay of Pigs. To talk to Cubans who lived through it, it was a moment in which individual fears were submerged in the collective, and national consciousness took on a peculiarly tangible form. They knew they were targets for a kind of attack that no one, if it came, would be able to escape, and although for the first time in history they had become masters of their own country, they were powerless to prevent it. Sergio, in his final voice-over, sandwiched between speeches on television by Kennedy and by Castro, expresses it in his own alienated fashion: "And if it started right now? It's no use protesting. I'll die like the rest. This island is a trap. We're very small, and too poor. It's an expensive dignity."

I believe it must have been this last sequence as much as anything that was responsible for the initial misreading of the film in the metropolis, where a number of critics were so surprised to find a Cuban picture handling the theme of

10. Michael Chanan, *The Cuban Image: Cinema and Cultural Politics in Cuba* (London and Indianapolis: BFI/Indiana University Press, 1985), pp. 236ff.

bourgeois alienation that they failed to perceive the critique which it levelled not merely at Sergio but by implication at anyone identifying too closely with him. These critics, insensible to the nature of Sergio's narcissism but narcissistically sharing his all-consuming sense of resentment, instead felt flattered at seeing such an accurate portrayal of their own reflection. And the epilogue is constructed with such understatement that it allowed them to identify completely with Sergio's own sentiments in the face of nuclear annihilation, failing to perceive the irony in his alienated response. They would have said, "And if it started right now? It would be no use protesting. I'll die like the rest. This island of Manhattan (or Britain) is a trap. We've got all the riches in the world and it won't do us any good. What price our dignity now?" They would have said this and not seen the difference.

And so they imagined that the film was meant to be critical of the political process that led up to the crisis. They assumed that the director of such a film could only be a kindred spirit, not a fellow traveler of the Fidelistas. They saw the film's critique of underdevelopment as a criticism of the stupidity of unselfcritical people, as if individuals were responsible and not history. Some critics, to be sure, escape these structures: Vincent Canby, for instance, who cited Antonioni in order to contrast the Italian and the Cuban.[11] But if there was a Vincent Canby there was also an Andrew Sarris, who, as president of the National Society of Film Critics, tried to turn Alea into a dissident of the type our imploded media love to find in the Soviet Union (but who now, in times of *glasnost,* has been rehabilitated).

That was when the U.S. State Department refused to grant Alea a visa to attend the Society's awards ceremony where he was due to receive a special prize for *Memories.* This was not the first time a Cuban filmmaker had been refused a U.S. visa (nor would it be the last). In 1972, entry had been denied to a delegation from ICAIC intending to visit the U.S.A. for a Cuban film festival planned by an independent distributor, ADF (American Documentary Films) in New York and other cities. On that occasion anti-Castro émigré terrorist groups threatened violence if the festival were allowed to go ahead, and there were indeed attacks on the Olympia Theatre in New York where the films were to be shown. But the biggest attack on the festival was by the U.S. government, which seized one of the films from the theater and raided the ADF office, thus bringing the festival to a halt. The grounds the government used for these actions were that the films had been illegally imported. But as Michael Myerson explained, "A meeting between a Festival spokesman and Stanley Sommerfield, Acting Head of Foreign Assets Control in Washington, was straight out of *Catch-22.* Sure, said Sommerfield, the government exempts the news media and universities from the Cuban embargo statutes because news gathering and a body of scholarship are in

---

11. See citation of Vincent Canby in *Granma,* "Elogian criticos norteamericanos filme cubano," 13 June 1973.

the national interest. But no, he continued, in answer to a question, it would not be in the national interest if the population as a whole had direct access to the materials instead of having selected elites act as middlemen in deciphering them."[12] This, of course, is exactly what the U.S. government accuses communist countries like Cuba of doing, while at the same time, it prohibits U.S. nationals from selling their own information and cultural products to Cuba. And this is what is called the free flow of information.

Protests were made, of course, by many distinguished people. At the very same moment the members of Film Institute delegation were refused their visas, President Richard Nixon was visiting China. Senator William Fulbright asked why the government should consider four Cuban filmmakers a security threat and not Mao Tse-tung and the People's Republic. Speaking in Congress when Alea was banned, he said, "I found it passing strange that the Treasury Department would be so terrified of the impact of Cuban films on the American people, while the State Department is encouraging such exchanges with the Soviet Union."[13] *Washington Post* columnist Nicholas von Hoffman, criticizing the aforementioned Treasury official, pointed to a more insidious anomaly: "Go every morning to your hutch in the Treasury Department, Mr. Sommerfield," he wrote, "drink your coffee, read your paper, and daily bring a full measure of aggravation into the lives of people who don't yet know your name. Keep out the movies. . . . The rest of the Treasury Department will let the heroin flow in."[14]

ADF was forced by the attacks into bankruptcy, though *Memories of Underdevelopment* was finally able to open commercially in New York in May 1973, to be selected early in 1974 by the *New York Times* as one of the year's ten best movies. The same newspaper, when Alea's visa was refused, again criticized the ridiculous behavior of the officials and declared it irrational to treat the offer of a prize to a film as a subversive act.[15] The Cubans took the whole affair stoically. It did not escape their attention that these responses did not all square up. As Alea made plain in the declaration he sent to be read at the awards ceremony, the Cubans were not surprised by any of it, for the film itself, the subject of the whole to-do, portrayed the aggressions directed by the U.S. government against the Cubans from the beginning, including the economic blockade, the disinformation and the gamut of actions intended to impede contacts between the two peoples, which kept the North Americans in a state of ignorance about Cuba and what was really going on there.[16]

It would seem to have been this kind of ignorance that led Andrew Sarris to

12. Meyerson, *Memories*, p. 34.
13. Ibid., p. 36.
14. Ibid., pp. 34–35.
15. See Pastor Vega, "Medida torpe y arbitraria de los imperialistas yanquis," *Granma*, 22 January 1974. Documents from the controversy are reprinted in the "Aftermath: Cinema and Politics" section of this volume.
16. Ibid.

misinterpret Alea's position. And what does Alea think of him? "His lack of information," he told the North American film critic Julianne Burton, "was such that one suspects a kind of tendentious ignorance if that's possible. It's hard to know in such cases where ignorance leaves off and stupidity or malice begins."[17]

In Cuba itself, because of the sophistication of its style, the film proved a difficult one for many of the audience. But Alea recalled later that it produced the very positive effect of sending people back to the cinema to see it a second and even a third time.[18] Here was evidence, then, that ICAIC's policy of treating the audience like grown-ups was beginning to bite. In the years since then it has not only come to occupy the position of a greatly loved black-and-white classic, but for all the reasons I have here reviewed, the film retains its vigilance.

17. Julianne Burton, Interview with Alea, *Cinéaste* 8, no. 1 (1977), p. 59. Reprinted in this volume.
18. Conversation with Alea, Havana, January 1980.

Tomás Gutiérrez Alea

A Biographical Sketch

Michael Chanan

In 1945, a U.S. Department of Commerce publication reported on the development of a new market in Cuba: "potentialities for the sale to amateur users in Cuba of United States motion-picture cameras and projectors are fair. It is estimated that upon termination of war about $3,500 worth of 16mm sound projectors . . . can be sold. Sales of 8mm motion picture cameras are expected to be somewhat higher."[1] A year later, Tomás Gutiérrez Alea was a seventeen-year-old student in Havana when one of these cameras fell into his hands, and he made his first forays into film.

Amateur cinematography was an accepted pastime in the kind of well-off, good Catholic family into which Alea was born, in Havana, in 1928. The Photographic Club of Cuba held its first amateur film competition in 1943, full of titles like *La vida de los peces* (*The Life of the Fishes*) and *Desfile gimnastico femenino* (*Feminine Gymnastics Display*). But Alea and the other young aficionados he soon teamed up with were made of sterner stuff than this. His first attempt to do "something serious," he says in an autobiographical reminiscence, was "a kind of comedy" based on a short story by Franz Kafka about the absurdities of daily life, called *Una confusion cotidiana* (*An Everyday Confusion*). "The film was about ten minutes long, I worked with actors, and the experience was exciting and fun. From then on, I knew what I wanted to be."[2]

Outwardly destined by social origins and intellectual ability for some kind of professional career, inwardly harboring a nascent desire to become a filmmaker, Alea went to university to study law. The University of Havana had been an arena of political ferment since the 1920s, and here, on the same campus as that other law student, Fidel Castro, he not only encountered Marxist literature but also activism. Bringing youthful artistic ambition and social conscience together,

---

1. U.S. Department of Commerce, *Industrial Reference Service,* August 1945, vol. 3, part 3, no. 7.
2. T. G. Alea, "I Wasn't Always a Film-maker," *Cinéaste* 14, no. 1 (1985), p. 36.

he worked on two films produced by the Cuban Communist Party (known at the time as the Partido Socialista Popular), though without becoming a party member. One was about a May Day demonstration which had been banned but still went ahead, the other about the world peace movement.

By long-standing cultural tradition, the young Latin American with artistic ambitions in search of worldly wisdom would generally gravitate to Madrid or Paris. For Alea, however, and a few others like him, the magnet was Rome and its pioneering film school, the Centro Sperimentale di Cinematografia. Here, to the fount of Italian neo-realism—the first movement of artistic renovation in postwar cinema—Alea came in 1951. Future film directors of the same generation sharing the same experience included his compatriot Julio García Espinosa, and from Argentina, Fernando Birri; there was also a young journalist from Colombia, Gabriel García Marquez.

The country to which Alea returned two years later—after a trip to Eastern Europe for a World Youth Festival—had fallen for the second time under the military dictatorship of Fulgencio Batista. Alea enrolled in a radical cultural club in Havana dedicated to cultural resistence, called Nuestro Tiempo (Our Times). Then, along with García Espinosa, he joined a group which formed itself in order to make a film that would protest the conditions of neocolonial underdevelopment. _El Megano_, a medium-length neo-realist story with nonprofessional actors, was filmed semi-clandestinely among the charcoal burners in the Zapata swamplands south of Havana; it took a year to make, shooting weekends on location and then borrowing facilities in Havana for postproduction. In 1956, the film became something of a _cause célèbre_ when it was seized by Batista's police after its first screening at the University of Havana, and the filmmakers were detained for interrogation.

Honest, gainful employment as a filmmaker in Batista's Cuba was hard to find. Feature film production was minimal, and mostly dominated by Mexican coproductions using Mexican directors and stars. There were several local newsreel companies, whose chief function, according to another U.S. trade survey, was "dissemination of propaganda and publicity for individuals, clubs . . . and the Government."[3] Alea has described them as an ideological protection racket, and a dirty business: "If a newsreel cameraman were to happen upon a car crash, he'd be sure to take shots of the smashed up car with its brand name in close-up, and blackmail the company to pay for them not to be shown."[4] It was not until 1956 that Alea finally found work (again along with García Espinosa) when the Mexican producer Manuel Barbachano Ponce set up a small outfit in Havana to produce a weekly ten-minute film magazine called _Cinerevista (Film-review)_, financed by advertising. Barbachano, says Alea, was young, cultured, and good

3. _World Trade in Commodities,_ November 1947, "Motion Pictures and Equipment," p. 4.
4. Quoted in Michael Chanan, _The Cuban Image: Cinema and Cultural Politics in Cuba_ (London and Indianapolis: BFI/Indiana University Press, 1985), p. 72.

at business. He had just won a prize at Cannes for a film called *Raices* (*Roots*), a neo-realist portrait of Mexican Indian life, which Alea says "had been made with very little money but a lot of feeling";[5] two years later he was to produce Luis Buñuel's *Nazarin*. *Cinerevista* consisted of short documentaries and humorous sketches, interspersed with the advertisements that paid for it. The sketches gave Alea a certain taste for comedy.

When Batista fled on the night of 31 December 1958 and Fidel Castro took power, artists and intellectuals of almost every hue were among his supporters. Filmmakers eager to make themselves useful were drafted by the Cultural Directorate of the Rebel Army, and Alea found himself directing a documentary, *Esta tierra nuestra* (*This Land of Ours*), with a script by García Espinosa about the proposed Agrarian Reform. Meanwhile, Alfredo Guevara, one of the group that made *El Megano* and a friend of Castro's from university days, was able to persuade Castro of the benefits that would accrue from setting up a film production house dedicated to supporting the Revolution. Hence the Revolutionary Government's first decree concerning cultural matters was to establish the Cuban Institute of Cinematographic Art and Industry, ICAIC, which took over the productions started by the Rebel Army. Alfredo Guevara became its chief, Alea one of its founding members. From the start, as Cuban films began to trickle out to international film festivals, his work began to be noticed abroad.

From this point on, Alea's personal development would be inseparable from that of the Revolution and its Film Institute. "The triumph of the Revolution," he has written, "gave us an opportunity to develop everything for which we had been preparing ourselves for years and that we had been attempting for so long without much success. . . . Not only would we make movies, but, after a few years, we would be able to speak of a cinematography, of an entire movement."[6] Within this movement, Alea himself would become the leading film dramatist, experimenting continually, molding and fashioning its language, exploring its thematics, creating paradigms of the new Cuban movie.

A year later, ICAIC made its first two feature films, Alea directing one and García Espinosa the other. Alea's debut as a feature director was a film in the neo-realist mold called *Historias de la Revolución* (*Stories of the Revolution*). Episodic, in the manner of Roberto Rossellini, and photographed by the Italian neo-realist cinematographer Otello Martelli, the first part portrays the 1957 revolutionary attack on the presidential palace; the second is based on an anecdote about the guerrilla struggle recounted to Alea by Che Guevara; and the third weaves a tale around the Battle of Santa Clara at the climax of the revolutionary war. This film won awards in Italy, the Soviet Union, Australia, and Cambodia. It was followed two years later by his first comedy, *Las doce sillas* (*The Twelve Chairs*), after the comic novel by Ilf and Petrov, dating from the early years of

5. "I Wasn't Always a Film-maker," p. 37.
6. Ibid., p. 38.

the Russian Revolution, which was also brought to the screen in 1970 by Mel Brooks in the United States.

Alea had already conceived the idea of this adaptation before 1959, at a time when it was hardly possible to make it. Now it was supremely apt, and the Cuban Revolution itself provided the setting. It was in the course of making this film, he has said, that he learned how rapidly the changes wrought by the Revolution were taking place. Between scouting for locations and arriving for the shoot, the places were transformed and the filmmakers were forced to improvise. A large private mansion would become an art school; a lonely country beauty spot now had a large hotel built by the Tourist Institute and full of tourists; where Cadillacs were once sold, they now sold furniture for workers who had been given houses by the Urban Reform.

By now, both the Film Institute and Alea had firmly found their feet, and stood on the approach slopes to the artistic high ground. Alea took an active part in the debates about the proper kind of cultural politics within the Revolution in which ICAIC was constantly engaged. A contribution he made in 1963, which was published in the journal of the artists' and writers' union, was characteristically entitled "Notes on a Discussion of a Document about a Discussion (of Another Document)." This wry and ironic sense of humor is already present in *Las doce sillas,* and reappears in all his later comedies.

His third film, in 1964, became a farewell to neo-realism. *Cumbite*—the Haitian word for a village assembly—is based on the novel *Les Gouverneurs de la Rosée* by Jacques Romain; set in the 1940s, it recounts, with sensitivity and objectivity, the return of a migrant worker to his home village in Haiti after fifteen years in Cuba. With this film behind him and the social transformations of the Revolution advancing, neo-realism takes its place as one stylistic option among others in Alea's developing artistry.

He returned to comedy for *La muerte de un burocrata (Death of a Bureaucrat)* in 1966. This is a black farce about a country which has made a revolution and decided to become socialist, and therefore insists that its bureaucrats provide streamlined equal treatment for all, including the dead: a corpse gets itself unburied for the sake of bureaucracy, and then finds that bureaucracy won't let it be buried again. The country where these events take place is a hilarious mixture of revolutionary Cuba and the land of Hollywood comedy, and the film is also a pastiche of the great comedy classics, a tribute to Chaplin, Keaton, Laurel and Hardy, Harold Lloyd, Jerry Lewis, and Marilyn Monroe.

It was this film that confirmed Alea in Cuba as the leading feature director, and began to establish his reputation abroad, where an Italian critic called *La muerte* "daring, objective, corrosive." One reason for its success was its multilayered language. On one level, it was Kafkaesque, on another as if Alea were exorcising Hollywood comedy, while on a third it echoed Castro's criticisms of bureaucracy. Abroad, it was praised as a sympathetic portrayal of a political system engaging in self-criticism with a sense of humor, and in Cuba it became very popular. It still is, whenever it is revived.

And then followed *Memories of Underdevelopment,* in which the Cuban intelligentsia confronted itself, discovered itself in the act of breaking down the vocabulary of its own existence. *Memories of Underdevelopment* is a film both *sui generis,* a singular exploration of individual consciousness in a revolutionary context, and also one of a series of films by different Cuban directors, in a period of great creative effervescence which lasted several years, all of which break with the stable perceptual categories of genre cinema. They are films where, in particular, the interpenetration of fiction and documentary becomes a distinctive preoccupation. It is a critical development not only for Cuban cinema but also for film art throughout the continent, where similar experiments were taking place in several countries. At this time, Latin American filmmakers were beginning to establish better contacts with each other. The year before *Memories* came out, the second meeting of a new generation of filmmakers from across the continent was held at Viña del Mar in Chile. Recognition soon followed that Alea's experimental openness was a model in a wider movement than that of Cuba alone.

In his next film, Alea moved from the immediate world of contemporary reality to the distant historic past. *Una pelea cubana contra los demonios (A Cuban Struggle against the Demons)* is in fact the furthest back that Cuban cinema has yet gone in historical reconstruction: a story of the mid-seventeenth century about smugglers, hellfire sermons, and Afrocuban shamans, based on the work of the pioneering Cuban anthropologist Fernando Ortiz. Less successful both at home and internationally, this is actually Alea's most experimental film. Its narrative style not only refuses all conventions of genre (and again denies the viewer a positive hero with whom to identify), but the fluid camera style involves long takes with an almost constantly moving hand-held camera, which allows few of the syntactical devices of established film languages—point-of-view shots, reaction shots, strategic close-ups, and so on.

It is also the first film of Alea's to be shot by Mario García Joya, the cinematographer on every film of his since; he has thus become the most important of Alea's artistic collaborators, responding to the open character of Alea's approach with a flexible and adaptable camera language. On the other hand, when it comes to scripts, Alea has tended to work with different writers, each especially apt to the subject in hand. He has found this combination to overcome the danger of the ossification of style. Every new script requires a fresh stylistic conception, and in this sense Alea has never made two films alike.

After *Una pelea cubana* in 1971, there was a gap of five years before his next feature, *La ultima cena (The Last Supper),* came out in 1976. But Alea was hardly idle during this period. He was kept busy with his responsibilities within ICAIC, guiding and advising the next generation of directors, and sometimes collaborating with them. He worked, for example, with others, on the script for

Alea and Daisy Granados, who plays Elena

the first of a trilogy of films about slavery by Sergio Giral, *El otro Francisco* (*The Other Francisco*). Answering the suggestion of a New York film critic, Andrew Sarris, that he was being blocked from working as a director, he replied, "Collective achievement is just as important as the personal one. . . . In order to avoid appearing saintly, like some extraterrestrial being removed from all personal interest, I would like to state that in order for me to fulfill my individual creative needs as a director, I need for there to be a Cuban cinema. In order to find my own personal fulfillment, I need the existence of the entire Cuban film movement as well."[7]

Indeed the work on *El otro Francisco* fed straight into Alea's next film, *La ultima cena*, another story of slavery, which develops the form of the historical allegory in the direction of black comedy. With a brilliant script by the young Cuban playwright Tomás González, the rich color photography of García Joya, and the great Chilean actor Nelson Villagra in the lead role, this is arguably Alea's second *chef d'oeuvre*, a subtle, ironic satire on the religious hypocrisy of a plantation owner toward his slaves, set in a time just after the Haitian revolution of 1795.

Before he began *La ultima cena*, however, a different responsibility intervened. In 1974 ICAIC mourned one of its most promising new directors when Sara Gómez died, leaving her first feature film unfinished. Alea and García Espinosa took on the task of completing it together, and it was finally released in 1977 under the title *De cierta manera* (*One Way or Another*): a study in sexual politics within the Revolution and critique of *machismo*, which further develops the fusion of fiction and documentary found in *Memories*. This film too produced a sequel by Alea, when after a slightly ponderous period comedy, *Los sobrevivientes* (*The Survivors*) in 1978, he came to make *Hasta cierto punto* (*Up to a Point*). A seemingly lightweight film, the research for *Hasta cierto punto* was carried out over a couple of years, using video, among Havana's dockworkers; this material was incorporated in the finished film, which was shot in 1983, and deals with the adulterous relationship of a playwright with an unmarried mother who works on the docks where he is researching a film script about dockworkers. Not only a homage to Sara Gómez, it also returns to some of the concerns in *Memories* with the individual consciousness of the intellectual.

In 1982, Julio García Espinosa had become ICAIC's new chief, succeeding Alfredo Guevara (who became Cuba's ambassador to UNESCO). To try and expand the film institute's output he encouraged a growing program of coproductions. Not all the plans for this endeavor have come to fruition, and it was not until 1987 that Alea was at work shooting again, becoming one of a number of Latin American directors to film a series of stories by Gabriel García Marquez,

7. Julianne Burton, "Individual Fulfillment and Collective Achievement: An Interview with T. G. Alea," *Cinéaste* 8, no. 1 (1977), p. 59.

partly financed by Spanish television. Alea's contribution was a gentle period love story called *Cartas del parque* (*Letters from the Park*), set in the Cuban provinces in 1913. A young man goes to a public scribe to have him write love letters on his behalf to a demure young woman, who goes to the same scribe to write her replies, only for the scribe to fall in love with her himself. It is a more successful realization of García Marquez than most, perhaps because it doesn't try too hard to be 'magical,' but relies on a pleasing magic of its own.

The same year, García Espinosa was preparing to restructure ICAIC in order to meet both the changing conditions of the film world and the demands of what is called *perestroika* in the Soviet Union and rectification in Cuba. After conversations with his counterpart in Moscow, Elem Klimov, production in ICAIC has been reorganized, and three new directors' workshops have been set up. Tomás Gutiérrez Alea is now, just turned sixty, the head of one of these workshops, and preparing new scripts of his own.

Chronology

March 1952: Fulgencio Batista seizes power and cancels planned elections, declaring himself head of a provisional government.

July 1953: Fidel Castro, challenging the legitimacy of Batista's power, leads a group of anti-Batista Cubans in an attempt to seize the Moncada Military Barracks in Santiago. The attack fails, many of the prisoners are killed by government forces, and Castro is tried and sentenced to jail.

March 1955: Castro, released from jail in an act of political amnesty, goes to Mexico where he organizes armed opposition to Batista.

November 1956: Castro lands in Cuba and establishes a small guerrilla military force in the Sierra Maestra.

January 1959: Batista, pressed by Castro's guerrillas and by mounting opposition in the cities, flees Cuba. Castro becomes the undisputed leader of the Revolution and takes command of the government.

February 1960: Cuba arranges trade agreements with the U.S.S.R., followed by similar agreements with other Eastern bloc countries. Friction with the United States leads to a U.S. embargo on virtually all trade with Cuba.

April 1961: Under the direction of the CIA, aircraft disguised with Cuban markings bomb Cuban airfields on 15 April. The following day Castro proclaims Cuba a Marxist-Leninist state. On 17 April a U.S.-sponsored invasion force of 1,300 men lands on the southern coast of Cuba at Playa Girón (Bay of Pigs). Cuban military forces quickly defeat the invaders, capturing large numbers of them who were then the subject of public interrogations and televised trials. They were later released in December 1962 in exchange for 53 million dollars' worth of food and medical supplies.

January 1962: The United States announces a full trade embargo against Cuba. The Organization of American States (OAS) expels Cuba from membership.

October 1962: The United States accuses the U.S.S.R. of establishing bases and installing missiles on the mainland of Cuba. The United States institutes a naval blockade of the island and threatens direct military action. The U.S.S.R. withdraws the missiles in return for a U.S. pledge not to interfere militarily in Cuban affairs.

Memories of Underdevelopment

Memories of Underdevelopment

The continuity script that follows is based on a print of the film, a copy of the director's continuity script, and other script materials, all made available by Tomás Gutiérrez Alea and by the Center for Cuban Studies in New York City. This account represents the film as it was presented for theatrical release in 1968. The notes referring to the earlier shooting script were also provided by Alea.

Camera distance is represented by the conventional abbreviations:

ELS   Extreme Long Shot
LS   Long Shot
MLS   Medium Long Shot
MS   Medium Shot
MCU   Medium Close-up
CU   Close-up
ECU   Extreme Close-up
POV   Point of View

These designations, as well as the descriptions of camera movement, are necessarily approximate.

The continuity script of the film is followed by notes which provide information about historical, cultural, and biographical matters pertinent to the film, and variations from the shooting script.

Credits

Director
Tomás Gutiérrez Alea

Producer
Miguel Mendoza

Assistant to the Producer
Jesús Pascaux

Production Company
ICAIC (Instituto Cubano del Arte e
Industria Cinematograficas)

Script
Tomás Gutiérrez Alea and Edmundo
Desnoes, based on the novel by
Desnoes

Director of Photography
Ramón F. Suárez

Assistant Directors
Ingeborg Holt Seeland
Jesús Hernández

Editor
Nelson Rodríguez

Music
Leo Brouwer

Conductor
Manuel Duchesne Cuzán

Special Musical Performance
Pello el Afrocán

First Assistant Cameraman
Alberto Menéndez

Script Girl
Babi Díaz

Sound Engineers
Eugenio Vesa
Germinal Hernández
Carlos Fernández

Musical Recording
Medardo Montero
EGREM Studios

Set Designer
Julio Matilla

Makeup
María Consuelo Ventura
Isabel Amezaga

Properties
Orlando González

Wardrobe
Elba Perez

Lighting
Enrique González

Grip
Juan García

Head of Construction
Luis Obregon

Stills
José Luis Rodríguez

Photographs
Luz Chessex

Titles
Umberto Pena

Animation
Roberto Riquenes

Optical Effects
Jorge Pucheux

Location
Havana

Process
Black and White

Length
104 minutes

Release Date
1968

Cast

Sergio
Sergio Corrieri

Elena
Daisy Granados

Noemí
Eslinda Núñez

Laura
Beatriz Ponchora

Pablo
Omar Valdés

Elena's Brother
René de la Cruz

With
Yolanda Far
Ofelia Gonzáles
José Gil Abad
Daniel Jordan
Luis López
Rafael Sosa

Continuity Script

Credits[1]

The film's titles and credits flash in white over images of carnival dancing to Pello el Afrokán's orchestra. It is night. The music and vocal refrain ("Where is Teresa? . . . / Maria Teresa . . . / Teresa . . . / Teresa . . .") continue until the end of the credit sequence.

1. MCU: *a musician is playing the* tumbadora *(conga drum), with the camera angled from the side looking down over his shoulder. Beyond him is the front of a stage and beyond, out of focus, an audience.*
2. MS: *the musician playing, now with the camera looking across his other shoulder. Women, seen from the rear, are dancing on the stage.*
3. MCU: *some faces cross very near the camera as people mill around and dance. Superimposed:* MEMORIES OF UNDERDEVELOPMENT
4. MCU: *the faces of dancers. Superimposed:* Script based on a novel by Edmundo Desnoes
5. MS: *a black woman, among the dancers, looks intently at the camera. Superimposed:* with Sergio Corrieri
6. MCU: *a couple, hand in hand, move very close to the camera. Superimposed:* Daisy Granados/Eslinda Núñez/Omar Valdés/René de la Cruz/
7. MCU: *a young mulatto woman laughs while dancing.*
8. MS: *a couple in the midst of another group of people dancing.*
9. MS: *a man in the midst of the dancers spreads his arms as two gunshots are heard.*
10. LS, *high angle: dancers scatter as a third shot is heard.*
11. MCU: *a man elbows his way through the crowd; the camera pans with him.*
12. CU: *hands beating* tumbadoras.
13. MS: *a group of people looking down. The camera tilts down to show a young man covered with blood lying on the ground.*
14. MCU: *the camera follows a man, seen from behind, forcing his way through the crowd until he disappears.*
15. MS: *the wounded man on the ground amid confusion. The camera looks down on him, but people pass in the foreground, blocking out the image.*
16. MS: *a young woman looking down.*
17. MS: *a couple look down while swaying to the music.*
18. MS: *people keep dancing around the body lying on the ground. Three policemen pick up the wounded man and carry him away on their shoulders, lifting the body above the crowd.*
19. MCU: *another musician playing the* tumbadora. *Superimposed:* Yolanda Far/Ofelia Gonzáles/José Gil Abad/Daniel Jordán/Luis López/Rafael Sosa

20. CU: *faces cross in front of the camera as people dance. Superimposed:* Director of Photography, Ramón F. Suárez
21. MS: *people dancing with raised hands.*
22. CU: *faces and hands moving confusedly to the rhythm of the music. Superimposed:* Editor, Nelson Rodríguez
23. MS: *a black man wearing a white hat and holding a glass of beer laughs and dances. Superimposed:* Music, Leo Brouwer/Conducted by Manuel Duchesne Cuzán/with a special performance by Pello el Afrokán
24. CU: *the black woman from shot 5 dances and looks at the camera. The frame freezes on the woman, who stares intently at the camera. Superimposed:* Direction, Tomás Gutiérrez Alea. *First the music, and then the image fade out.*

25. MS: *José Martí International Airport in Havana. The camera follows a cart loaded with suitcases being pushed by a porter. The camera tilts up to include passengers lining up in front of a Pan American Airways counter. Superimposed:* HAVANA, 1961. MANY PEOPLE ARE LEAVING THE COUNTRY.
26. MS: *the hands of two employees at the ticket counter as they check tickets and passports.*
27. MS, *high angle: the two clerks, their faces now visible.*
28. MCU: *the hands of one of the clerks, returning documents to a young man.*
29. *The camera travels in* MS *over a pile of baggage on the floor until it rises and shows in* LS *a waiting room full of people.*

30. MS: *a boy, embraced by his mother, looks at the camera, then turns toward her, his back to the camera. The camera moves up to the mother's face; she is about to burst into tears.*
31. MS: *a seated woman, coat over her arm and satchel on her lap, wipes her eyes with a handkerchief.*
32. MS: *a camera looks over the shoulder of a man and through a glass partition that separates passengers from people who have come to say goodbye to them. The man in the foreground waves at a woman behind the glass and then taps on the glass with a fan. She begins to cry.*
33. MCU: *the camera pans with a girl moving right, carrying a doll. She turns, faces the camera, looks at another girl who is sticking her tongue out, and giggles. The camera tilts up to a man wearing sunglasses who taps the second girl on her head with his fan.*
34. MS: *the camera pans right with three young men walking around the passenger lounge.*
35. LS: *the camera tracks left on passengers waiting to have their passports stamped. It holds on a table where three officials are checking passports.*
36. MCU, *high angle: the camera looks over an official's shoulder down to his hands. He gives a receipt to a passenger who signs it. The receipt is stamped with the word* "Departure."
37. MS: *Sergio is saying goodbye first to his father, then to his mother, his face visible over their shoulders as he embraces them. He is evidently unmoved. Then he turns to his wife Laura.*
38. MS: *Sergio approaches Laura. He mouths what looks like* "Well, bye, bye" *(in English) and shrugs. She looks at him for a second, then turns her back on him without uttering a word. Sergio watches her as she moves away.*
39. MS, *Sergio's* POV: *Laura's back as she walks toward the runaway. She hesitates for a second, as if to look back, then keeps walking.*
40. ELS: *the runway from the airport balcony, crowded with people waving. The camera pans with the airplane, which taxis past in the background. Sergio enters the frame in* CU *with his back almost completely turned to the camera. The camera pans to show Sergio's face; he starts to whistle.*
41. LS: *inside a moving bus, looking through the windshield at the avenue leading from the airport to the city. At left of frame, the driver's back.*
42. CU: *Sergio's mother's face, over his shoulder, as she says goodbye to him at the airport.*
43. CU: *Sergio's father's face, also in the airport, as in 42.*
44. CU: *Laura, now seen from behind Sergio. She turns her back on him, as in 38.*
45. MS: *Sergio seated in the bus. He yawns.*
    SERGIO: *(voice-over):* She'll really have to go to work there . . .

46. *High angle* MS: *Laura's back as she walks along the airport runway. She
    moves away sobbing until she reaches the steps of the plane, where she
    stands in* LS. *A sign beside the steps reads:* Flight 422—Miami.
    SERGIO (*voice-over*): . . . well, that is, until she finds some dumb guy
    who'll marry her. To tell the truth, she's still something to look at.
    She'll remember me when things get bad. After that . . . I'm the one
    who's really been stupid. Working so that she could live like someone
    who had been born in New York or Paris, and not on this under-
    developed island . . .

47. MS: *Sergio making way for a militiaman who has been sitting at his side.
    The bus has come to a stop.*
    SOLDIER: Excuse me.
    The bus starts again.

48. LS, *Sergio's* POV: *through the window we see a large billboard display-
    ing a poster that celebrates the Cuban victory at Playa Girón (Bay of
    Pigs).*[2] *The bus continues along the avenue.*

49. MS: *the camera tracks, continuing the lateral movement of the last shot.
    It adopts Sergio's* POV *as he steps into his apartment. The camera moves
    through the hallway and living room. It is a handsome, modern, not
    particularly luxurious apartment. The furniture is solid, American in
    style; there are some Cuban paintings on the walls as well as some
    framed family pictures; also, scattered around, some copies of American
    magazines (*Vogue, Life, Harper's Bazaar*). Offscreen, Sergio whistles
    "Adelita," a song from the Mexican Revolution. The whistling continues
    on the soundtrack through shot 54.*

50. MS: *the coffee table in the living room laden with several bottles and
    half-filled glasses.*

51. ELS: *the city seen through the balcony's glass doors.*

52. MCU: *two tropical birds in a cage.*

53. MS, *Sergio's* POV: *the camera tracks through a messy bedroom, with the
    bed unmade and clothes scattered around.*

54. CU: *Sergio tosses his jacket aside. He walks over to the bed and sits on
    the edge while the camera reframes him in* MS. *He removes his shoes and
    tie, continuing to whistle, and then collapses backward on the bed. His
    head hits a wooden hanger hidden under the scattered clothes. He tosses
    it aside.*

55. CU: *a blank piece of paper is inserted in a typewriter. The following
    words are typed:* All those who loved and fucked me over up to the last
    moment have already gone

56–57. MS: *tracking camera shows different objects in Sergio's apartment:
    paintings, small sculptures, pottery, books, photographs, posters.*
    SERGIO (*voice-over*): I've been saying for years that if I had the time I

would sit down and write a book of stories or a diary; now I'll find out if I have anything to say.

58. CU: *Sergio's hands spreading butter on toast with a knife; he picks up a cup of café au lait and moves from the counter to the kitchen table, as the camera reframes him in* MS. *He is in his undershirt and his hair is mussed. He slowly eats his breakfast, smoking a cigarette at the same time.*

59. MS: *Sergio steps onto the balcony. He goes to a telescope attached to the railing and peers through it.*[3]

60. *A shot through the telescope: a couple in* LS *kissing as they lie on a chaise by the edge of a rooftop pool at the Hotel Capri.*
    SERGIO (*voice-over*): Everything remains the same.

61. MS: *Sergio changing the position of the telescope.*

62. ELS: *through the telescope, tilting upward and panning rapidly across the whole city.*

63. ELS: *through the telescope, the camera pans more slowly to the left across the city and its harbor; ships entering the harbor can be glimpsed between tall buildings.*
    SERGIO (*voice-over*): Here everything remains the same. All of a sudden it looks like a set, a city made of cardboard.

64. ELS: *through the telescope, the camera pans across a rooftop play-ground of a school, then moves across other rooftops and tilts upward to Maceo's statue.*[4]
    SERGIO (*voice-over*): The Bronze Titan . . .

65. ELS: *through the telescope, the foundation of the monument to the Maine.*[5] *The camera tilts upward to the top of the monument from which the eagle has been torn down.*

     SERGIO (voice-over): . . . Cuba, free and independent . . . who would have thought that this could happen? Without the imperial eagle. And what about the dove Picasso was going to send?

66. ELS: *the telescope pans to the left to focus on a freighter in the harbor.*

67. ELS: *the telescope pans left and then right to focus on a small torpedo boat in the harbor.*

     SERGIO (*voice-over*): It's very comfortable being a communist millionaire in Paris.

68. ELS: *the telescope focuses on a large building in the dock area. On a wall one can read:* ESTA HUMANIDAD HA DICHO BASTA Y HA ECHADO A ANDAR.

     SERGIO (*voice-over*): "The people have said enough and are now on the move."[6]

69. ELS: *the camera pans slowly left across the docks, where belching smokestacks suggest industrial activity.*

     SERGIO (*voice-over*): Like my parents, like Laura, and they won't stop until they get to Miami. Yet today everything looks so different. Have I changed, or has this city changed?

70. MS: *Sergio, hearing his birds chirp, turns away from the telescope and goes to the cage to feed the birds. One of them is dead.*[7] *Sergio lifts it out by its feet and lets it fall from the balcony to the street. He watches it fall.*

     SERGIO (*voice-over*): "It's the time of departure. Oh! abandoned like the wharves at dawn. Everything in you was shipwrecked."[8] (*Sergio yawns and leans on the railing while looking impassively at the city below him.*)

71. MCU: *a reel-to-reel tape recorder. Sergio's hand presses a button and a casual conversation between him and Laura is heard.*

     SERGIO (*on the tape*): What are you doing?

     LAURA (*on the tape*): Can't you see?

     SERGIO (*on the tape*): I mean, what are you reading?

72. CU: *Sergio listening to the tape. He is in the living room. In a glass jar he stows a rolled-up magazine whose cover displays a photograph of Brigitte Bardot. (The taped conversation between Sergio and Laura continues.)*

     LAURA (*on the tape*): Something ordinary, trivial, and decadent. (*In English.*) The best of everything. (*Returning to Spanish.*) The best of the world, the best of everything, whatever you like.

     SERGIO (*on the tape*): Oh yes. That film . . .

     LAURA (*on the tape*): Yes. Let me alone, please.

73. MS: *Sergio before a closet full of Laura's clothes. He takes a fur stole out and drapes it around his shoulders.*

SERGIO (*on the tape*): Me?

LAURA (*on the tape*): Yes, you're looking at me as if I were some strange insect. I can't read like this.

SERGIO (*on the tape*): Why don't we talk a little?

LAURA (*on the tape*): (*In English.*) What's come over you? (*Returning to Spanish.*) What's bugging you?

SERGIO (*on the tape*): Is that all you can talk about—bugs?

74. MCU: *a dresser drawer Sergio has opened, filled with Laura's things. Sergio's hands pick up and discard several objects: a powder puff, a pearl necklace, a monocle . . .*

LAURA (*on the tape*): What am I supposed to talk about when I'm surrounded by bugs all the time—filthy people, pigs. . . . It's a backward country, as you rightly say.

SERGIO (*on the tape*): What do you think?

LAURA (*on the tape*): Why do you ask that? You've never been interested in what I think about anything. (*In English.*) What's come over you?

SERGIO (*on the tape*): You're practicing your English a lot lately. I think you really intend to leave.

LAURA (*on the tape*): What's it to you, baby!

75. CU: *Sergio trying on the monocle he took out of the drawer.*

76. MS: *a very brief shot of Laura lying on the bed, reading. She raises her eyes to the camera and lifts her glasses, a gesture that echoes Sergio's action with the monocle.*

77. CU: *Sergio, as in 75. The monocle almost falls off.*

SERGIO (*on the tape*): Common, that's the way I like you. . . . You know that always excites me, when you're halfway between shabbiness and sophistication, between rags and tuxedos.

78. ECU: *Sergio's hands playing with a lipstick; he twists it up and down several times.*

79. CU: *Sergio looks at the lipstick and half-smiles.*

LAURA (*on the tape*): I've been looking at you for a long time now and you're looking really weird. I don't know, but the thing is you're really horrible lately.

80. MS: *with the lipstick, Sergio draws a face on the dressing-table mirror, over the reflection of his own face.*

SERGIO (*on the tape*): The thing is I haven't got any Yardley's hair oil, any Colgate toothpaste, any imperialistic after-shave lotion. . . . As you know, all that helps a lot.

LAURA (*on the tape*): Yes, it must be that . . .

SERGIO (*on the tape*): And yet you get more attractive each day.

LAURA (*on the tape*): You think so?

SERGIO (*on the tape*): Yes, you're more artificial. I don't like natural beauty. I like women like you, made of nice clothes, good food, makeup, massages. Thanks to all that you've stopped being a slovenly Cuban girl and have become a beautiful exciting woman.

81. MCU: *Sergio's hand opening a drawer full of lingerie. His hand touches various pieces, finally holding and stretching a pair of underpants.*

82. LS: *Laura, naked, her back to the camera, steps into the shower.*

  LAURA (*on the tape*): You're unbearable! I never know when you're serious and when you're making fun of me.

  SERGIO (*on the tape*): A little of both, darling.

  LAURA (*on the tape*): Well, do a number on your little mother, darling.

  SERGIO (*on the tape*): Yeah, yeah.

83. MCU: *Sergio's hands remove a nylon stocking from the drawer. The camera follows the movement of his hands until it locks on a* CU *of his face. He rubs the stocking close to his ear and then caresses his own cheek with it.*

  LAURA (*on the tape*): Go to hell!

  SERGIO (*on the tape*): That's very good, very good!

  LAURA (*on the tape*): Are you crazy, you idiot? Let me go, let me go! I can't stand you! I can't stand living here any longer, I can't stand the heat, the sweat. . . . You sweat too much, you stink. . . . Let me go!

  Sergio pulls the stocking down over his head and face.

  SERGIO (*on the tape*): Do you know that everything you said is being taped?

  LAURA (*on the tape*): What?

  SERGIO (*on the tape*): Everything. Word for word. It'll be a lot of fun later, when you hear it.

84. MS: *Sergio looks at himself in the mirror. His reflection is superimposed on the face he drew with the lipstick. His face is disfigured by the stocking.*

  LAURA (*on the tape*): You're a monster! You're sick! Give it to me!

  Slowly Sergio moves away from the mirror.

  SERGIO (*on the tape*): Watch out! You're going to break it! Let go!

  LAURA (*on the tape*): Let go of me!

  SERGIO (*on the tape*): No, no. What are you doing?

85. MCU: *Sergio's hand turns off the tape recorder. The camera tilts up to* MS *of Sergio standing in the middle of the living room. He gently removes the stocking from his head and sits down, leaning back on the couch as if exhausted.*

86. MS: *people stepping off a bus onto a crowded street in downtown Havana.*

87. LS: *people walking as the camera, after a bus passes, tracks forward and crosses the street, facing people who are crossing in the opposite direction.*

88. LS: *people moving along the sidewalk across the frame to the right and to the left.*

89. CU: *the camera pans left to follow a woman wearing metal rollers in her hair.*

90. CU: *the camera pans right to follow a young woman who passes, licking an ice cream cone.*

91. MS: *the camera pans right,˙then left, to follow an* "iyabó,"[9] *dressed in white, who approaches the camera and passes it, continuing down the street.*

92. MS: *the camera tracks behind a voluptuous young woman. It focuses first on her legs and then tilts up along her body to the back of her head. The woman stops at a stall where lottery tickets are sold. The camera closes in and veers a little toward her. When the camera is alongside her, the woman turns slightly and looks directly at the camera for a moment. The camera does not hold on the woman's look, but moves on past her.*

93. MS: *Sergio is walking along the sidewalk, with the camera tracking backward. He looks at people, shop windows, buildings. He stops to look at a bookstore display rack, then walks into the store. The camera follows him.*

94. MS, *Sergio's* POV: *books on a shelf. They are recent publications (a novel by Mikhail Sholokhov, a book on Yuri Gagarin, the works of José Martí). The camera travels along the bookrack and finally tilts up to show on the other side, in* MS, *a young woman, also browsing. The woman raises her head, looks Sergio in the eye for a moment, then goes back to her browsing.*

95. MS: *Sergio also looks away from the woman. He takes a last look at the books and walks away a few steps.*

    SERGIO (*voice-over*): Here women look straight into your eyes as if they want to be touched by your look.

96. MS: *Sergio taking a book from a shelf and leafing through it. The woman approaches him from the back. He turns around, and again they look briefly into each other's eyes. The woman leaves the frame, crossing past the camera.*

    SERGIO (*voice-over*): That doesn't happen anywhere else in the world. Maybe Italian women stare a little more, but no, it's never like here. (*Sergio closes the book he has been looking at and hands it to the cashier to indicate he wants to buy it. The camera moves forward to a* MCU *of the book. It is* Bourgeois Morality and Revolution *by Leo Rozitchner.*)[10]

97. LS: *Sergio walks in the street surrounded by people. He passes by the park where* "El Encanto" *used to be.*[11] *He stops to look.*

98. LS: *the park with its benches, rather impersonal and relatively empty. People are passing by. The ambient sound is gradually drowned out by the noise and shouts of the night* "El Encanto" *burned down.*

99–102. *Stock shots of the fire at "El Encanto." The last shot shows the charred ruins seen from above. (Little by little the sound of shouts, sirens, etc., stops, and the previous muffled ambient sound returns.)*

103. MS: *Sergio continues to walk. He leaves the park behind, crosses the street and moves toward the camera, which has panned right and now holds him in* CU *range.*

> SERGIO (*voice-over*): Since "El Encanto" burned down, Havana seems like a country town. When you think they used to call it the "Paris of the Caribbean"! At least, that's what the tourists and the whores used to call it.

104. MS: *the camera follows a woman who moves along the sidewalk, stopping in front of an almost-empty shop window. It displays a Fidel Castro poster and a bust of José Martí flanked by a vase filled with paper flowers. Next to the bust, there is a line by Martí, copied on a piece of cardboard: "Our wine is bitter, but it is our wine." Far off, one hears the Orquesta Aragon playing the danzon "Angoa." The music continues through shot 110.*

105. LS: *a man stands in front of a store window inscribed with a circular logo and the word* SECCIONAL.

106. LS: *an empty store window with a hand-printed sign attached to the glass in front of a large photograph of Fidel in battle dress: "Ophelia and Chiqui have moved to Federigo between Neptune and St. Mark."*

107. LS: *an empty store window displaying a sign advertising Kodak film.*

108. LS: *a store window displaying a photograph of Fidel Castro against a cloth backdrop. Next to it is a crudely lettered sign: "Aquilimbo. This concern is united in fulfilling the golden rule."*

109. LS: *an empty store window with strips of tape forming an "X" across the window, a picture of José Martí in the background.*

> SERGIO (*voice-over*): Now it looks more like a Tegucigalpa of the Caribbean—not only because they burned down "El Encanto" and there are so few good things in the stores. It's also because of the people.

110. LS: *several objects displayed in a store for religious relics: a naked "Santa Barbara," an image of Christ, and a photograph of Fidel.*

111–119. *Faces of people in the streets. (The music of the* danzon *dissolves into a slow, delicate melody played on the harpsichord through shot 120.) Sad, worried faces of humble people; faces of old people; faces that somehow reflect Sergio's feelings of solitude and sadness.*

111. CU: *the camera pans right with an elderly man.*

112. MS: *the camera pans left with a bald, overweight man in an open shirt who is eating a sandwich.*

113. MCU: *two men are facing the camera, looking in different directions.*

114. MCU: *a man with his back to the camera, but seen in profile. A woman is facing the camera.*

115. MCU: *two women, both looking anxiously to the right.*
116. MS: *a black woman wearing sunglasses and with a cross around her neck is seated in front of a tree trunk.*
117. MCU: *a middle-aged black man wearing a hat. He strokes his chin.*
118. CU: *an older man, unshaven, with a heavily lined face.*
119. CU: *a younger woman stares with a frown of concentration toward something beyond the camera.*
120. MS: *Sergio walking along. The camera is stationary and he moves into a* MCU.[12]

    SERGIO (*voice-over*): What meaning does life have for them? What meaning does it have for me? . . . But I'm not like them! (*Sergio's face looks contorted, somewhat wasted, grave, sad, as the ones just seen. When he is close to the camera, the frame freezes.*)
    Fade out.[13]

121. LS: *Havana's Malecón highway from a moving car. The camera shows the point of view of the driver. Superimposed:* PABLO[14]

    PABLO (*off*): These people say they're making "the first socialist revolution in America." . . .
122. MS: *Sergio and Pablo in Pablo's convertible, seen from the side, with Sergio in the passenger seat closer to the camera.*

    PABLO: So what? . . . They're going back to the jungle. . . . They're gonna go hungry . . . just like the Haitians. They toppled Napoleon and . . . so what? They used to have the biggest sugar crop in the world before the Revolution, and look at them now. Barefoot and walking around like zombies.

SERGIO: Times change.

PABLO: Besides, Sergio, this is not our problem. This is a problem between the Russians and the Americans. We haven't lost a thing. And listen, Sergio, this whole thing is going to blow up. . . . We're going to catch the first punch either of them throws, and you know why? Because we're so small, a teeny tiny island. It'll be you guys who'll catch the punch, because I won't be here.

123. LS: *a cabaret full of people. Sergio and Laura sitting at a table with Pablo and his wife. Pablo is telling a funny story. The women look amused. (The sound of traffic from the previous shot remains.)*

SERGIO (*voice-over*): To think that we've been running around together all the time for more than five years.[15]

124. LS: *night. The four people in the previous shot come out of a theater where the film* Hiroshima, Mon Amour *is playing. A section of the film poster appears on camera.*

125. *Sergio and Pablo, as in 122.*[16]

PABLO: It's true that with Batista things had gotten to the point where one just couldn't go on any longer.[17] Not me, because I never messed around in politics. I've got a very clear conscience.

126. MS: *Pablo and Sergio sunbathing at the edge of the Hotel Nacional pool. Two young women in bathing suits cross in front of the camera and both men turn and follow them with their eyes.*

PABLO (*voice-over*): The only thing I've done all my life is work. Work like an animal . . .

PABLO (*referring to one of the young women*): Can you imagine Anita? So beautiful, and yet her stomach is stuffed with black beans. I saw her eating lunch today on the terrace.

127. MS: *Sergio and Pablo, seen from the back seat of the convertible. They pull into a gas station on the Malecón and stop the car in front of the pump. Pablo asks for the tank to be filled and then continues his conversation with Sergio.*

PABLO: They really do have all the means, Sergio, the "know-how," to develop this country's economy. (*To the attendant.*) Fill it up.

SERGIO: The "know-how," no?

PABLO: Yeah, the "know-how," the "know-how," the Americans really know how to do things, they know how to make things run.[18]

128. MS, *Sergio's* POV: *the garage attendant finishes filling up the tank. He hangs up the hose and moves to the car to collect payment. The camera pans with him until he stops on Pablo's side.*

PABLO (*to the attendant*): Check the oil.

ATTENDANT: Haven't got any. If you like, I can check it anyway.

PABLO: No . . . what for? (*Pablo makes an "I told you so" gesture to Sergio and starts the car.*)

The camera leaves Pablo and pans to frame the landscape seen through the windshield.

129. MS: *Pablo and Sergio, as in 125. Sergio is almost amused at Pablo's predicament.*

PABLO: I wish I could smash it. Shit! Now it turns out that I have got to hand it back in the same condition it was before.

SERGIO: Why?

PABLO: It's been inventoried, baby. If I don't hand it in just as it was, they won't let me leave.

Sergio laughs. Pablo looks at him, puzzled.

130. LS: *Sergio walking through an auto body repair shop. He approaches a small shrine to Our Lady of Charity on the wall of the shop and inspects it. He then walks over to Pablo, who is having an argument with one of the workers in the shop.*

131. MS: *the mechanic and Pablo, looking at the front of Pablo's car, which is dented. Sergio moves closer, paying attention. The camera moves over to him, until he is in MCU range.*

MECHANIC: The thing is that I can't get the sealed-beam unit, you'll have to find one yourself. Things aren't what they used to be . . .

PABLO: Yes, I know that.

MECHANIC: And the paint job won't look the same. If you can't get wood alcohol, you'll have to use synthetic paint, which isn't the same. You'll have to paint all this part, at least, so it doesn't look so bad.

Sergio yawns. (The mechanic's voice gradually fades.)

SERGIO (*voice-over*): He says the only thing that Cubans can't stand is to go hungry. With the hunger people have suffered here ever since the Spaniards came!

132–137. *Documentary photographs of hungry people in Cuba during different historical periods.*

138–144. *Other photographs with images of hunger in Latin America.*

143. SERGIO (*voice-over; cold, impersonal*): In Latin America four children die every minute due to illnesses caused by malnutrition. In ten years 20 million children will have died, the same number of deaths as were caused by the Second World War.[19]

144. *The last image ends with a slow zoom into a foreshortened casket being carried on the shoulders of poor people.*
Fade out.

145. MS: *Pablo and Sergio in the convertible arriving at the garage in the basement of Sergio's apartment building. They get out and Pablo stops for a moment to stare at Sergio's car on blocks in the background.*

PABLO: It's the symbol of decadence!

SERGIO: I can almost say I feel happier with things as they are. I don't have to keep on fixing it or anything like that.

This time it is Pablo who laughs at Sergio's broken-down car. They both walk over to it, followed by the camera.

PABLO: Well, if you like walking . . .

SERGIO: No, but I feel more at ease. I don't have to worry about it.

Sergio and Pablo laugh.

146. MCU: *Pablo unscrewing one of the headlights in Sergio's car to replace the broken one in his own. Meanwhile, he keeps on talking.*

PABLO: Listen, they say the latest American cars are incredible. I was reading a magazine Julio Gómez lent me. Sealed motors with two spark plugs and a two-year guarantee. If it breaks down, they give you another one. You don't have to fix it. . . . Imagine, with the kind of mechanics we have here, that's the solution. (*Pablo's voice gradually grows fainter.*)

The camera pans up from Pablo to hold Sergio in MS *as he leans on the hood of the car.*

SERGIO (*voice-over*): People seem to me more stupid every day.

147. LS: *the two couples, as in 123. The camera slowly approaches the table. Some people cross in front of the table.*

LAURA: Pablo's right, all the French smell bad.

PABLO: They're just pigs by nature, Laura. (*They laugh.*)

148. MS: *Pablo is washing his hands and face in Sergio's bathroom, his image reflected in the bathroom mirror. He looks at himself while wiping his hands dry and talking.*

PABLO: I couldn't care less if they take it all. It's not going to last long. But now it's different, my friend . . .

149. MS: *Sergio turning the pages of the book by Rozitchner he bought in shot 96. He walks to the bed and sits on it. The camera pans to follow him and shows Pablo in the background, who finishes wiping his hands and moves over to* MS *range while he talks.*

PABLO: But now I'm not going to stay at home and do nothing like when they were fighting Batista, because the truth is, I never thought they were going to win. Now I know that if I don't get moving somehow, I'll never be able to function when this thing blows up.

150. MCU: *Sergio leaning back on the bed and leafing through the book.[20] He sits up and the camera follows him, bringing Pablo into the frame on the left.*

SERGIO: That's what they said.

PABLO: Who?

SERGIO: The Bay of Pigs prisoners. Listen . . .

PABLO: Oh, Sergio . . .

151. LS: *a group of prisoners immediately after being captured at the Bay of Pigs. They walk along a dusty road, their hands raised and clasped behind their heads. Superimposed:* THE TRUTH OF THE GROUP IS IN THE MURDERER

152. LS *(from above): prisoners now seen as they advance toward the camera. Some armed Cuban soldiers stand guard at the side of the road.*

153. *Prisoners move from left to right, crossing past the camera in* MCU. *The camera pans with them to follow them from behind.*

154–155. *Hand-held camera moves backwards to keep the advancing groups of prisoners in* MCU.

    SERGIO *(voice-over; reading)*: We found in the military organization of the invading brigades a hierarchy of social functions which epitomizes the division in the moral and social work of the bourgeoisie:

156. MCU: *photograph of Father Lugo. (Shots 156–161 are linked by a series of dissolves, so that each face merges with the adjoining ones.)*

    SERGIO *(voice-over)*: the priest . . .

157. MCU: *photograph of Fabrio Freyre.*

    SERGIO *(voice-over)*: . . . the businessman . . .

158. MCU: *photograph of Felipe Rivero.*

    SERGIO *(voice-over)*: . . . dilettante official . . .

159. MCU: *photograph of Ramón Calviño.*
    SERGIO (*voice-over*): . . . the torturer . . .
160. MCU: *photograph of José Andreu.*
    SERGIO (*voice-over*): . . . the philosopher . . .
161. MCU: *photograph of Carlos Varona.*
    SERGIO (*voice-over*): . . . the politician . . .
162. MS: *a prisoner still dressed in uniform stands facing the camera as it pans slowly up from feet to head.*
163–165. MS: *separate shots of three different prisoners, apparently in a detention yard. The yard is crowded and behind each man other prisoners stand casually in the background.*
    SERGIO (*voice-over*): . . . and the innumerable sons of good families. Each one of them carried out specific duties . . .
166. MS: *the camera pans to the right along a group of prisoners standing in line; a guard carrying a rifle passes in the foreground.*
    SERGIO (*voice-over*): . . . and yet, it was the whole, the group, which gave meaning to . . .
167. *High angle* LS: *prisoners grouped in a circle, as guards patrol around them.*
    SERGIO (*voice-over*): . . . each individual activity.
168. ECU: *Calviño.*
    SERGIO (*voice-over*): Calviño was a murderer who horrified even the bourgeoisie.
169. MLS: *witness Maria Elena, during Bay of Pigs trial of prisoners. She is displaying a housecoat, holding it up in front of her.*
    MARIA ELENA: . . . and this is the housecoat I was wearing. There are still bloodstains on the front, because he kicked me . . .
170. MCU: *Calviño, listening and nodding. Someone is holding a microphone in front of him.*
    MARIA ELENA (*off*): . . . in the stomach and I had a hemorrhage. That wasn't enough for him.
171. MLS: *Maria Elena, the housecoat now folded up in her hand. With her other hand, she points to her lower back.*
    MARIA ELENA: I had to fight so they wouldn't do that, and they broke two of my vertebrae. . . . Do you remember?
172–176. *Human bones and implements of torture, displayed on tables. In 172–174, members of the Revolutionary Army are partially visible as they examine the implements.*
    WITNESS (*voice-over*): When they started hitting him with sticks, he fell on his knees and you . . .
177. *The camera pans from weapons on a table to Batista and the chief of police in* MLS *smiling as they inspect the captured weapons.*
    WITNESS (*voice-over*): . . . kicked him in the side and he sprawled on

the floor. Don't you remember? And after you murdered him, you
violated him too, because you're a dirty murderer.

178–179. MLS: *captured weapons being exhibited by the police.*

180. *Low angle* MS: *the chief of police inspects a howitzer. Freeze frame.*

181. MS: *photograph of high military officials, smiling, behind a desk. One
displays a pistol, pointed toward the ceiling.*

> PILAR (*voice-over*): Coward! You killed a man in front of me, I
> saw you!

182. MS: *photograph of prisoners, crowded in a single cell, seen through the
bars of the cell.*

> CALVIÑO (*voice-over*): In front of you?

183. MS: *a photograph of prisoners, standing behind a table piled with confiscated ammunition.*

184. LS: *a photograph of a group of men, apparently prisoners, standing
against a wall and facing the camera.*

185. MLS: *a photograph of a group of men, stripped to the waist and standing
against a wall with their backs to the camera. They show visible signs of
torture.*

> PILAR (*voice-over*): I saw you, you killed him in front of me, you shot
> him and then you laughed at the way he died.

186. CU: *film of the scarred back of one man. A hand at the left of the frame
points to marks of torture.*

> CALVIÑO (*voice-over*): Excuse me . . .
> PILAR (*voice-over*): At 106 Avellaneda! The sixth of October, at seven in
> the evening! Tell me you didn't! Tell me you didn't! Say it isn't so,
> that . . .

187. *High angle* LS: *a photograph of a bullet-riddled corpse lying in the
street.*

188. *High angle* LS: *a corpse lying face up, shirt torn away. His throat has
been cut.*

189. MS: *a photograph of another corpse, lying under some shrubbery, so
that only the head, badly battered, is visible.*

> PILAR (*voice-over*): . . . after you killed Morua, nine days later, you
> arrested me and you sat down to tell me how you had killed him! Say
> you didn't! Say it, Calviño!
> CALVIÑO (*voice-over*): I can't answer her.

190–191. ELS: *police cars driving at high speed down largely deserted
streets.*

192. ELS: *a large group of uniformed policemen clustered for protection close
to the wall of a building. They fire their handguns to the right.*

193. ELS: *a crowd of civilians runs to the right down a street, trying to
escape gunfire.*

194. LS: *the crowd running, now seen from the sidewalk. In the foreground, a*

uniformed man rushes past and the camera pans to see him striking a civilian with his nightstick.

195. MS: *two uniformed policemen in an office, apparently at a news conference. The man in the foreground, the chief of police, is sweating profusely and keeps wiping his face with a handkerchief.*

     SERGIO (*voice-over*): In all capitalist societies, there is this same type of man at the disposition of the bourgeoisie, who is in charge of such special duties.

196. LS: *a couple in formal evening dress are dancing as other couples form a circle around the ballroom floor to watch.*

197. LS: *more dancers in formal dress crowd the floor at what appears to be the same party.*

198. MS: *two middle-aged men and a woman seated at a table at the party. The men are smiling and drinking.*

199. LS: *an overhead shot of the crowded dance floor.*

     SERGIO (*voice-over*): In the division of moral work, the contract murderer allows those to exist who are not directly involved with death, and who want to display their clean souls.

200–203. MCU: *a photograph of Rivero in profile dissolves into two other profile shots, then one full face.*

     RIVERO (*voice-over*): I'm talking for myself and for those who think like me; we might be in the minority. I'm not talking for Ventura nor for those miserable creatures you've named.[21] I didn't even know Calviño at that time. I was just interested in living my own life.

204. *Dissolve to a photograph of a large group of prisoners in* MCU, *seated as if in an auditorium. The camera zooms in slowly on the photograph.*

     SERGIO (*voice-over*): They appear like disjointed elements in a totality which nobody embraces completely.

205–206. *Dissolve to a photograph of Andreu in* MCU; *dissolve to a photograph in* CU.

     ANDREU (*voice-over*): In the end, I can't answer for the others, because everybody answers for himself.

207. *Dissolve to a photograph of Father Lugo in* MCU.

208–209. *Scenes filmed by the Bay of Pigs invaders before arriving in Cuba.*

208. LS: *a priest displays a small crucifix.*

209. *High angle* LS: *a priest offers communion on a ship.*

     FATHER LUGO (*voice-over*): It seems as though you want to accuse me of being the originator of the invasion and all those things. I want to insist that my mission was purely spiritual. I have never handled a weapon, before or after. The fact that one is mixed up in a conspiracy doesn't make one a conspirator.

210. MS: *the camera pans over two captured and beached landing boats.*

211. CU: *a skull and crossbones painted on the side of one of the boats.*

212. MLS: *a photograph of Lugo, testifying before a panel.*
213. MCU: *photograph of Freyre.*
     FREYRE (*voice-over*): Well, for a start, I've told you that I have been a perfectly . . . (*Coughs.*) . . . apolitical person all my life. I've never had anything to do with any political party . . .
214. *Dissolve to a photograph of Andreu; the camera moves in to* CU.
     ANDREU (*voice-over*): . . . and, secondly, it's your personal behavior that frees you from responsibility.
215. *Dissolve to a photograph of a group of prisoners seen from behind in* ELS. *They are seated in rows at a large outdoor assembly. The camera again moves in.*
     SERGIO (*voice-over*): Everybody refers to his own individuality when he wants to get away from another person's . . .
216. *Dissolve to a photograph of Calviño, as camera moves in to* CU.
     SERGIO (*voice-over*): . . . contaminating misery, or he sinks into the . . .
217. ELS: *the assembly of prisoners from 215, but now seen from the front. The camera pans across them.*
218. LS: *another group, also seated in rows, in a night assembly.*
     SERGIO (*voice-over*): . . . group when he has to hide his own responsibility and then infects everybody else.
219. CU: *photograph of Calviño, as in 216.*
     CALVIÑO (*voice-over*): You see, now we are a group. I'm not alone.
220. LS: *the prisoners, as in 218. One man stands, then sits down as the man sitting next to him stands.*
     SERGIO (voice-over): Thus it can be seen how that responsibility, rejected by everyone, is brought back and vindicated again by . . .
221. CU: *Calviño's hands.*
     SERGIO (*voice-over*): . . . a single member of the same group.
222. ECU: *the upper part of Calviño's face.*
     CALVIÑO (*voice-over*): No, you're talking about the group's . . .
223. *High angle* MS: *the body of a militiaman killed during the invasion is being lifted into a truck.*
224. *High angle* MS: *the camera pans over the body of another dead militiaman.*
     CALVIÑO (*voice-over*): . . . cause, which is not my cause.
     SERGIO (*voice-over*): In fact, the murderer-torturer resorts to the . . .
225. *High angle* LS: *photograph of two murdered women lying on the ground.*
     SERGIO (*voice-over*): . . . category of totality in order to avoid claiming . . .
226. MS: *Calviño, seen speaking.*
     SERGIO (*voice-over*): . . . moral responsibility.

227. LS: *invaders at Bay of Pigs standing in relaxed attitudes in a thicket of woods.*

CALVIÑO (*voice-over*): Listen, I'm telling you that I've committed no direct crime.

MODERATOR (*voice-over*): The meeting is over.

228–232. *Previously seen photographs of Lugo, Freyre, Rivero, Andreu, and Varona, linked by dissolves.*

SERGIO (*voice-over*): But in none of the cases under review was there a recovery of the true dialectical relationship between individuals and the group. The others who came with Calvino in the invasion don't recognize themselves as part of the system which entangles them in their own acts.

233. *A formal party in an elegant mansion. The guests are seen from above in* ELS, *as the camera looks down from the top of a marble staircase.*

234. LS: *young women in white ball gowns together perform a formal dance.*

SERGIO (*voice-over*): In the accounts of Freyre, the land baron; . . .

235. MS: *a priest, seen only partially, is celebrating a mass.*

SERGIO (*voice-over*): . . . in the extreme unctions of Lugo, the priest; in the inheritance of the Babum brothers; in the delicate ideas of Andreu, the philosopher; . . .

236. LS: *a group of older men and women in formal dress are gathered for some social event.*

SERGIO (*voice-over*): . . . in the dismissals and in the book of Rivero, the dilettante; . . .

237. ELS: *a public square crowded with people. Batista's campaign placards and banners hang from surrounding buildings.*

238. LS: *the speakers' platform at a Batista rally.*

239. LS: *an overhead shot of Batista among cheering crowds, waving.*

SERGIO (*voice-over*): . . . in the "representative democracy" of Varona, . . .

240. CU: *a wounded man; the top of his head is bandaged.*

SERGIO (*voice-over*): . . . you cannot read clearly the death . . .

241. *High angle* LS: *a corpse lies in an empty field. Several bystanders look at it.*

242. ELS: *two corpses in open countryside. Again bystanders are looking at them.*

243. *High angle* LS: *the camera pans slowly over a group of corpses sprawled on the ground.*

SERGIO (*voice-over*): . . . that through them spread over Cuba, . . .

244. LS: *several young women dressed in white evening gowns are seated in a semi-circle. They seem to constitute a queen and her court at a society ball. They clap their hands politely.*

SERGIO (*voice-over*): . . . death by hunger, . . .

245. MLS: *a student climbs a telephone pole to tear down a political poster.*
246. LS: *men and women marching, with arms linked, up a broad avenue. They move toward the camera.*
247. LS: *a crowd of marchers, now seen at a distance, approach several automobiles from which policemen are emerging.*
248. LS: *police and civilians jostle one another on a sidewalk.*
249. ELS: *police train hoses on a crowd of marchers in a street and force the marchers toward the sidewalk. The camera is located behind the police lines.*
    SERGIO (*voice-over*): . . . by sickness, by torture, by frustration.
    Fade out.

250. LS: *Sergio preparing the coffeepot in the kitchen. Noemí enters. Superimposed:* NOEMÍ [22]
    SERGIO (*voice-over*): She comes three times a week to clean the apartment.
    Noemí starts helping him make the coffee. Sergio takes out another cup and places it on the kitchen table. The camera follows him in MS.
    SERGIO (*voice-over*): She's been coming for more than a year and I've never noticed her. If she would fix herself up and dress better, she would be very attractive. She's as thin as a *Vogue* model. I like her. Born in Matanzas and a Protestant. A Baptist, I think.
251. MS: *Noemí gets a pitcher and moves back to the coffeepot.*
252. MS: *Sergio and Noemí at a table in the kitchen having breakfast. She is seen over Sergio's shoulder.*
    SERGIO: Did they baptize you in a river?
    NOEMÍ: Of course.
    SERGIO: What's it like?
    NOEMÍ (*looking embarrassed*): Well . . .
    SERGIO: Don't you want to tell me?
    NOEMÍ: People gather at the edge of the river, . . .
253. CU: *Sergio looks over at Noemí as he drinks coffee and eats some buttered bread.*
    NOEMÍ: . . . the minister and I go into the water. Afterwards, he told me what baptism means. It symbolizes the death of sin, the resurrection of a new life . . .
254. ELS: *Noemí's baptism as imagined by Sergio. A group of people dressed in white robes are slowly going into a river.*
    NOEMÍ (*voice-over*): . . . full of faith, of hope, of dignity. Then he took me to the deepest part and put me under. If you could have seen how scared I was!
255. MS: *Sergio and Noemí alone in the river. He holds her in his arms, keeping her upper body above the water. The white robe clings to her and*

her nipples show through the wet cloth. The movement is extremely slow,
unreal, and is accompanied by Vivaldi's music.
   NOEMÍ (*voice-over*): But everything happened so quickly that I didn't
      even notice. All that anxiety and all that fuss, for nothing.[23]
256. MCU: *a book open to a picture of Botticelli's* Birth of Venus. *Sergio's*
      hand caresses Venus's body.
257. MS: *Sergio sitting in front of his typewriter. When he realizes that Noemí*
      is approaching, he abruptly closes the book.
258. MS, *Sergio's* POV: *Noemí crosses in front of Sergio and steps into an-*
      other room; she is preparing to clean the house.
259. MS: *Sergio, as in 257. He is deep in thought.*
260. LS: *Noemí is making the bed in Sergio's bedroom.*
261. CU: *very brief shot of Sergio embracing Noemí in the bedroom.*
262. MS: *Sergio, as in 257, before the typewriter. He digs in his ear with a*
      paper clip.
263. CU: *very brief shot of Sergio and Noemí collapsing on the bed in an*
      embrace.
264. LS: *very brief shot of Noemí, naked, lying on the bed.*
265. MS: *Sergio, as in 257, in front of the typewriter, hears Noemí approach-*
      ing and pretends to be working.
266. LS: *Noemí, as in 258, crosses in front of Sergio and says goodbye.*
267. MS: *Sergio, as in 257, scratches himself with a china scratcher in the*
      form of a hand.

268. CU: *Sergio wearing a bathing suit and a pullover. He is on a walkway above the outdoor pool at the Riviera Hotel, with the hotel visible in the background. He looks down toward the pool and when he pauses and looks directly below him, the camera pans down to show a young woman sunbathing. The camera then pans up to Sergio who walks away. His back is now turned and the logo of Kent State University is visible on his pullover.*
   SERGIO (*voice-over*): Almost everybody is an exhibitionist. They generally give the impression of defenseless, almost hairless animals, balanced precariously on two legs.
269. MS: *a man in a bathing suit, seen from the back, walking along the edge of the pool.*[24]
270. LS: *a swimmer climbs to the top of the diving board.*
271. MS: *two athletic young men at the top of the springboard.*
272. MS: *three boys at the top of the springboard. Two of them dive into the pool. The camera follows one of them into the water.*
   SERGIO (*voice-over*): Someone once said, man's intelligence and physical imperfection are due to the fact that he is the premature fetus of the monkey.
273. MS: *Sergio is lying on a lounge chair, with an unlit cigar in his mouth. He puts down the book he is reading, removes his sunglasses, and looks around him.*
274. MS: *three older women sit fully dressed in the shade and chat.*
275. LS: *a young woman in a bathing suit walks by the side of the pool.*
276. MS: *three young women sunbathing, seen partially from ground level near their feet.*
277. MS: *an attractive woman of about thirty-five is stepping into the pool with a little girl.*
   SERGIO (*voice-over*): There is an exquisite moment between thirty and thirty-five when Cuban women suddenly go from maturity to decay. They are fruits that rot at an amazing speed.
278. LS: *three somewhat flabby women in bathing suits walk by the edge of the pool.*

279. *Television screen with a succession of images:*[25] *a) Marilyn Monroe singing the closing bars of the song "Baby, I'm Through with Love." b) The entrance to the U.S. Naval Base at Guantánamo.*[26] *c) Cuban employees having their identification checked by U.S. military as they enter the Naval Base. d) An American plane flies over the base. e) A sign seen through a cyclone fence surrounding the base. The sign announces in English and Spanish:* DANGER　THIS AREA PATROLLED BY VICIOUS DOGS. *f) A U.S. soldier behind the cyclone fence wiggles his hips in a*

vaguely sexual gesture, waves at the camera, and throws rocks over the fence.

TV ANNOUNCER: And the domination of the Yankee empire having been ended by the Revolution, the United States now uses the Guantánamo Naval Base as an espionage center against Cuba. ICAIC cameramen film some of the provocations and violations committed by military personnel and counterrevolutionaries given asylum on the base.[27]

The television set is turned off.

280. LS: *Sergio walking along La Rampa, a major boulevard in Havana. He crosses the street and continues along the other sidewalk, as the camera tracks backward. He is wearing glasses, a jacket, and a tie. He moves into* MS *range. Superimposed:* ELENA

281. LS, *Sergio's* POV: *Elena stands at the foot of the stairs to El Mandarin Restaurant. The camera moves toward her.*

282. MS: *Sergio removes his glasses and stares at Elena as he moves closer to her.*

283. LS, *Sergio's* POV: *the camera moves into* MS *of Elena as it passes her.*

284. CU, *Elena's* POV: *the camera pans with Sergio as he climbs the stairs. He speaks to Elena as he passes her.*
SERGIO: You have beautiful knees.

285. CU, *Sergio's* POV: *Elena appraises Sergio out of the corner of her eye, then turns away, as he continues to climb the stairs.*

286. MS: *Sergio continues to climb, the camera tracking him from behind. When he reaches the restaurant doors, he turns to look at Elena.*

287. LS, *Sergio's* POV: *Elena seen from above inspecting her left knee. She looks up.*

288. MS: *Sergio looks at Elena and smiles.*

289. LS: *Elena, as in 287, shifts her eyes again and touches her hair self-consciously. She moves toward a nearby stairway.*

290. MS: *Sergio, as in 288, sees Elena walking away and decides against going into the restaurant. He follows her.*

291. LS, *Sergio's* POV: *Elena climbs to the top of the stairs, as the camera follows her. She moves to the right along the walkway, as two men who pass her stop and look back appreciatively.*

292. LS: *Sergio walks along the passageway to the right. He comes closer to the camera, into* MS *range.*

293. MS, *Sergio's* POV: *the camera moves toward Elena to hold her in* MS *as she walks along. She stops momentarily as Sergio speaks.*
SERGIO (*off*): Do you want to have dinner with me?
ELENA: Are you crazy?
SERGIO (*off*): No, it's just that I don't like to eat alone.

Elena walks away. The camera tilts down to her legs, then up again, holding in MS. *She stops in front of a shop window. The camera moves forward to hold her in* CU.

SERGIO (*off*): What are you doing here? Are you waiting for someone?
She nods without looking at him.
SERGIO (*off*): Your boyfriend?
Elena looks at him flirtatiously but with mock disapproval, then walks away again, only to stand at a nearby railing overlooking the street.
ELENA: Are you crazy?
SERGIO (*off*): At your age it's dangerous to be alone around here.
The camera follows Elena, moving to show her from the side in CU.
ELENA: You are crazy!
The camera pans left to show a dwarf passing by; he is carrying a contrabass. The camera then pans back to Elena who looks toward Sergio. They both laugh.
SERGIO (*off*): No, look, really. I swear I can't digest properly when I eat alone.
ELENA: I'm waiting for someone from ICAIC who called me about a job.
SERGIO (*off*): From ICAIC?
ELENA: Yes, the Film Institute. They're going to give me a film test.
The camera tracks with Elena, holding her in CU *profile, as she retraces her steps, walking now to the left.*
SERGIO (*off*): Oh, really. I have a friend who's a director there. He's pretty important.
ELENA: At ICAIC?
SERGIO (*off*): Yes. If you want, tomorrow morning I'll take you there and have you meet him.
She looks at him disbelievingly.
ELENA: What time is it?
SERGIO (*off*): Around six-thirty.
ELENA: He's late. I'm sure he's not coming. (*Elena stops again and stares down at the street.*)
SERGIO (*off*): So, are you coming?
She glances at him, turns back to the street, then looks at him again.
294. MCU: *a Chinese waiter in a restaurant. He finishes taking the order and starts moving away from their table.*
SERGIO (*off*): Oh, look . . .
295. MCU: *Sergio orders something else. He looks across the table.*
SERGIO: But first bring me a dry martini.
296. MCU: *Elena sitting across the table.*
SERGIO (*off*): Why don't you have something to drink before dinner?
ELENA: I can't drink. They're giving me shots for my nerves.
Look . . . (*She stares at him for a moment, then shows him her arm.*

The camera focuses on Sergio's hand traveling along Elena's arm and trying to hold her hand while he looks at the scars left by the injections.)

297. MCU: *Elena, unsmiling, removes her arm.*
298. MCU: *Sergio, as in 295, looks at Elena and smiles.*
     SERGIO: Why do you want to be in films?
299. MCU: *Elena, as in 297.*
     ELENA: Because I'm tired of always being the same. That way I can be someone else without people thinking I'm crazy. I want to be able to unfold my personality.
300. MCU: *Sergio, as in 295. He tries to sound serious.*
     SERGIO: But all those characters in theater and film are like broken records.
301. MCU: *Elena, as in 297. She is still distracted, but listening to Sergio.*
     SERGIO (*off*): The only thing an actress does is to repeat the same gestures and the same words thousands of times. The same gestures and the same words . . . the same gestures and the same words . . .

302–307. *Looped clips with original soundtrack, each with very different musical accompaniment.*
302. LS, *from above: a man and a woman lying on a blanket at a beach. The man has only trousers on, the woman is in a bathing suit. They are embracing, and the man begins to roll on top of the woman (the sequence repeated four times).*
303. LS: *a naked woman seen from the back stepping into the bathtub in a luxurious apartment (the sequence repeated three times).*
304. MS: *the legs of a woman removing her underpants (the sequence repeated three times).*
305. MS: *an old man fondling the breasts of a beautiful woman wearing a low-cut evening gown who is sitting on his lap.*
306. MS: *a woman removing her bra and whirling around to music, as part of a striptease (the sequence repeated twice).*
307. MS: *Brigitte Bardot and a male actor performing a love scene in bed and speaking the following lines:*
     BARDOT (*dubbed in English, with Spanish subtitle*): Don't waste your time, I'm not giving in.
     MAN (*dubbed in English*): Is that so?
     The camera slowly closes in. They look at each other for a moment and then start kissing passionately.
308. LS: *Sergio, Elena, the film director, the director of photography, and an editor in a small screening room at ICAIC.*[28] *They have just finished watching shots 302–307. Elena combs her hair.*

SERGIO: Where did you get the clips?

DIRECTOR: They showed up one day. These are the cuts the commission made.

SERGIO: What commission?

DIRECTOR OF PHOTOGRAPHY: The Film Review Commission.[29] The one that we used to have before the Revolution. Those are the cuts they made before showing the films.

EDITOR: They said they were offensive to morals.

DIRECTOR: Morals, good breeding, all that . . .

SERGIO: Yes, I remember that. It looks like those people also had their moral preoccupations.

DIRECTOR: At least they worried about keeping up appearances.

Elena yawns.

309. LS: *they leave the screening room, Sergio and the director talking. The camera tracks backward, preceding them down the hall. Elena follows them, paying no attention to their conversation.*

SERGIO: What are you going to do with them?

DIRECTOR: I'm thinking of using them.

SERGIO: In a film?

DIRECTOR: Yes. It'll be a "collage" that'll have a bit of everything.

SERGIO: It will have to have some meaning.

DIRECTOR: It's coming along. You'll see.

SERGIO: Will they approve it?

DIRECTOR: Yes. (*The director ushers Sergio and Elena into an office in the Actor's Department.*)

310. MCU: *Elena, as she is being interviewed by an employee in the Actor's Department.*

EMPLOYEE (*off*): What's your experience? Have you worked in the theater, T.V., or something?

ELENA: No, it seems that I haven't had any luck.

EMPLOYEE (*off*): Have you studied with anybody?

ELENA: I was going to take some classes once, but . . . I didn't.

EMPLOYEE (*off*): Well, write all that on the form.[30]

311. LS: *Elena and the employee at a desk in a small room. Sergio and the director are also present.*

ELENA: Aren't you going to give me an audition today? I can sing, too.

Sergio and the director look at one another.

312. MCU: *Elena, as in 310.*

ELENA (*breaking ineptly into song*): This sadness rejects oblivion/Like darkness rejects light . . .

313. MCU: *the employee looks at Elena with a puzzled expression.*

ELENA (*off; singing*): . . . I hope destiny lets you return . . .

314. MCU: *Sergio contemplates the situation, a cigar in his mouth. He raises his eyebrows ironically in resignation.*
ELENA (*off; singing*): . . . one day, to remember . . .

315. MS: *Sergio and Elena walk through an old residential neighborhood. They look at each other and smile. The camera tracks backward to hold them in* MS *as they talk. Sergio looks slightly amused.*
SERGIO: If you say so . . . and you?
ELENA: No.
SERGIO: Really? . . . Look, what a nice house. Do you like it?
They pass by the camera, then turn to stop in front of a seemingly abandoned house. Elena shrugs.
ELENA: I don't know.
Sergio stares at Elena. He strokes her hair and her neck. She lets him do that for a moment, then takes his hand to prevent him from going on.
ELENA: Don't think that we'll get to anything.
Sergio watches her with irritation as she walks away. Then he follows her. She pretends to be annoyed. As if playing, he takes her hand; she smiles and becomes playful. She pulls at his hand and forces him to cross the street at a run. The camera slows its movement so that they walk away in LS.

316. MCU: *Sergio and Elena on the sidewalk in front of his apartment building. The camera holds on Elena, with Sergio at the right of the frame turned toward her.*
SERGIO: Look, there's where I live. Come on. What's the matter?
ELENA: I don't . . .
SERGIO: Don't what?
ELENA: And your wife?
SERGIO: Didn't I tell you I was divorced, that my wife left me?
ELENA: Well, even then . . .
SERGIO: Even then, what?
ELENA: What'll the neighbors think?
SERGIO: Well, if you don't trust me . . .
ELENA: It isn't that.
SERGIO: What is it then?
ELENA: Well. You go up first. I'll come in afterwards.
Sergio gives her a doubtful look, then makes up his mind and walks toward the building.
SERGIO: It's the top floor, apartment K-L.
Elena watches him walking away.

317. LS: *Sergio walks rapidly toward the building doors.*[31]

318. MS: *Sergio enters his apartment whistling a tune. He leaves the door ajar. He goes into the living room and inspects it. He places a magazine*

that is lying on the floor in a rack. He picks up a bottle of brandy and a glass, then turns on the radio. He removes his jacket and looks at himself in the mirror, rearranges his hair, and rubs his hands together in anticipation, sticking out his tongue. Looking very excited, he carries the bottle and glass into the kitchen. (The radio begins to play Renaissance music for lute.)[32]

319. MS: *Sergio in the kitchen as the doorbell rings. He puts down the bottle and goes to answer the door, the camera tracking with him. It is Elena, looking frightened. They do not speak. She glances around the apartment pretending she is not interested, while he watches her. The camera tracks backward to precede them as they enter the living room, with Elena in* CU, *Sergio, behind her, in* MS.

SERGIO: Make yourself comfortable. I'll make some coffee.

320. MS: *Sergio steps into the kitchen and begins to prepare coffee.*

321. MS: *Elena sits down on the living room couch and relaxes; a wall hung with oil paintings is visible behind her. She gets up, with the camera following her movements. She walks to the radio and changes stations, picking up a popular song by Elena Burke.*[33] *Several photographs are on top of the radio; two are bridal pictures of Laura. Elena looks toward the photographs and a mirror and pats her hair. Sergio returns with the coffee and begins talking about the photographs on the radio.*

SERGIO: They're my parents, and that's Laura. They left the same day.

(The camera follows Sergio as he walks away from Elena and sits on the couch. He places the coffee tray on the table in front of him.)

ELENA (*off*): And you?

SERGIO: What about me?

322. MS: *Elena remains near the pictures and the radio set, touching various objects on top of the console. She turns toward Sergio.*

ELENA: Aren't you going to leave?

SERGIO (*off*): No, I'm fine right here.

ELENA: Are you a revolutionary?

SERGIO (*off; laughing*): What do you think?[34]

The camera follows Elena as she comes to sit on the couch with Sergio. She now seems in a playful mood.

ELENA: That you're neither a revolutionary nor a counterrevolutionary.

SERGIO: Then, what am I?

ELENA: Nothing. You're nothing. (*Elena stands up while Sergio remains on the couch looking thoughtful.*)

323. MS: *Elena stands close to a window leafing through a magazine. Sergio approaches her. She looks at him for a moment, then walks away. The camera pans to hold her in* CU.

ELENA: They'll send you things from there.

SERGIO: What for?

ELENA: Nice shoes. What do I know about it! They could even send a car over if they wanted to.

324. MCU: *Sergio smiles.*

SERGIO: Hey, you know Laura had a figure like yours.

325. MCU: *Elena, as at the end of 323. She looks toward him cautiously, even suspiciously. She is paying attention.*

SERGIO (*off*): If you want I can show you some of her dresses.

326. MCU: *Sergio, as in 324.*

SERGIO: If you like them you can keep them.

327. MCU: *Elena, as at the end of 323.*

ELENA: But . . .

328. MCU: *Sergio, as in 324.*

SERGIO: Look at them anyway.

329. MS: *Sergio waits in the bedroom for Elena, examining some of Laura's dresses that he has thrown on the bed. He straightens up and walks to the window.*

330. MLS: *Elena steps out of the bathroom in one of Laura's dresses. She looks very attractive.*

331. MS: *Sergio, as at the end of 329. He looks at Elena, pleased by what he sees. The camera follows him as he moves to her side.*

SERGIO: It looks good on you. Take a look.

ELENA: You'll have to button me up.

She stands in front of the mirror while, behind her, Sergio buttons the dress. MS *of both of them looking at each other's reflection in the mirror.*

They smile. She stops smiling and turns to face him. The camera shifts away from the mirror and includes Sergio in the frame. They look intently at one another, then they embrace and kiss for a long time. After having aroused Sergio, Elena disengages herself from his arms as if she suddenly feels trapped.

332. MCU: *Sergio watches Elena move away. He follows and leaves the frame at the right.*

333. MCU: *Elena lowers her head and covers her face with her hands as if she were going to cry. Sergio enters the frame from the left. He looks at her and does nothing. Since she does not move, he gradually approaches her. He puts his hands on her shoulders and touches her gently. Suddenly, she turns and kisses him. They sit down on the bed. He slips his hand through the opening at the back of her dress and unbuttons it hurriedly.*[35]

334. CU: *Elena draws back frightened and straightens her dress.*

335. MCU: *Sergio has fallen off the bed. While still lying on the floor he starts kissing her legs.*

336. MCU: *Elena pushes him with a pillow.*

337. MCU: *Sergio falls again.*

338. MS, *Sergio's* POV: *Elena laughs and slips off the other side of the bed to the floor. She grins back at Sergio.*

339. MCU: *Sergio moves purposefully across the bed toward the camera into* CU.

340. CU, *Sergio's* POV: *the camera moves in on Elena to hold her in* ECU. *Smiling, she sticks out her tongue at Sergio.*

341. CU: *Sergio, lying across the bed, leans over and kisses her. Elena draws back, kisses him, draws back until Sergio loses his balance, since his upper body is now stretched so far beyond the edge of the bed.*

342. CU: *Sergio looks sternly at her from the floor.*

343. CU: *Elena giggles and suddenly moves out of the frame as she heads toward the bedroom door.*

344. MCU: *the camera pans with Sergio as he reaches the bedroom door first and blocks the way. He and Elena are now standing beside the mirror on the back of the door. In the mirror she is seen to withdraw to the other end of the room while he slowly follows her, now in* LS. *She is laughing and she wiggles her fingers in her ears.*

345. MS: *Elena stands besides the curtains. Sergio moves into the shot and embraces her. They fall on the bed; at first she resists him, then they kiss. He starts to undo her clothes.*

346. MS: *the bedroom window. It is sunset. The sound of Elena's sobbing can be heard.*

SERGIO (*off*): Come on, baby, don't cry anymore.

The camera pans to an MS *of Sergio sitting on the edge of the bed. He*

has just put on his shoes. He gets up and moves toward Elena who is standing in front of the dressing table.
SERGIO: Please don't . . .
ELENA: You've ruined me!
Elena moves toward the bed, continuing to sob. The camera stays with Sergio in MS.
SERGIO: Who, me? Take it easy. We haven't done anything wrong.
  (*Sergio approaches her once more, strokes her back, and tries to calm her down.*)
ELENA: What am I going to tell my mother?
SERGIO: Don't tell her anything.
Elena bursts into tears. Sergio, exasperated, stands up and moves away, with the camera following him in MS.
347. MS: *the radio in the living room is still on. It is dark. The radio is tuned to Radio Reloj Nacional. First the station identification, then the time and the news are heard. Sergio and Elena leave the bedroom and walk toward the apartment door in* MS. *Sergio is carrying Laura's dresses on his arm. Elena is somewhat calmer. Sergio disappears into another room, then reappears stuffing the dresses into a shopping bag. He offers her the shopping bag. At first she refuses to take it, but then she accepts it.*
SERGIO: If you wait a minute, I'll go with you.
ELENA (*with downcast eyes*): No, I want to be alone.
SERGIO: Well . . .

They do not kiss. Sergio opens the door for her, and Elena slips out.

SERGIO (*before closing the door*): Well . . . give me a call.

He finally shuts the door and remains thoughtful for a moment. He lights a cigarette and smokes. The radio is still on; now it carries news of subversive activities in Venezuela. Sergio shuts off the radio and moves toward the balcony. The camera continues to follow him in MS *until he reaches the balcony's glass doors.* CU *of his profile, wet with perspiration, as he stares out at the city by night.*

SERGIO (*on the tape*): Thanks to that you've stopped being a Cuban slob, and have become a beautiful, exciting woman.

348. *The camera pans slowly around Sergio's bedroom; in contrast to 347, it is now daylight.*

LAURA (*on the tape*): You're unbearable! I never know when you're serious and when you're making fun of me.

SERGIO (*on the tape*): A little of both, darling.

LAURA (*on the tape*): Well, do a number on your little mother, darling!

SERGIO (*on the tape*): Yeah, yeah.

LAURA (*on the tape*): Go to hell!

SERGIO (*on the tape*): That's very good, very good!

LAURA (*on the tape*): Are you crazy, you idiot? Let me go, let me go! I can't stand you! I can't stand living here any longer. I can't stand the heat, the sweat. . . . You sweat too much, you stink. . . . Let me go!

SERGIO (*on the tape*): Do you know that everything you said is being taped?

LAURA (*on the tape*): What?

SERGIO (*on the tape*): Everything. Word for word. It'll be a lot of fun later, when you hear it.

LAURA (*on the tape*): You're a monster! You're sick! Give it to me!

SERGIO (*on the tape*): Watch out! You're going to break it! Let go!

LAURA (*on the tape*): Let go of me!

SERGIO (*on the tape*): No, no. What are you doing?

LAURA (*voice-over*): Give it to me!

The camera suddenly pans across the room to a CU *of the tape recorder. Laura's hands are seen trying to break it, but Sergio prevents this from happening. As she struggles, she is pushed to the floor; the camera follows her in* MS. *Laura is wearing a diaphanous white nightgown. She gets up from the floor, extremely upset, and staggers backward, away from Sergio, with the camera following her. When she reaches the other side of the bedroom, she bends over, covering her face with her hand.*

LAURA (*hysterically*): Let me go! We're through! I never want to see you again! I'm leaving. I'm going alone. I don't want you to come with me. I can't take one more day here!

SERGIO (*off*): So, you want to leave me?

LAURA: I don't care. Find another woman who can put up with you! I
   can't.
SERGIO: (*off*): Didn't you use to say . . .
The camera circles with Laura as she moves around the bedroom.
LAURA: I won't be a guinea pig for your tricks and little games.
SERGIO (*off*): My little games?
LAURA: I'm going to live my own life! I'm getting old! Do you hear!
   Old! I'm going alone! I'm leaving! I don't want to be with you! I'm
   leaving! (*She cries hysterically, and falls upon the bed. The camera
   moves to hold her face in* ECU.)[36]
Fade out.

349. MCU: *Sergio in his undershirt brushing his teeth. He looks at his reflec-
   tion in the bathroom mirror. The doorbell rings. Without hurrying too
   much he goes toward the door, stopping to put his trousers on. The
   camera follows him in* MS.
350. MS: *Sergio opens the apartment door.*
   SERGIO: What's this?
   *Elena kisses him and steps through the door. She is wearing one of
   Laura's dresses and she is in a sunny mood, humming a tune.*
   ELENA (*singing*): Before your lips confirmed/That you love me,/I al-
      ready knew it,/I already knew it.
   *She proceeds to the living room while the camera holds on Sergio, who
   looks extremely puzzled.*
   SERGIO: Are you all right now?
351. MS: *Elena in the living room, standing beside the glass doors to the
   balcony.*
   ELENA: Who, me?
   SERGIO (*off*): I thought you were feeling bad last night.
   *Elena suddenly becomes serious, then she recovers her happy manner.
   The camera pans with her as she crosses the room and sits down on the
   couch.*
   ELENA: I was, but I'm all right now. I came to see how you were. If you
      like I can help you make lunch and clean the house.
352. MCU: *Sergio, still silent and looking tense.*
353. MS: *Elena, on the couch, as at the end of 351.*
   ELENA: What's wrong with you?
   Sergio enters from the right and sits next to her.
   SERGIO: Nothing at all.
   *Elena moves closer to caress him. She feels his coldness, so she walks
   over to the radio, while singing theatrically. The camera follows her in*
   MS.

ELENA: Go on and say it,/It couldn't last,/It's all finished,/It couldn't be,/You don't love me anymore.

354. MCU: *Sergio bursts into laughter.*

355. MS: *Elena is smiling. She starts to inspect the phonograph records stored in the radio console and takes out one by Elena Burke.*

ELENA: Do you like the song?

SERGIO (*off*): Then all that crying last night?

Sergio enters from the left. Elena stops smiling for a moment.

ELENA: Don't make fun of me.

SERGIO: I'm not making fun of you.

Elena has another abrupt change of mood. She is frivolous once more.

ELENA: You just don't have any feelings. Besides . . . (*Singing.*) You don't have to criticize/The way I live/If all I have now . . .

Sergio silences her with a kiss. The frame freezes.

356–371. *Still photographs of Elena at different moments in the previous scenes (in reverse order of time: in Sergio's bedroom, in the living room, at ICAIC, at the restaurant, on La Rampa).*

SERGIO (*voice-over; thoughtfully*): One of the things that really gets me about people is their inability to sustain a feeling, an idea, without falling apart. Elena turned out to be totally inconsistent. It's pure deterioration, as Ortega would say. She doesn't connect one thing with another. That's one of the signs of underdevelopment: the inability to connect things . . .

372. MS: *faces—mainly women's—crossing in front of the camera.*

SERGIO (*voice-over*): . . . to accumulate experience and to develop. . . . It is difficult here to produce a woman shaped by sentiments and culture.

373. LS: *people strolling in a park. The camera tracks with the crowd until it holds one woman in* MS.[37]

SERGIO (*voice-over*): It's a bland environment. Cubans waste their talents adapting themselves to every moment. People aren't consistent. And they always need somebody to do their thinking for them.[38]

374. LS: *a billboard displaying Fidel's face and the words "Playa Girón." It is seen from a car that is moving along the avenue that leads to the airport. The car passes the billboard and leaves it behind. The camera pans to a* CU *of Pablo who is sitting in the back seat, then pans to a* CU *of Sergio in the front seat.*

PABLO: I hope to see you soon over there, Sergio.

SERGIO: I don't think so. I already know the States; on the other hand, what's going to happen here is a mystery to me.

375. *Pablo and Sergio walking together through the airport lobby. Pablo is on*

crutches; he looks tense and angry. The camera tracks backward, holding them in a low angle MS.

PABLO: This is no mystery for anybody, Sergio. Everybody knows what's going to happen here.

SERGIO: Well, I don't. I really don't.

PABLO: Well, look. I can tell you that now it's not going to be like the Bay of Pigs.

SERGIO: Maybe, but that might turn out to be interesting.

PABLO: That's true, but when it happens I want to be on the other side.

SERGIO: You'll be safer. And you'll also be able to see old friends.

PABLO: I know what you're driving at.

SERGIO: Yes?

PABLO: Yes. But there are also decent people among them. Did you hear me? Really decent people.

SERGIO: At least that's what they say.

PABLO: I don't know if they say that or not. I've got a clean conscience.

SERGIO: You, yes.

376. MS: *Pablo is in the passengers' waiting room, seen through a glass partition and over Sergio's shoulder. He approaches the partition, gesturing to Sergio and trying to tell him something. Sergio is unable to understand.*

377. CU: *Sergio, seen through the partition, still unable to make out what Pablo is saying.*

378. MS: *Pablo gesturing, as at the end of 376.*

379. CU: *Sergio, as in 377. He gives up trying to understand.*

SERGIO (*voice-over*): Was I like him, before? It's possible. Although it may destroy me, this revolution is my revenge against the stupid Cuban bourgeoisie. Against idiots like Pablo.

380. MS: *Pablo, as in 378. He is joined by his wife and they both say goodbye to Sergio as they are called to go on board.*

SERGIO (*voice-over*): I realize that Pablo is not Pablo, but my own life.

381. MS: *Sergio, as in 377, waving to Pablo and then walking away from the camera.*

SERGIO (*voice-over*): Everything I don't want to be.

382. CU: *Sergio's back. He is facing the airport runway. The camera revolves around him to show his face, which is now very grave.*

SERGIO (*voice-over*): It's good to see them leaving. Just as if I vomited them up. I keep my mind clear. It's a disagreeable clarity, an emptiness. I know what's happening to me but I can't avoid it. He, Laura, and everybody . . .[39]

383. MS: *Sergio is walking along a shady street in an old residential district, the camera following him.[40] Two Asians coming out of a stately mansion*

cross in front of him. They are elegantly dressed, possibly diplomats. The camera pans to follow them as a chauffeur ushers them into an expensive car.

384. MS: *Sergio, his back to the camera, stares at them. He turns to face the house from which they came. The camera pans to follow Sergio's gaze and holds on a* LS *of the courtyard of the house.*
Dissolve.

385. LS: *the formal garden of the house.*
SERGIO (*voice-over*): Francisco de la Cuesta used to live here.
Dissolve.

386. MCU: *the camera pans over the front of a luxury car.*
SERGIO (voice-over): We were eight or ten years old.
Dissolve.

387. ELS: *two boys are running along the terrace above the garden.*
Dissolve.

388. LS: *the camera pans across a child's room, showing all kinds of toys. The camera then holds on an open door and looks out into the formal garden.*
SERGIO (*voice-over*): Where is Francisco now? Does he remember what games we used to play?
The camera shows in ELS *two boys in the background, on the porch, playing an unidentifiable game.*
SERGIO (*voice-over*): I try to and I can't.
Fade to white.

389. MS: *Sergio strolls along the sidewalk, with the camera tracking ahead of him. He looks to one side.*

390. LS: *the façade of what used to be La Salle School. Boarding students are streaming out. They all wear military uniforms.*
Dissolve.

391. LS: *the schoolyard as it used to be: priests and children crowding the yard during recess.*

392. MS: *a young priest playing with a group of boys in the schoolyard.*

393. MS: *the priest and the boys from another angle.*

394. MCU: *a notebook in which a boy is drawing a naked woman.*

395. MS, *high angle: Sergio as a twelve-year-old in the classroom snatching a notebook from the boy sitting in front of him to see what he has drawn.*

396. MCU: *the teacher, a priest, standing at the blackboard, catches Sergio with the notebook.*
SERGIO (*voice-over*): When we were at school, the priests were always right. They were the ones who had the power then. I hadn't done anything, but it was all the same.

397. MS: *both Sergio and the other student are being punished. They stand at the blackboard, their faces to the board, their backs to the camera.*

SERGIO (*voice-over*): I understood then, for the first time, the relationship between Justice and Power.

398. MS: *both students strolling along at night in a red-light district. The camera tracks alongside them. The other boy, Armando, looks very self-confident. Sergio seems somewhat frightened. Armando leads the way into a brothel.*

SERGIO (*voice-over*): Armando's father was a freethinker. Every week he'd give him a peso so he could go to a whorehouse. He took me for the first time . . .

399. CU: *the camera focuses on the faces of two half-dressed prostitutes inside the brothel. Armando moves into the background with one woman and a fat prostitute leads Sergio through a narrow, dingy corridor and into a room. The camera follows her in* MS.

SERGIO (*voice-over*): . . . to a fat woman who charged fifty cents. He told her to be nice to me.

400. MCU: *the camera looks down on the fat prostitute lying on a bed. She has removed her blouse and is wearing only a brassiere.*

401. MS: *Sergio is undressing. He puts his jacket on a chair.*

402. MCU: *Sergio and the prostitute naked on the bed, lying next to one another and seen from the side. She seems to ask him what the matter is. He shrugs his shoulders, then takes some money from his trousers and gives it to her. He pulls himself up and leaves the bed and the frame at the right.*

SERGIO (*voice-over*): But I couldn't do anything with her. I had to find another.

403. *The camera pans along a wall with peeling paint, focuses on a bedside lamp and then, in a high angle* MS, *on Sergio in bed with another prostitute.*

SERGIO (*voice-over*): After that I went every week.

404. MS: *Sergio browsing through some shelves in a bookstore. He picks up a book (*Lolita *by Nabokov) and leafs through it.*

SERGIO (*voice-over*): All of a sudden I discovered that Elena didn't think the way I did. I had expected more of her. I thought she was more complex and interesting. I always try to live like a European.

405. LS: *Elena, standing in the bookstore, is looking bored while she waits for Sergio to buy some books.*

SERGIO (*voice-over*): And Elena forces me to feel underdeveloped at every step.

406. LS: *Elena and Sergio are attending an exhibition of paintings by Acosta León at Havana's Bellas Artes Museum.*[41] *Sergio is studying one of the paintings. He gestures in Elena's direction and starts walking until he leaves the frame at the right. Elena enters the frame from the left, showing some reluctance, then leaves at the right.*

407. MS: *Elena is not paying much attention to Sergio's remarks about one of the paintings.*
    SERGIO (*voice-over*): I also tried to change Elena, just like I tried with Laura . . . but she doesn't understand anything. She has another world in her head, very different from mine.
    Elena is evidently not listening to what Sergio is telling her; she straightens his tie knot.
408. LS: *a different part of the gallery. Sergio stares at Elena from the background. Elena, in* MS *range, looks bored.*
    SERGIO (*voice-over*): She doesn't see me.

409. MS: *The head of an impala gazelle hanging from a wall. Superimposed:* A TROPICAL ADVENTURE. *The camera tilts down to show in* MS *a group of Soviet and Czech tourists. A guide is explaining and the interpreters translate.[42] The camera pans over the group of tourists, then holds on Sergio who stands at the back of the group. He then shifts his gaze away from the guide. They are all gathered in Ernest Hemingway's house, near Havana, which was turned into a museum after the writer's death.*
    GUIDE: This gazelle was shot by Hemingway during his last trip to Africa in 1953. He made that trip with Mary, his fourth wife. This is one of the fastest gazelles in Africa. . . .

410. LS: *Elena walks aimlessly through the living room. Sergio enters the frame in* MS, *his back to the camera, and stares at her.*
GUIDE (*off*): Besides being very fast, it's constantly jumping.
Elena leaves the frame and Sergio turns and concentrates his attention on the exhibits.
SERGIO (*voice-over*): He said he killed so as not to kill himself . . .
411. LS: *a corner of the living room: two of Hemingway's armchairs, and between them a table filled with bottles of liquor.*
SERGIO (*voice-over*): . . . but in the end he couldn't resist the temptation.
412. MS: *Sergio approaches the tourists, who have formed a semicircle around the guide. They are now looking at photographs of the Spanish Civil War. He peers over their shoulders.*
GUIDE: . . . some shots taken by Hemingway himself and some by Robert Capa.[43] We know Hemingway made several trips to Spain as a war correspondent . . .
413–423. *A series of photographs by Robert Capa of the Spanish Civil War.*
GUIDE: . . . later he joined the International Brigade. (*The voice is replaced by music.*)
424. MS: *Elena, her back to the camera. She crosses behind Sergio who is looking at some books and she runs her finger down his back. The camera pans with her as she moves away, glancing around the room and occasionally fingering an object.*
ELENA: Is this where Mr. Way used to live? I don't see anything so special. Books and dead animals. Just like the American house in Preston.[44] The same furniture and the same American smell.
SERGIO (*off*): What is an American smell?
ELENA: I don't know. You feel it.
SERGIO (*off*): Which do you like best, the smell of the Russians or the smell of the Americans?
Elena crosses beside Sergio once more.
ELENA: Leave me alone. I don't know anything about politics. (*She tweaks his nose and leaves the frame at the right.*)
425. MS: *Elena leans out of a window that looks into the garden. She is posing for a foreigner who is taking her picture.*
RUSSIAN TOURIST (*off; in Russian*): Please!
426. MCU: *the tourist, his camera raised, taking another picture.*
427–429. *Three stills of Elena posing in the window, slight variations of 425.*
430. MS: *a group of tourists looking at Elena.*
SERGIO (*voice-over*): The tropics. That's what backward countries are for: to kill animals, to fish, and to sunbathe.
431. CU: *the Russian tourist, as in 426, taking his last picture.*
RUSSIAN TOURIST (*in Spanish*): Many thanks!

432. MS: *Elena, as in 425. Now she looks in both directions, searching for Sergio.*

  SERGIO (*voice-over*): There you have her: the (*in English*) beautiful Cuban señorita.

443. *The camera pans slowly over Hemingway's desk, cluttered with many objects. It then pans up to hold in MS on Sergio, who is reading a book. The soundtrack identifies it as the Hemingway story "The Short Happy Life of Francis Macomber." The pan continues up the wall where, above Sergio, is an enormous buffalo head. To one side, a shotgun.*

  SERGIO (*voice-over; reading*): "You know I don't think I'd ever be afraid of anything again," Macomber said to Wilson. "Something happened in me after we first saw the buff and started after him. Like a dam bursting. It was pure excitement." (*Sergio raises his head and looks at the buffalo. He puts down the book, walks toward the gun and touches it.*)

  SERGIO (*voice-over*): As if running after a buffalo was enough to conquer fear. Anyway, there are no buffalos in Cuba. I'm an idiot. He conquered the fear of death but he couldn't stand the fear of life, of time, of a world that was beginning to get too large for him. (*He walks away from the gun, but turns, hearing Elena approaching.*)

434. MCU: *Elena, irritated, is looking for Sergio.*

  ELENA: Why did you leave?

  SERGIO (*off*): You were amusing yourself.

  Elena turns her back on him.

  ELENA (*singing*): Jealousy . . .

  SERGIO (*off*): Oh, please!

  She turns to face him.

  ELENA: Does it bother you?

435. LS: *Sergio continues to wander around the room, examining objects. He looks over his shoulder at Elena.*

  SERGIO: No, it doesn't.

  ELENA (*off*): You don't care.

  SERGIO: About what?

436. MS: *Elena, as at the end of 434.*

  ELENA: Me. Nothing matters to you.

  SERGIO (*off*): You're the one who doesn't care.

  ELENA (*turning away*): What?

437. LS: *Sergio, as in 435.*

  SERGIO: You don't care about anything.

438. MS: *Elena walks toward Hemingway's typewriter and examines it. She doesn't know how to answer. In order to do something, she picks up a pencil.*

439. MCU: *Sergio, now watching and listening to Elena.*

440. MS: *the guide, who has entered the room, speaks to Elena.*
The camera pans from the guide across a table with a typewriter to hold on Elena, in profile.
GUIDE: This is Hemingway's private study. He could always be found working in front of this old typewriter, standing up, with bare feet.
Elena tries to show interest in the guide's recitation.
GUIDE (*off*): He never sat down to write, nor did he wear shoes. He'd get up very early and would work until eleven or eleven-thirty. Very few people could come into this room and I was one of the few. I would walk . . .

441. MS: *Sergio, as in 439.*
GUIDE (*off*): . . . very quietly. The rest of the day Hemingway would spend his time . . . (*The guide's voice fades away.*)

442. MCU: *photograph of the guide; the photo illustrates a magazine article on Hemingway.*

443. MS: *another photograph of the guide flanked by Hemingway and his wife.*
SERGIO (*voice-over*): His name is René Villarreal. Hemingway found him when he was a little boy playing in the streets of San Francisco de Paula.[45]

444. LS: *the square and church of San Francisco de Paula.*
SERGIO (*voice-over*): I read that somewhere.

445. MS: *photograph of Hemingway and Villarreal looking into a cockfighting ring.*

446. MS: *a photograph of Hemingway seated, with Villarreal standing near him.*
SERGIO (*voice-over*): He molded him to his needs. The faithful servant and the great lord. The colonialist and Gunga Din.

447. LS: *a street in San Francisco de Paula. The camera tracks over a row of shabby houses.*
SERGIO (*voice-over*): Hemingway must've been unbearable.

448. ELS: *the camera slowly pans over the view from the tower on Hemingway's estate. There are green fields and small cottages in the foreground, smokestacks on the horizon.*
SERGIO (*voice-over*): This was his refuge, his tower, his island in the tropics.

449. CU: *Sergio stands in the tower, gazing out at the view.*

450–455. *Several* MCU *shots of Hemingway's belongings kept in the house and in the tower.*

450. *Hunting hats on a shelf, above them mounted animal heads and a photograph of Hemingway displaying a large game fish as a trophy.*

451. *Racks of hunting guns mounted on the wall; above them are mounted animal heads.*

452. *A bookcase with bullfight sketches on the wall above.*
453. *Another taller bookcase. On the wall beside it is a large poster announcing a bullfight.*
454. *Hemingway's typewriter, with a writing clipboard propped up next to it.*
455. *A book on a desk with a pair of Hemingway's eyeglasses placed on top.*
    SERGIO (*voice-over*): Boots for hunting in Africa, American furniture, Spanish photographs, magazines and books in English, a bullfight poster.
456. *The camera pans over several miscellaneous objects on a shelf (animal skulls, a barometer, a portable radio) and holds in* MCU *on a photograph of the yacht* Pilar.[46]
    SERGIO (*voice-over*): Cuba never really interested him. Here he could find refuge, entertain his friends, write in English, and fish in the Gulf Stream.
457. MS: *Sergio seen from behind looking out a tower window. The camera pans with him as he walks from window to window in the tower. He stops and looks down toward the ground outside.*
458. ELS, *Sergio's* POV: *Elena and the guide have left the house and proceed down a flagstone walk. The guide is explaining to her as they go.*
    GUIDE: In 1947 many journalists came to see Hemingway in order to interview him.
459. CU: *Sergio hides behind the windowcase and listens.*
    GUIDE (*off*): They never left him in peace to write in this room.
460. ELS: *the guide keeps talking to Elena, as in 458. She is not paying too much attention.*
    GUIDE: She thought that by building that study . . .
461. LS: *the tower seen from the outside, as if from the guide's point of view.*
    GUIDE (*off*) . . . he would be able to isolate himself and she tried to make it as comfortable as possible.
462. CU: *Sergio, as in 459.*
    GUIDE (*off*): She had ten double windows put in so that the air could circulate and he could . . .
463. ELS: *Elena and the guide, as in 458.*
    GUIDE: . . . enjoy the view . . . simple and comfortable furniture . . . *Suddenly Elena believes that she has spotted Sergio in some corner of the garden. She leaves the guide in mid-sentence and goes back up the walk.*
    ELENA: Sergio! Sergio!
464. MS: *Sergio watches her from his hiding place, moving from window to window to follow her movements.*
465. ELS, *Sergio's* POV: *Elena runs onto the front terrace of the house, which borders on the driveway. Two cars filled with tourists are getting ready to leave. Elena runs toward them to ask if anyone has seen Sergio. When nobody has, she is undecided what to do.*

466. CU: *Sergio looks on, seen from outside a tower window.*
467. ELS: *Elena, as in 465. She calls again.*
    ELENA: Sergio!
    The cars with the tourists start. Elena, now by herself, makes up her mind and calls to one of the drivers.
    ELENA: Wait a minute! (*She runs down to the driveway, climbs in the car, and leaves with the tourists.*)
468. CU: *Sergio, as in 466. He watches Elena leave. He gazes at the view for some time and then withdraws from the window.*

469.[47] *Screen title (in white letters over a black background) that reads:*

ROUND TABLE   LITERATURE AND UNDERDEVELOPMENT

René Depestre   Gianni Toti

Edmundo Desnoes   David Viñas

Moderator: Salvador Bueno

Tuesday at 7   Salón de Actos

ENTRANCE FREE

DEPESTRE (*voice-over*): Culture, in an underdeveloped country, is the sometimes painful and costly operation . . .
470. LS: *part of the audience at the meeting, seen from the side. Sergio is among them.*
    DEPESTRE (*off*): . . . by which a people becomes conscious of their ability to change their social life, . . .
471. MS: *René Depestre is reading his paper.*[48]
    DEPESTRE: . . . to write their own history, and to gather the best of their traditions in order to make them bear fruit and in order to enrich them with the conditions created by the struggle for national liberation.
472. LS: *a view of the panelists from the audience. Desnoes is reading his paper. To the right of the panel an employee in overalls fills glasses with water.*
    DESNOES: We were just a few steps removed from the Negro cooks and servants of the school. I found out I was a "spick," a derogatory term used in order to look down on Latin Americans . . .
473. MS: *Desnoes reading. Behind him, the employee continues filling the glasses.*
    DESNOES: . . . or brown people, or people almost black.
474. MS: *Sergio is listening. He rubs one of his eyes with his fingers, then puts his glasses back on.*
    DESNOES (*off*): Now I know that, although I look white, Anglo-Saxon, and Protestant, I am really a Southern Negro.
475. LS: *the entire panel as seen from the center aisle in the auditorium. The employee distributes the water glasses to the panelists and leaves, crossing in front of the panel.*

DESNOES: All Latin Americans are Negroes, discriminated against, op-
pressed, rejected, ignored, strangers in this new swindle which has
pretensions of universality. The American way of life, the great white
dream of the United States.

476. MCU: *Gianni Toti begins to speak.*[49]

TOTI: Now it's the turn of the devil's advocate, he who piles doubt upon
doubt and who asks you: But, gentlemen . . .

477. MS: *Salvatore Bueno*[50] *and René Depestre sit and listen, both taking
notes.*

TOTI (*off*): . . . don't you realize that the words you are using—underdevelopment, underdevelopment, underdevelopment—are sick, . . .

478. MS: *David Viñas nods in agreement.*[51]

TOTI (*off*): . . . or at least, sickly.

479. MCU: *Toti speaking.*

TOTI: Don't you realize that these words might be language-traps, ac-
complices of an already wasted culture, a stratagem, a linguistic alibi, a
linguistic-ideological entanglement, that can lead us to the mental peace
of clichés?

480. CU: *Sergio, seen from above and placed in the corner of the frame. He is
paying close attention.*

TOTI (*off*): It is useless to flee from the linguistic continent of underdevelopment and forget that the basic contradiction of our times is not
the contradiction . . .

481. MS: *Jack Gelber*[52] *and another man, seated in the audience, listening.*

TOTI (*off*): . . . between North American imperialism and the three underdeveloped continents, . . .

482. MS: *a notebook in a woman's lap in which she is doodling.*

TOTI (*off*): . . . but the contradiction between the impetuous development of the productive forces . . .

483. MS: *two young men listening attentively.*

TOTI (*off*): . . . of all the world and the forms . . .

484. CU: *a young woman in the audience, part of her face initially obscured
by the head of someone seated in front of her.*

TOTI (*off*): . . . and the relations of the production of capitalism; . . .

485. CU: *another young woman in the audience, smoking and listening.*

TOTI (*off*): . . . that is to say, between the socialist revolution and the
capitalistic system in its ultimate imperialistic phase.

486. MCU: *David Viñas is speaking, arguing with Toti. The camera pans to a*
MCU *of Desnoes, who sites beside Viñas.*

VIÑAS: For example, you speak of the basic contradiction between the
proletariat and capitalism. I believe that what you have said is entirely
abstract.

487. MS: *Toti takes notes, then covers his chin with his hand.*

VIÑAS (*off*): The fundamental contradictions are verified in reality and when the fundamental contradiction is embodied, it is converted into war. I mean to say that for me . . .
488. MS: *Depestre is nodding and smoking his pipe.*
VIÑAS (*off*): . . . the fundamental contradiction is not to be found between the European proletariat and European capitalists, but in an area where the war embodies, materializes, . . .
489. MS: *Toti nervously scratches his head while listening.*
VIÑAS (*off*): . . . and shows what the fundamental contradiction is, in other words, Vietnam.
490. MS: *Viñas listens to Toti who has begun to respond.*
TOTI (*off*): Then that problem cannot be separated from the other . . .
VIÑAS (*interrupting*): The problem is . . .
The camera pans to show Toti who tries to restate the problem differently.
TOTI: This discussion is based only on whether the fundamental contradiction is of one kind or another.
VIÑAS (*off*): No, no no. . . . On a level derived exclusively . . .
491. MS: *Desnoes lights a cigar.*
VIÑAS (*off*): . . . from Marxist scholastics, I do agree with you, but in the concrete embodiment I see it as something else. (*Gradually the voice fades away.*)
SERGIO (*voice-over*): What are you doing up there with that cigar? You must feel pretty important because there's not much competition here.

492. CU: *Sergio watches from the audience, smoking a cigarette.*
> SERGIO (*voice-over*): Outside Cuba, you'd be a nobody. . . . But here, you're well placed.

493. CU: *Desnoes is smoking his cigar.*
> SERGIO (*voice-over*): Who's seen you, and who can see you now, Edmundo Desnoes?

494. MS: *a section of the audience. Jack Gelber asks for the floor. Sergio is seated next to him.*
> GELBER (*in English*): Could I ask a question in English?
> *The panelists agree (off).*
> GELBER (*in English*): It's all right? Ah . . . ah . . . (*He stands up.*)
> Why is it that if the Cuban Revolution is a total revolution, they have to resort to an archaic from of discussion such as a round table, and treat us to an impotent discussion of issues that I'm well informed about, and most of the public here is well informed about, when there could be another more revolutionary way to reach a whole audience like this?

495. MCU: *Desnoes, seen in profile, translates.*
> DESNOES: Jack Gelber says that if the Cuban revolution is an original revolution, why does it make use of conventional means like round tables and why doesn't it develop . . .

496. LS: *Gelber is now seated again, reacting to Desnoes's translation by smiling. The comment is met by smiles in the audience.*
> DESNOES (*off*): . . . a more dynamic method of establishing a relationship between the panel and the public?

497. ELS: *Sergio walks through the square near the library. The camera tracks with him and then zooms in until his image covers the entire screen and becomes a meaningless blur.*[53]
> SERGIO (*voice-over*): I don't understand a thing. The American was right. Words devour words and they leave you in the clouds or on the moon. A thousand miles away. How does one get rid of underdevelopment? It marks everything. Everything. What are you doing down there, Sergio? What does all this mean? You have nothing to do with them. You're alone. In underdevelopment nothing has continuity, everything is forgotten. People aren't consistent. But you remember many things, you remember too much. Where's your family, your work, your wife? You're nothing, you're dead. Now it begins, Sergio, your final destruction.

498. MS: *Sergio opens his mailbox in the lobby of his building. He takes out an envelope with U.S. stamps and a notice that he has a package from abroad to be picked up. He opens the letter.*
> SERGIO (*voice-over*): Every time my old lady writes it's the same thing.

499. CU: *a stick of chewing gum and a Gillette razor blade slip from the envelope into Sergio's hand.*

SERGIO (*voice-over*): She knows I don't chew gum and that I use an electric shaver.

500. CU: *Sergio stares at the gum and the blade, then puts them in his pocket. He unfolds the letter and reads it while walking toward the street and away from the camera.*

SERGIO (*voice-over*): The only thing I've asked her for are books and magazines, but she doesn't send these things.[54] I can't read her handwriting. They're crazy. We don't understand each other.

501. CU: *Sergio strolls along the sidewalk, wet with a recent rain. The camera tracks backward in front of him. He looks to the side.*

502. LS, *Sergio's* POV: *an altar in the yard of what used to be a French Dominican school in Havana. The altar is now covered by a large picture of Lenin. On top, there is a sign that reads:* LENIN, SPECIAL SCHOOL. *Dissolve.*

503. LS: *the altar as it used to be, with a statue of Our Lady of Fatima. The camera pans over the building, then holds on a group of uniformed students streaming out through the gate in bright sunshine.*

504. MS: *Sergio, age twenty. He waits for somebody, leaning on the wall that surrounds the school.*

505. LS: *Hanna, in her school uniform. She comes out of the school surrounded by her classmates. She leaves them to join Sergio. They walk away, hand in hand, crossing beside the camera.*

506. LS: *Sergio and Hanna are walking in a park. He has his arm around her.*

SERGIO (*voice-over*): Hanna was more mature, more of a woman than the underdeveloped girls here.

507. CU: *Sergio and Hanna on a chaise lounge. She is trying to pencil in a false moustache on his upper lip. He pushes her away playfully.*

SERGIO (*voice-over*): How long were we together? I can't remember. It's the best thing that has ever happened to me.

508–511. LS: *the camera tracks through trees in successive dissolves; in the final shot the camera tracks over water, focussing on small cabins on a wooded embankment.*

SERGIO (*voice-over*): Why did I let her go? Why didn't I run after her?

512. MS: *Sergio and Hanna are kissing under the branches of trees.*

513. MCU: *Hanna, naked, is combing her hair.*

514. MS: *Sergio is lying in bed and Hanna is sitting on the edge of the bed with her back to the camera, combing her hair. Both are naked. Sergio raises himself to a sitting position and they embrace.*

515–517. *Three photographs of Hanna in New York, all street scenes with tall buildings in the background. In the third photograph her mother appears with her.*

SERGIO (*voice-over*): When she left for New York with her parents we thought we were going to be married.

518–528. *Stills of Sergio and Hanna together, embracing or kissing. Several are taken from earlier moments in this sequence.*

SERGIO (*voice-over*): We didn't believe in formalities, but we thought it would be best. We had plans. I was going to go to New York, make my life with her. I wanted to be a writer and she believed in me. She was the only one who believed in me. She was going to help me. Then my father gave me a furniture store.

529. CU: *a priest's hands brandish an aspergillum and Sergio's mother's hands cut the symbolic ribbon at the opening ceremony of the furniture store. The camera tilts up to give a full view of the store as people start entering. Through shot 531 harsh and foreboding music plays.*

530. LS: *the camera pans over the guests to focus on a priest who is blessing the store.*

531. *The camera pans slowly from the priest, now seated and accepting a glass of wine, across a group of guests attending the ceremony and holds Sergio in* MS. *He looks uncomfortable.*

SERGIO (*voice-over*): I buried myself behind a desk.

532. MS: *Sergio sits by himself in his office at the store. He is checking some bills. The lighting suggests it is late at night.*

SERGIO (*voice-over*): I worked like mad for two years.

533. MS: *Sergio in the office at night; he is writing a letter.*

SERGIO (*voice-over*): "Hanna, darling, I can't leave now. Please understand. I don't want to arrive there with empty hands."

534. MS: *Sergio driving his convertible.*

SERGIO: (*voice-over*): Hanna, darling, one day it was too late. I look for you, I'll always look for you.

535. MCU: *Hanna sits in a cafeteria. She is looking at the camera. Outside it is dark and raining.*

SERGIO (*voice-over*): Where are you now? What do you think of me now?

536. MS: *Hanna stands up and crosses beside Sergio who has been sitting at the table across from her. She pats his shoulder lightly and leaves the frame. The camera holds in* CU *on Sergio, deep in his thoughts, his head lowered.*

537. MCU: *rain falling heavily on a sidewalk.*

538. MCU: *Sergio, as when he left his building in 501. He has taken shelter from the rain, together with several other people, in the porch of a grocery store. At the beginning of the shot, he appears to be looking at the sidewalk of 537.*

539. LS: *a person steps out of a taxi.*

540. MS: *Sergio runs through the rain to catch the free taxi.*
The camera pans, following him until he is in LS.
541. MCU: *Sergio inside the taxi, looking worried by something he sees*
through the window.
SERGIO (*to the driver*): Wait, stop, stop right here.
542. LS, *Sergio's* POV: *Elena is in the entrance of his building, waiting for*
him.
543. LS (*from inside the taxi*): *Sergio runs toward the basement door of the*
building, trying to avoid Elena. She sees him and begins to run toward
him.
ELENA: Sergio! (*Because it is raining heavily, Elena turns back and*
runs into the lobby.)
544. *Sergio crosses near the camera as he runs through the basement to the*
elevator. As he leaves the screen, Elena can be seen in LS *in the back-*
ground running down the basement stairs. She runs toward the camera
which pans with her as she then moves toward the right to the elevator
whose doors are now closed. Elena hammers with her fists on the doors.
ELENA: Sergio! Sergio!
545. MS: *Sergio, wet from the rain, leans out from his apartment's balcony,*
his back to the camera. The doorbell rings loudly and persistently. Sergio
does not move.
546. MS: *Sergio enters his hallway with his back to the camera. He stops in*
front of the door. The camera follows him as he turns back to the living

room, adjusts the T.V. set so that it shows the image but produces no
sound, and sits to watch it in MCU. The camera pans to the T.V. screen
to show images of racial violence in the United States.
Fade out.

547. MCU, *Sergio's* POV: *two members of the Committee for the Defense of
the Revolution*[55] *interview Sergio and fill out forms.*[56] *The man is wearing
a militia uniform. The woman openly stares at the furnishings of the
apartment.*

MAN: Principal occupant. Surname?
SERGIO (*off*): Carmona.
MAN: Second surname?
SERGIO (*off*): Bendoiro.
MAN: First name?
SERGIO (*off*): Sergio.
MAN: Occupation?
SERGIO (*off*): None.
WOMAN: You don't work?
SERGIO (*off*): No.
WOMAN: How do you live?
SERGIO (*off*): From the rent of several apartments.
MAN: An ex-landlord. Age?
SERGIO (*off*): Thirty-eight years old.
MAN: Total net income?
SERGIO (*off*): Six hundred pesos.

MAN: Income from other members of the family?

SERGIO (*off*): I live alone.

MAN: Do you pay the Urban Reform?[57]

SERGIO (*off*): No.

MAN: The last month you paid?

SERGIO (*off*): I've never paid anything.

MAN: Nature of occupancy? Owner, renter, free tenant, squatter . . . ?

SERGIO (*off*): No, no, owner.

MAN: Any liens?

SERGIO (*off*): No.

MAN: Approximately how many square meters?

SERGIO (*off*): Your guess!

MAN: More or less.

SERGIO (*off*): Yes, but . . .

WOMAN: It's pretty large.

MAN: Shall we say . . . one hundred? . . . two hundred meters?

SERGIO (*off*): I think it's more than that. Do you want to measure it?

MAN: No, no. I'll take your word for it. Let's say three hundred. If that's not right we'll change it afterwards. Type of construction? Brick.

SERGIO (*off*): Yes, I think so.

MAN: It's one apartment. How many rooms?

SERGIO (*off*): A bedroom and a study.

WOMAN: Servant's quarters.

SERGIO (*off*): Ah, yes, two.

WOMAN: Ah . . .

MAN: How many toilets?

SERGIO (*off*): It has . . . one, two, three . . . four . . . it has five.

MAN: How many baths?

SERGIO (*off*): Three.

MAN: Elevators? Two. State of upkeep? Good. Sign here.

548. MCU, *man's* POV: *Sergio puts on his glasses before signing.*

SERGIO: And what's all this for?

MAN (*off*): We're just verifying.

SERGIO: Yes, but . . .

549. *Filling the whole screen is a picture of an eye such as one used for* santería *practices. Underneath is the inscription:* I AM HUNTING FOR YOU.[58]

MAN (*off*): Don't worry, if there's anything wrong, we'll let you know.

550. MS: *from inside a taxi in which Sergio is riding, a traffic policeman is seen blocking the way.*

POLICEMAN: Hey, wait! You can't turn there.

DRIVER: We're only going two more blocks.

POLICEMAN: No, you have to go straight ahead.
The camera pans to Sergio in the back seat.
SERGIO: That's all right, I'll get off here. (*Sergio pays for the ride and leaves the taxi. He walks away and the camera pans to follow his movements from inside the taxi.*)

551. MCU: *Sergio walking to the right with the camera tracking at his side. He is wearing a jacket and tie. The camera pans to show people walking in the opposite direction.*[59]
SERGIO (*voice-over*): In the midst of all this I'm living off rents.

552. CU: *Sergio walking to the left; he crosses by the camera as it pans with him.*
SERGIO (*voice-over*): I still have thirteen, no, twelve, eleven years to collect. It's been two years since they took away my apartment house.

553. MS: *the camera tracks left in the midst of a crowd of people who carry flags and drums and move to the left.*
PEOPLE (*singing*): We are socialists/Up and down/And whoever doesn't like us/Let them suffer and suffer.

554. MCU: *Sergio with his back to the camera. He makes his way through the crowd and keeps walking. The camera keeps him at a constant distance.*
SERGIO (*voice-over*): Everything comes to me either too early or too late. In another time, I would've been able to understand what was going on here. Now, I can't.[60]

555–571. *A series of shots from the dancing shown during the opening credits.*[61] *The music is disassociated from the images. Sergio intermittently appears amid the dancers as he watches what is taking place, including the removal of the wounded or possibly dead man, first seen in 18. Sergio appears isolated in the crowd.*

572. LS: *Sergio strolls in Havana's Central Park. He approaches the camera into* MCU *and wipes his brow.*
SERGIO (*voice-over*) I'm thirty-eight years old and I'm already an old man. I don't feel wiser or more mature. More stupid. More rotten than mature . . .

573. MS: *a street photographer adjusts his camera to take Sergio's picture. The camera pans left as the photographer moves from behind his apparatus in order to prepare the sitter. The photographer takes the picture.*
SERGIO (*voice-over*): . . . like a piece of rotten fruit. Like refuse. It might have something to do with the tropics. Here everything matures and rots easily. Nothing lasts.

574. *Several photographs spread on the floor. The camera pans over them until it holds in* MS *on Sergio sitting on the floor. An open wardrobe drawer shows several boxes full of pictures. Sergio is looking at some of them.*

575. *A photograph of Sergio as a child.*
576–582. *Family pictures showing Sergio at various stages of his life, arranged chronologically.*

> SERGIO (*voice-over*): I'm already an old man. In the whorehouses since I was thirteen. At fifteen I thought I was a genius. At twenty-five I owned a fashionable furniture store.

583–584. *Photographs of the store opening.*
585–589. *Photographs of Laura, some with Sergio, at different places.*
585. *Laura at a zoo, feeding an emu.*
586. *Laura with Sergio, on the steps of a public building in New York.*
587. *Laura in a café with Sergio and another couple.*
588. *Laura in her wedding dress.*
589. *Laura and Sergio posing with friends for a photograph in an amusement arcade.*

> SERGIO (*voice-over*): . . . and then Laura. . . . My life is like a monstrous and pulpy vegetable, with huge leaves and no fruit.

590. MCU: *Sergio stares at a passport-size photograph.*
591. CU: *the photograph of 590, held in Sergio's fingers. It is the one he posed for in 573.*

> SERGIO (*voice-over*): I believe that I project a certain dignity.

592. CU: *Sergio stops staring at the picture and looks directly at the camera.*

593. MCU: *Sergio opens the door to a man in a checked shirt who scowls at him.*

> BROTHER: Are you Sergio?

594. MCU: *Sergio, in his doorway.*

> SERGIO: Yes.
> BROTHER (*off*): I'm Elena's brother.

595. MCU: *the brother, still scowling, steps into the apartment without an invitation.*
596. MCU: *the camera follows the brother from behind as he moves into the living room. Sergio follows him and the camera holds on Sergio as he stops and turns to face Elena's brother.*

> SERGIO: Is she sick?
> BROTHER (*off*): No, my sister is a very healthy girl. She's never sick. It's something else . . .
> *Sergio looks at him and says nothing.*
> BROTHER (*off*): She says you took advantage of her.
> SERGIO: That's not the way it is.
> BROTHER (*off*): I don't know whether that's the way it is or not. You've ruined her and that's got to be fixed.
> SERGIO: What?

597. MCU: *Elena's brother as he confronts Sergio.*

BROTHER: This must be made right.

SERGIO (*off*): I don't know what Elena might have told you, but . . .

BROTHER (*angrily throwing several dresses down*): This is not something that can be paid for with dresses or can be paid for with anything.

598. CU: *a chair in the apartment as the dresses land on it.*

599. MCU: *Sergio, as in 596. He first looks down toward the dresses, then toward the brother.*

SERGIO: Please, take it easy.

BROTHER (*off*): She says that you first promised to marry her . . .

SERGIO: I promised?

BROTHER (*off*): . . . and then you took advantage of her and now you won't even open your door to her.

SERGIO (*taking off his glasses and raising his voice*): Look, that's not the way it is. I didn't . . .

BROTHER (*off; breaking in excitedly*): I don't know if it is or not!

SERGIO: But . . .

SERGIO (*voice-over*): Elena would do anything. I should have thought of that.

600. MCU: *the brother, seen from behind, turns to look toward the camera.*[62]

SERGIO (*voice-over*): I didn't want any trouble with the police.

601. MCU: *the camera pans partly up the body of the brother during the moment, earlier in the scene, when he was throwing the dresses on the chair.*

SERGIO (*voice-over*): I was willing to marry her if she asked me.

602. MS: *the brother leaves the apartment angrily.*

SERGIO (*voice-over*): I was afraid.

603. MCU: *the brother sits at a table on the porch of a cafeteria. It is nighttime.*

BROTHER: Tell him what you told Mother. Go on, tell him.

The camera pans to a MCU *of Elena, who hesitates before starting to talk. Her head is lowered and she does not look up.*

ELENA: You deceived me.

604. MCU: *Sergio, sitting across the table.*

SERGIO: You? (*He is reacting to her use of the formal Spanish "usted" rather than the intimate "tu."*)

605. MCU: *Elena, as at the end of 603.*

ELENA: You deceived me.

SERGIO (*off*): Why?

ELENA: You said you were going to give me some of your wife's dresses and then you took advantage of me.

606. MCU: *Sergio, as in 604.*

SERGIO: If you say so. . . . But you know it isn't true.

607. MCU: *Elena, as in 605. She raises her eyes to Sergio.*
    SERGIO (*off*): Besides, you're not a virgin.
608. MS: *Sergio and the brother at the table. The brother, angry, slams his fist on the table and stands up.*
    BROTHER: You're not treating her with respect!
    SERGIO: Look, please . . .
    BROTHER: I know my sister's no whore, damn it!
609. MCU: *Elena, as in 605. She turns to look at her brother.*
610. MS: *two ladies at a nearby table stare at Sergio's table.*
611. LS: *Elena's parents arriving in front of the store where they will meet Sergio in shot 615.*
612. LS: *Elena and her brother arriving at the cafeteria where we have already seen them meet with Sergio.*
    SERGIO (*voice-over*): How could I get mixed up in all this?
613. LS: *several arrested men sitting on benches at the police station Sergio will later be taken to. The camera pans left across the room.*
    SERGIO (*voice-over*): I resigned myself.
614. CU: *Elena sitting at the table in the cafeteria, slowly lowering her head.*
    SERGIO (*voice-over*): I was going to let myself be dragged along to the end. I was afraid.
615. MS: *Sergio is flanked by Elena, her brother, and her parents in front of a shop window that displays wedding dresses. It is evening. The camera, hand-held, moves among them.*
    MOTHER: Girls must go to the altar as virgins! That's the greatest treasure a woman can bring to a marriage.
    SERGIO: That was before. Now women are liberated.
    BROTHER: Don't start talking as if you were a revolutionary because you're not.
    The father tries to grab Sergio by the lapels of his jacket.
    FATHER: If you don't marry her, I'll kill you.
    Sergio pulls away to the right. The brother holds the father back.
    BROTHER: Keep quiet! Damn!
    Sergio is now free of the father and stands apart from the group.
    SERGIO: If I marry her it's because I want to. You're not going to force me into it.
    The father tries to attack Sergio once more, but the brother prevents it.
    FATHER: Nobody can make fun of my daughter!
    BROTHER: Be quiet!
616. MS: *Elena turns to Sergio. The mannequins with their wedding dresses are clearly visible behind them.*
    ELENA: Why didn't you want to see me? Did you want to get rid of me?
    SERGIO: It isn't that. I'll marry you. I've got to think . . .
    ELENA: Think about what?

The camera pans to hold the brother and mother in MS.
SERGIO (*off*): I've got to get the permit, don't I?
617. MS: *the brother is in the foreground, turned toward Sergio, Elena to one
side, Sergio in the background facing the camera.*
SERGIO: I've got to get the . . . the divorce papers.
The camera pans left to include the mother.
MOTHER: You're divorced?
The camera pans to the mother.
SERGIO (*off*): Yes, I'm divorced.
FATHER: Then you have to marry her! Immediately!
*The father tries to attack Sergio again. The brother holds him back and
the two men struggle.*
BROTHER: Listen, Papa, keep quiet. We will deal with the papers. (*To
the mother.*) Why did you bring him along? You didn't have to bring
him.
MOTHER: That night she came home late. She told me. She came home
with her underpants stained with blood.
618. MS: *Sergio, standing apart. He moves toward the others.*
SERGIO: That's not true, señora!
The camera pans to the other participants, then back to Sergio.
619. MS: *Elena is crying and her mother holds her to comfort her. The brother struggles to hold back the father. They are all screaming. The camera
makes a swish pan to Sergio.*

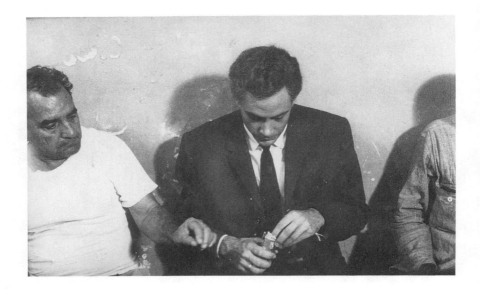

SERGIO (*voice-over*): I was sure she was not a virgin.

620. MS: *Elena's family getting into a taxi, seen from inside the back of the cab.*

SERGIO (*voice-over*): Poor devils! What could they get out of all this?

621. MCU, *Sergio's* POV: *a typewriter on which a deposition is being typed. The camera tilts up to show the policeman who is typing.*

POLICEMAN: Have you anything to say?

622. MCU: *Sergio is making his statement.*

SERGIO: It isn't true. I have had relations with her, but they were voluntary. There was no abuse and certainly no rape. All that is a lie.

623. LS: *Elena and her family sitting on a bench at the police station.*

624. MCU: *the policeman, as at the end of 621. He places the typed statement in front of Sergio.*

POLICEMAN: Sign here, Sergio.

625. MCU: *Sergio, as in 622. He takes out his pen and signs the papers. In the background, there is a guard at the door.*

POLICEMAN (*off*): Guard!

A man enters, led by a policeman. Another policeman leads Sergio out of the frame at the right.

626. MS: *Sergio sits in another room among other detainees. His appearance and attire makes a sharp contrast with those of the others. He takes a cigarette pack out of his pocket. Everyone asks for a cigarette before Sergio can keep one for himself, so he is unable to smoke. The camera slowly moves into a* MCU.

627. MS: *Sergio walking along the center hall of the empty courtroom, led by a clerk who motions him to sit in the front row. The camera tracks backward to precede him. Sergio sits down.*[63]

    BAILIFF (*off*): The accused, Sergio Carmona Bendoiro, planned to seduce Elena Josefa Dorado, age sixteen, and to that effect through a ruse took her to his apartment . . .

628. MS: *the members of the court in their seats.*

    BAILIFF (*off*): . . . located at Linea, Vedado . . .

629. MS: *the prosecutor, paying close attention to what is being said.*

    BAILIFF (*off*): . . . where he abused her virginity . . .

630. MS: *three lawyers, one a woman, are talking among themselves.*

    BAILIFF (*off*): . . . although knowing that said young girl was mentally disturbed . . .

631. MCU: *the bailiff, as he finishes reading the indictment.*

    BAILIFF: . . . and therefore incapable of resisting.

632. MCU: *Sergio faces the camera. He is ready to answer the lawyers' questions.*

    MEMBER OF THE COURT (*off*): Answer the questions of the prosecutor.

633. MS: *the prosecutor starts the cross-examination.*

    PROSECUTOR: Do you know Elena Josefa Dorado?

634. MCU: *Sergio, as in 632. He answers the prosecutor.*

    SERGIO: Yes.

    PROSECUTOR (*off*): When you answer, look at the court.

    Sergio turns to face the members of the court.

    SERGIO: Yes.

    PROSECUTOR (*off*): Yes, sir.

    SERGIO: Sorry. Yes, sir.

    PROSECUTOR (*off*): Where did you meet her?

    SERGIO: On Twenty-third Street, in Vedado.

    PROSECUTOR (*off*): Is it true that you took her to your apartment and had sexual intercourse with her?

    SERGIO: Yes.

635. MS: *the defense attorney begins his examination.*

    DEFENSE ATTORNEY: Tell me, on the night in question, did the plaintiff confess to you whether she had had sexual intercourse with another man?

    SERGIO (*off*): No, never.

636. MS: *Sergio sits in the front row of the courtroom. In the background, Elena is being led into the court by a clerk.*

    SERGIO (*voice-over*): I was the only one who spoke with some coherence. That finished me. They treated me as if I had cheated some unfortunate "woman of the people."

637. MCU: *Elena is sitting and facing the members of the court. She is being cross-examined.*

ELENA: Yes, also to give me some dresses which he offered me. Those that belonged to his wife who had gone north.

SERGIO (*voice-over*): Now everything is "the people" . . .

638. MCU: *Elena's mother answering the lawyer's questions.*

MOTHER: She had these black-and-blue marks and she told me that this man . . . (*The sound becomes muffled.*)

SERGIO (*voice-over*): Before I would have been the respectable one, and they the damned guilty ones.

639. MS: *the mother walks down the courtroom aisle, leaving the trial. As she passes Sergio, she attacks him with her handbag. Sergio cowers.*

SERGIO (*voice-over*): I saw I was lost . . .

MOTHER: The bastard! He has nerve! . . .

The clerk holds the mother back and succeeds in leading her, still struggling to break free, to the door in the background. She keeps on insulting Sergio and screaming hysterically.

640. MCU: *Elena's father is being cross-examined.*

DEFENSE ATTORNEY (*off*): Did you threaten Sergio's life?

FATHER: Yes, if he didn't marry her.

DEFENSE ATTORNEY (*off*): Your threatened to kill him?

FATHER: Yes, sir.

DEFENSE ATTORNEY (*off*): What did Sergio say?

FATHER: He said he would get the permit, that he would marry her, but in the end he didn't marry her.

641. MCU: *Elena's brother is being cross-examined.*

DEFENSE ATTORNEY (*off*): When did they take Elena to the doctor?

BROTHER: I don't know exactly. My mother says she took her some months before all this happened.

DEFENSE ATTORNEY (*off*): Do you know what the doctor said?

BROTHER: No, I don't.

642. MS: *the prosecutor is delivering his closing statement.*

PROSECUTOR: . . . and from the results of the tests . . .

SERGIO (*voice-over*): Then came the verdict.

PROSECUTOR: . . . we arrive at the conclusion . . .

The synchronous sound becomes markedly lower, but it can be faintly heard interspersed with the reading of the verdict by the bailiff. After the prosecutor's closing statement, the defense attorney delivers his own statement.

BAILIFF (*off*): The accused, Sergio Carmona Bendoiro, . . .

643. MS: *the lawyer for the defense making his statement.*

BAILIFF (*off*): . . . invited Elena Josefa Dorado, age seventeen, for a walk on the evening of the 25th of January, 1962, and during said walk they proceeded to the home of the accused located at Linea Street, where they had sexual intercourse. According to tests performed, there

is no proof that Elena Josefa Dorado shows any signs of mental distur-
bance nor that she was insane or unconscious at that time. Secondly:
the district attorney has sustained his conclusions as definite and they
have been duly recorded in folio 6 and 7.

644. MS: *the three members of the court retire to deliberate. The camera pans
left with them as they leave the room.*

BAILIFF (*off*): Thirdly: the defense sustained as definite its conclusions
in which it concretely denied every charge placed by the district attorney, pleaded the acquittal of the accused and the absolvement from
court costs. Finally: In the facts proved as true there are no grounds to
sustain the crime of rape as charged by the district attorney.

645. MCU: *the bailiff is reading the verdict.*

BAILIFF: Due to the above and executing Articles 142, 240, 741, and
742 of the Social Defense Code and the Criminal Prosecution Law, we
render the following verdict:

646. MCU: *Sergio is paying close attention.*

BAILIFF (*off*): We hereby absolve the accused of the crime of rape as
charged by the district attorney.

647. LS: *the defense attorney is shaking Sergio's hand, while the judges file
out in the background. Sergio leaves the courtroom, with the camera
tracking back to keep him in MS. He removes his glasses and wipes his
eyes with his handkerchief.*

SERGIO (*voice-over*): It was a happy ending, as they say. For once justice
triumphed. But was it really like that? There is something that leaves
me in a bad position. I've seen too much to be innocent. They have too
much darkness inside their heads to be guilty. I haven't seen them
again. I hope they haven't locked her up.

648. MS: *Sergio is in his apartment wearing pajama pants and an undershirt.
He picks up the newspaper delivered under his door.*[64] *He stands reading
the headlines and some articles. The camera moves in to hold him in CU.*

649. CU: *newspaper headlines:* MORE PLANES AND BATTLESHIPS TO
FLORIDA / KENNEDY RETURNS SUDDENLY TO WASHINGTON / AT-
MOSPHERE OF WAR HYSTERIA GRIPS U.S. CAPITAL

650. *Newspaper headline:* YOUNG MOTHER GIVES BIRTH TO TRIPLETS

651. *Newspaper headline:* DOG WITH TWO HEARTS

652. *Newspaper headline:* TRADE UNIONS COMPETE TO GAIN RENOWN

653. *Newspaper headline:* BULLETIN BOARD MATERIAL. POST IT WHERE
YOU WORK. CUT OUT AND PASTE.

654. *Newspaper headline:* HOW TO PREVENT TETANUS. Anyone can become infected with the tetanus bacillus. Most cases are fatal. Vaccination
is the only sure protection.

655. *Newspaper headline:* WORDS OF MAO TSE TUNG. Trying to solve ideo-

logical problems and the problem of what is right or wrong through administrative regulation or by repressive methods is not only useless but also harmful.

656. *A fragment of a letter from a reader of the newspaper complaining about the lack of attention on the part of the Institute of Urban Reform paid to the problem of masonry falling from the façades of buildings.*

657. *A fragment of a headline:* WORK WITH JOY AND . . .

658. *The camera pans across a newspaper comic strip by Chago titled "Salomón." In the first four panels a glum-looking figure is shown with a question mark suspended over his head. The question mark gets larger in each panel and in the fifth panel it comes crashing down on the figure's head.*

659. MCU: *Sergio finishes with the newspaper, puts it down, and moves away to the left.*

660. MCU, *Sergio's* POV: *Noemí's hand advancing to give him some photographs. The camera tilts up to hold Noemí in* MCU *as she talks to him with her head lowered. Her words are inaudible.*

  SERGIO (*voice-over*): She brought me a stack of photographs. They were taken when she was baptized in the river.

661–667. *Photographs of Noemí's baptism, evidently taken by an amateur, all in* MLS. *They dissolve into one another.*

661. *A group of people gathered on a rise of ground. Noemí is barely visible in the midst of the group.*

662. *Noemí and the minister in the lower foreground. The rest of the group stands at a slight distance behind him.*

663. *Noemí and the minister are now several steps farther away from the others. She is dressed in white.*

664. *The setting now becomes clear. The group is standing on a riverbank and Noemí and the minister have entered the water.*

665. *Noemí and the minister are now knee-deep in the water. The group is no longer included in the picture.*

666. *The minister holds Noemí on her back in the water.*

667. *Noemí and the minister emerge from the water to the bank, where the group awaits them.*

  SERGIO (*voice-over during 661–667*): It wasn't like I thought it would be. It's nothing. The clothes didn't cling to her body. There were lots of people. I hadn't thought about them. Witnesses who are always everywhere.[65]

668. MCU: *Sergio is lying back comfortably on a sofa, his hands crossed above his head. He closes his eyes and daydreams.*[66]

669–674. *Several brief shots in* CU *and* ECU *of Sergio and Noemí kissing passionately. The camera revolves around them, always keeping them in close range. During the last shot the camera slowly withdraws to* MS. *The last shot is accompanied by radio static.*[67]

675. MCU: *Sergio on the sofa. He opens his eyes. Superimposed:* OCTOBER 22, 1962/KENNEDY SPEAKS

676. LS *(from a moving vehicle): Artillery weapons deployed along the Malecón.*

677–689. *Photographs taken during the Missile Crisis. The shots dissolve into one another and the camera often pans over the photo or slowly zooms in on a detail.*

677–679. *Three aerial pictures of the missile sites, each successive picture from a lower altitude.*

680. *Aerial photograph of a ship loaded with missiles, seen from directly above.*

681. MS: *John Kennedy, wearing sunglasses, in a navy boat.*

682. LS: *U.S. soldiers and combat equipment lined up for inspection.*

683. MS: *a group of U.S. soldiers in combat dress.*

684. MCU: *U.S. civilians, examining weapons, apparently to suggest combat readiness.*

685. LS: *small landing boats filled with soldiers are leaving a larger ship.*

686. LS: *soldiers in silhouette as they land on a beach.*

687. LS: *an aircraft carrier and other ships in silhouette.*

688. LS: *a tank pointed to the left with foot soldiers accompanying it.*

689. LS: *a tank pointed to the right with foot soldiers accompanying it. During the sequence 677–689, John Kennedy's voice can be heard on the soundtrack, but with a good deal of static interference, as if heard over a short-wave transmission. A Spanish translation in typescript is scrolled over the photographs.*

KENNEDY (*voice-over*): . . . a series of offensive missile sites is now in preparation on that imprisoned island. . . . Additional sites not yet completed appear to be designed for intermediate range ballistic missiles . . . capable of striking most of the major cities in the Western Hemisphere, ranging as far north as Hudson's Bay, Canada, and as far south as Lima, Peru.

In addition, jet bombers, capable of carrying nuclear weapons, are now being uncrated and assembled in Cuba while the necessary air bases are being prepared.

. . . To halt this offensive build-up a strict quarantine on all offensive military equipment under shipment to Cuba is being initiated.

Should these offensive military preparations continue, thus increasing the threat to the hemisphere, further action will be justified.

I have directed the armed forces to prepare for any eventualities . . .

690. ELS: *aerial view of an atomic bomb explosion.*

691–696. *People on the street in Havana during the Missile Crisis.*

691. MS: *two militiawomen stop in front of a shop window to gaze at a wedding dress.*

692. CU: *a smiling man wearing a military cap.*

693. CU: *two smiling young men talking.*
    SERGIO (*voice-over during 691–693*): It makes no sense. The people behave and talk as if war were a game.
694. MCU: *two militiawomen walking along a street; the camera pans with them.*
695. MCU: *a young black man with a sombrero.*
    (The opening bars of a Charles Mingus composition, with the lyrics—in English— as follows: "Oh, Lord, don't let them drop that atomic bomb on me.")[68]
696. LS: *a wall that displays a half erased piece of graffiti whose only complete word, written in bold letters, is* DEATH. *A man walks alongside the wall.*

697. CU: *the book with the reproduction of Botticelli's* Birth of Venus. *Sergio's right hand partially covers the page; his left hand strokes the image of Venus. It is already dark. The camera pans up to* MCU *of Sergio, in his pajamas and unshaven; he raises his head.*[69]
    SERGIO (*voice-over*): And if it all were to start right now?
698. LS: *a nighttime scene on the street. A truck towing a piece of artillery passes from right to left.*
699. CU: *Sergio, from his apartment, watches the trucks pass by.*
700. LS: *another truck, silhouetted against bright floodlights behind it, passes from left to right.*

701. CU: *Sergio continues to look.*
702. MS: *a farm truck, with men standing in its open back, moves to the right, silhouetted in bright light.*
703. LS: *more equipment passing close to the camera from right to left in semi-darkness.*
704. CU: *Sergio, increasingly tense.*
 SERGIO (*voice-over*): It's no use protesting. I'll die like the rest. This island is a trap. We're very small, and too poor. It's a very expensive dignity.
705. *A television screen. Castro in* MLS *is delivering a speech.*[70]
 CASTRO: We definitely reject any intention of inquiry, any intention . . .
706–709. *Photographs on the television screen.*
706. *Photograph of the United Nations Security Council.*
707. *Photograph of U Thant, the secretary general.*
708. *Photograph of Russian delegates arriving at the United Nations.*
709. *Photographs of U.S. delegates, including Adlai Stevenson, in a limosine.*
 CASTRO (*voice-over*): . . . of inspecting our country. Nobody inspects our country.
710. *Castro in* MCU *on the television screen.*
 CASTRO: We know what we are doing and we know how to defend our integrity and we know how to defend our sovereignty.
711. LS (*on the T.V. screen, from a moving vehicle*): *artillery weapons are deployed in the city.*
712. *On the T.V. screen, militia members are shown on guard duty in the city. The camera, hand-held, moves over to a building entrance. It holds in* ECU *on a poster that reads:* TO ARMS.
 CASTRO (*voice-over*): They threaten us by saying we'll be nuclear targets. They don't scare us. We have to know how to live in the age into which we are born, with the dignity with which we should know how to live. All of us, men and women, young and old, are one in this hour of danger!
713. *Castro on television, as in 710.*
 CASTRO: It is the same for all of us, revolutionaries and patriots, and victory will be ours! Our country or death! We shall triumph!

714. LS: *very high waves are visible beyond the Malecón.*
715. LS: *Sergio walks by himself along the Malecón. There is a strong wind and the waves break forcefully along the sea wall. Sergio approaches the camera.*
716. CU: *soapy water going down the drain.*
717. CU: *Sergio looking down.*
718. CU: *as in 716, with Sergio's hands wiping the washbasin's edge, where some soap suds have remained.*

719. LS: *the city by night, seen as from Sergio's balcony.*
720. CU: *Sergio, on the balcony of his apartment, scans the sky with his telescope.*
721. *The moon seen through the telescope.*
722. MS: *Sergio collapses face down on his unmade bed.*
723. ECU: *the poster that says* TO ARMS, *as at the end of 712.*
724. CU: *the tip of a cane moving very close to a crystal rooster on top of a tiled living room table.*
725. CU: *Sergio is putting on his glasses. In semi-darkness he makes a brief motion with the cane.*
726. CU: *as in 724. A sweeping blow with the cane shatters the rooster.*
727. LS: *soldiers lowering the back ramp of a large truck that carries a tank. It is still dark and the scene is flood-lit.*
728. LS: *the tank starts to roll down the ramp.*
729. MCU: *a restless Sergio paces the apartment.*
730. MCU: *as 729, from a different angle. The camera follows Sergio.*
731. MCU: *Sergio shuts the balcony door.*
732. LS: *another tank rolls down the slope onto the city street.*
733. MS, *Sergio's* POV: *the camera tracks through the apartment.*
734. MCU: *Sergio continues to pace in the apartment, and the camera follows him.*
735. MS: *a tank driver seen from the back as he stands in the open hatch of a moving tank.*
736. MCU: *Sergio, looking troubled, steps into his bedroom.*

737. *Zoom in to* CU *of drawings hanging on the apartment wall. A big eye stands out.*
738. MCU: *Sergio comes into the living room.*
739. *Zoom in to* CU *of a drawing in which a figure holds by the hair a decapitated head.*
740. MCU: *Sergio in profile. He sits in the living room playing with a cigarette lighter that he keeps opening and closing. The only sound is that of the lighter; it resembles the ticking of a clock.*
741. LS: *the camera tracks along a street flanked by troops and artillery. It is still dark. The clicking of the cigarette lighter continues through this shot.*
742. LS: *the railing of the balcony, with Sergio's telescope prominent on the left. In the background, the city and the sea. It is dawn.*
743. LS: *the city as seen from Sergio's apartment. The camera slowly pans to the left across the buildings by the harbor until it finally holds on soldiers on a rooftop deploying antiaircraft weapons. Then the camera pans slowly back to the right, now at a lower level. Some cars and a convoy of army trucks loaded with heavy artillery move along the Malecón. The camera slowly moves in closer to the roadway and to the trucks. The noise of the trucks gradually drowns the music. Fade to white. The noise is replaced by music.*

Notes on the
Continuity Script

1. In the shooting script the title of the film is *Pages of a Diary*. The prologue—the credits sequence—is explained in the following manner:

   A cold voice, without inflection, mechanical, reads the police report on the discovery of a corpse in a Vedado apartment on a day in October 1962. The body shows signs of poisoning and the death is presumed to be a suicide. Among the documents found (some can be mentioned) which may be of interest in the investigation is a diary.

   The scene (silent, without effects) as follows:
   Interior, Apartment
   Men at the moment they take the body from the house.
   Exterior, Building
   Curious bystanders.
   Surroundings.
   They put the body in the car and drive off.
   People in the street, curious bystanders disperse: each goes on with his own affairs. (This scene should reflect some of the same feeling as the Prado street dance scene near the end of the film.)
   Artillery Emplacement
   The car passes by the artillery emplacement: the scene freezes.
   Here the music (timpani) comes up, TITLE and successive credits roll over:
   Street
   A group of very active militiamen (still photo).
   Faces (photos).
   Studio
   An ID photo of Sergio, full screen.
   A series of stills of the military mobilization we will see at the end of the film.

Some CUs *(stills) of Sergio.*
All the stills appearing after the title will be taken from scenes that will be seen later in the film.

The phrase above, "the Prado dance scene," refers to a street dance attended by Sergio and Noemí. The scene is similar to the one shown in the credit sequence of the film (shots 1–24), but without Sergio and Noemí; that sequence is partially repeated later in the film (shots 555–571) with a different sound treatment and with the presence of Sergio.

2. The billboard refers to the April 1961 defeat of invading counterrevolutionary forces sponsored by the U.S. government at Playa Girón (Bay of Pigs).

3. The idea of Sergio having a telescope on his balcony was not part of the shooting script. It was conceived only a few days before shooting started, in order to characterize visually the role of "spectator of reality" which defines the protagonist: a character who sees and judges reality from afar and above rather than becoming part of it.

4. General Antonio Maceo (1845–1896), a black who as a young man participated in the first armed insurrection for Cuban independence (1868–1878). He died in combat against Spanish forces, having become a legendary Cuban leader.

5. In 1898, there was an explosion on the U.S. battleship *Maine* outside Havana Bay. The sinking of the *Maine* was blamed, without clear proof, on Spain and was President William McKinley's pretext for declaring war on Spain and intervening militarily in Cuba. Near the site of the explosion, a monument topped by the figure of an imperial eagle was erected, and shortly after the success of the Castro Revolution, the eagle was knocked down. At that time there was talk that Picasso was going to donate a dove, the symbol of peace, to take the eagle's place, but the top of the monument remained vacant.

6. The phrase comes from the last paragraph of the Second Declaration of Havana, proclaimed by Castro on 4 February 1962.

7. The cage with the two birds that appears in shot 52 was included only for decorative purposes. The day the telescope scene was shot one of the birds was found dead. Therefore this sequence was improvised and in a sense it emphasizes the protagonist's solitude and ironic attitude.

8. Lines from "Todo en tí fue naufragio" ("Everything in You Was Shipwrecked") from the book *Veinte poemas de amor y una canción desesperada* (*Twenty Love Poems and a Desperate Song,* 1924) by the Chilean poet Pablo Neruda.

9. *Santería* is a popular religion in Cuba, the syncretic product of the West African Yoruba cult and Spanish Catholicism. A person being initiated into santería (an *iyabó*) must dress in white for a year.

10. This essay by an Argentine writer is based on information provided by prisoners taken at Playa Girón (Bay of Pigs). It analyzes the responsibility of those whose well-being depends on exploitation and crime and who at

the same time claim to have clear consciences. The book, *Moral burguesa y revolución,* was published in Buenos Aires (Ediciones Procyon) in 1963.

11. "El Encanto," the most celebrated department store in Havana, was burned down in an act of sabotage in April 1961.

12. The shot of Sergio walking toward the camera from the back of the frame appears in the shooting script as a repetition of another shot placed after Sergio begins to write in his diary, "Now I'll know if I really have something to say . . ." (before shot 58).

13. Between this sequence and the one that follows (PABLO) the shooting script includes Sergio's evocation of his childhood, including his visit to the brothel (shots 383–403). The evocation ends with the following scene:
Classroom
Brother Leon in the midst of a lecture. Visual aids, etc.
SERGIO'S VOICE: The last year Brother Leon looked like a porcupine. He talked in detail about the effects of venereal diseases: sores, twisted and rotten bones, unbearable pain, deformed children . . .
Sergio and Armando among the students. They look at each other and giggle about something. They're nervous.
SERGIO'S VOICE: I stopped going to brothels for over a year. Then I forgot about it.

14. In the shooting script the scene begins with the following dialogue:
PABLO: . . . and I don't see why we had to end up on the Russians' side.
SERGIO: Well, we already know what it's like to be on the American side.
PABLO: It doesn't matter! No matter how bad they were. . . . With a little skill, a little common sense, we could have utilized the triumph of the revolution to get things from them.
SERGIO: The thing is, it looks like what these people want is a real revolution . . .
PABLO: So what? They could have had agrarian reform and thousands of other things without losing the Americans' support. The problem is they didn't know how to maneuver. The United States is more interested in Cuba's political backing, its vote at the U.N., than in the few dollars it stands to lose in this game.
Then the dialogue continues as it appears in the film.

15. In the shooting script a short scene from *Hiroshima, Mon Amour* is shown full screen, between this and the next shot.

16. According to the shooting script, the scene in shot 126 (on the beach rather than at the Hotel Nacional pool) is placed here. Shot 125 follows.

17. Fulgencio Batista, then an army sergeant, led a military mutiny in 1933. Several years later (1940–1944), he was named president of the Republic. In 1952 he returned to power through a coup d'état and maintained a repressive policy which served the interests of U.S. monopolies. He was overthrown on 31 December 1958 by the revolutionary movement led by Fidel Castro. He died in Madrid on 6 August 1973, age seventy-three.

18. The whole first part of the dialogue at the gas station does not exist in the shooting script.
19. This information appears in Rozitchner's book on p. 109. (See note 10.)
20. In the shooting script the dialogue between Sergio and Pablo continues as follows:

> SERGIO: I was reading here that you and I are also responsible for the crimes.
> PABLO: What crimes?
> SERGIO: The crimes, the tortures, . . . everything, during Batista's time.
> PABLO: My conscience is clear. I never got involved in politics.

Then the shooting script continues as in the film.

21. Esteban Ventura was one of Batista's most infamous and feared associates. He escaped to Miami after the revolutionary government came to power.
22. In the shooting script this sequence begins as follows:

Sergio's Apartment
Noemí is cleaning the living room.
SERGIO'S VOICE: She comes three times a week to clean the apartment.
In the study Sergio is absorbed, poking his ear with a paper clip. When he hears Noemí's footsteps he rushes over to his typewriter and sits down.
SERGIO'S VOICE: Someone's glance can change your life completely. And turn every day into a masquerade . . .
Noemí passes by the door. She half-smiles.
SERGIO'S VOICE: . . . an act put on for others. That's what my life was like until everyone went away and left me all alone. . . . And now Noemí . . .
Sergio looks at her out of the corner of his eye. He can't write any more after that.

The scene continues with Sergio making breakfast in the kitchen, as appears in the film.

23. The next shots (256–267) are different in some ways from the shooting script. The shooting script does not contain the Botticelli print, but instead "Noemí dressed up like a *Vogue* model" and then a photograph from *Vogue*. Further on, before Sergio senses that Noemí will walk by him again, two photos appear, one of a *Vogue* model, the other of Noemí modeling Laura's clothes, wearing his glasses, and carrying a book in her hand.
24. Shots 269 through 278 were done with a hidden camera, except 273 of Sergio.
25. Instead of this shot 279, the shooting script contains:

Sergio's Apartment
Television screen: a Soviet film or a T.V. news program. Or one of those live programs that are clear displays of underdevelopment. It is turned off.

Movie Theatre

Movie screen: sex scenes from Hiroshima, Mon Amour.

The film's sound in the background; in the foreground:

SERGIO'S VOICE: I've never felt anything exists beyond my body. I think we're more machines than souls incarnate, electronic machines . . .

Sergio watching the movie.

SERGIO'S VOICE: . . . machines . . . our bodies are all we have or want to hate others . . .

Oculist's Cabinet

Oculist's eye chart.

(*Conversation between Sergio and the oculist.*)

Street

A blind man on the street.

Sergio walks down the street. He stops in front of a store selling religious objects.

SERGIO'S VOICE: Forgetting nothing . . . Knowing how to piece things together. . . . I think that's what civilization is all about.

Objects used in santería (*Afro-Cuban religion*).

People on the street. Dolly: an iyabó.

SERGIO'S VOICE: But this is a country without a memory. It lives in the present.

Sergio among the crowd on the street. He stops in front of a showcase. He looks . . .

An optician's showcase: the two eyes that serve as its ad, full screen.

Sergio's Apartment

Sergio doing exercises:

> *pushups*
> *deep knee bends*
> *exercises for the torso*
> *Sergio in front of the mirror. He pulls in his chest.*
> *He takes a shower.*

(As can be seen, some of these elements were incorporated into other parts of the film: the religious objects store in shot 110 and the *iyabó* in shot 91.)

26. When the war with Spain ended on 10 December 1898, U.S. troops occupied Cuba for three years. Before formally handing administration over to a Cuban government President McKinley convened a constituent assembly in 1900 for Cubans to draft a constitution. An amendment to the constitution (the Platt Amendment), included under strong pressure from the United States, stipulated that Cuba sell or lease the United States necessary lands for a naval installation. The key provision of the Platt Amendment gave the United States the right to intervene in the internal affairs of the island whenever it deemed U.S. citizens or property to be at

risk. Later Guantánamo Bay became the site of a U.S. naval base which is still in existence.

27. The Cuban Film Institute (ICAIC) was created less than three months after the formation of a revolutionary government. It established the basis for a national film industry which produces feature films, documentaries, short subjects, animated films, and a weekly newsreel.

28. The director and the director of photography for *Memories of Underdevelopment* play these respective roles in this scene.

29. The Film Review Commission was replaced in October 1959 by the Commission for the Study and Classification of Films, part of ICAIC, whose purposes included classifying films according to recommended ages for viewing.

30. In the shooting script the scene ends here. In other words, the following shots—311 through 314—were not planned.

31. The following appears in the shooting script:
Before entering he looks at her again. An old couple enters and say hello to Sergio. They go up in the elevator together.
Elevator
The couple get off one floor before Sergio. Everyone courteously says goodbye. When they get out, Sergio is alone and makes a face at them.

32. In the shooting script the sound is Radio Reloj, giving news on the situation in Cuba before the Missile Crisis. Similar background sounds occur in the film in shot 347.

33. One of the most popular of Cuban singers, especially of romantic songs.

34. In the shooting script Sergio responds:

SERGIO (*laughs*): What do you think? . . . No! But I'm fine here.

The rest of the dialogue in this shot (until Elena says "Nothing. You're nothing") was not included in the shooting script.

35. The sequence in the following shots—to 345—is not included in the shooting script.

36. The shooting script returns to a CU of Sergio smoking and looking out the window at night, just as when we leave him after he says goodbye to Elena.

37. After these shots the shooting script indicates a series of archive shots of people shouting in Revolution Square.

38. This last phrase is not in the shooting script.

39. In the shooting script there is the following short scene in the park:

Sergio and Elena are walking in a Vedado park. She is tired. Her feet hurt.
SERGIO'S VOICE: I suddenly realized that Elena didn't share any of the ideas that passed through my head.
He invites her to sit down on a bench. but she refuses. They look for a taxi.

Then Sergio's thoughts in a bookstore are heard, as in shots 404–405 of the film.

40. In the shooting script this remembrance of Sergio's childhood appears much earlier. See note 13.

41. A Cuban painter (1932–1964). His first individual show was in Havana in 1959.

42. The guide speaks in his own words; he is really Hemingway's former servant. The rest of the dialogue and the structure of the sequence (shots 409–488) have followed the shooting script relatively faithfully.

43. Hungarian-American (1913–1954), renowned as a photographer of war. Some of his most memorable photographs were taken during the Spanish Civil War.

44. Founded in 1906 in Mayari, eastern Cuba, by the Nipa Bay Company, this was one of Cuba's most important sugar mills. It was bought by a man named Preston, an intermediary of United Fruit. The mill was nationalized in August 1960.

45. A small town founded in the late eighteenth century some nine miles south of Havana. Hemingway bought the Vigia estate there in 1941; after his death it became the Hemingway Museum.

46. The *Pilar* was designed and built by Hemingway in 1934; he named it for his second wife, Pauline ("Pilar") Pfeiffer.

47. This sequence (shots 469–496) has been totally improvised. The shooting script reads as follows:
    A group of writers present their views, one at a time, to the audience. This whole scene is to be filmed with direct sound, like a newsreel. What they say will be easy to understand when it's interesting. Some things will be said with the camera on Sergio's face. Especially the end.

48. Haitian poet born in 1926. He lived in exile in Cuba from 1959 on. Later he moved to Paris where he worked as a UNESCO official.

49. Italian poet, novelist, and playwright (1924–   ). Editor of *Carte Segrete* magazine.

50. Cuban literature professor, critic, and essayist (1917–   ).

51. Argentine professor, critic, and novelist (1929–   ).

52. American playwright (b. 1932), best known for *The Connection* (1956), a play about drug addicts.

53. The shooting script reads:
    Sergio's thoughts turn to something he heard at the library. Along general lines, after a bitter refutation of the most revolutionary viewpoints (Fanon), Sergio considers his current confusion and frustration. He would have liked to be born in a large country "where history happens." Maybe that way he would have become something more than a furniture salesman and frustrated dilettante.
    His personal solution: being alone,

keeping a diary
to clarify his thoughts
and face death.

Then a billboard with a quote from Tran-Duc-Tao or someone similar
appears briefly.

Finally, before shot 498 of the film, the following scene appears in the
shooting script:

Sergio's Apartment

Sergio wakes up. He stretches. The telephone rings. He automatically gets
up to answer the phone but when he gets there he decides not to answer it.
He turns around and goes into the bathroom.

54. Sergio's voice reads part of the letter: "I'm sending you some sleeping
    pills. I always take them when things get hard, when problems overwhelm
    me. At those times the best thing is to sleep, to forget everything. They
    could help you a lot in Cuba."
55. The Committee for the Defense of the Revolution (CDR) was established in
    September 1960.
56. This scene (shots 547–549) does not appear in the shooting script. Instead
    there is a scene in a bank. Sergio is in a line of former apartment house
    owners waiting to pick up the rent money the state continues to pay them
    as compensation for a certain number of years. Sergio's thoughts as he
    waits in line appear in the film—with slight modifications—in shots 551,
    552, and 554. At the end of the scene one of the old people comments with
    contained indignation: ". . . and now they say I'm an exploiter and a thief.
    And I worked so hard all my life, because everything I had came from the
    sweat of my brow . . . everything!"
57. The Urban Reform Law (October 1960) prohibited private individuals from
    renting out housing. Subsequently all housing units were transferred to the
    ownership of the renters occupying them. The rent they had been paying
    was turned into time payments to the state toward permanent ownership of
    their housing. The former owners continued to receive a maximum of 600
    pesos a month from the state for a stipulated number of years as compensa-
    tion for the loss of their property.
58. Afro-Cuban syncretic symbol. The eye symbolizes God's observance of all
    human actions and the tongue pierced by a poniard represents the destruc-
    tion of all maledictions.
59. This shot and the ones following—through 554—do not appear in the
    shooting script.
60. Next in the shooting script is a scene with a sweaty Sergio inside a crowded
    bus on a very hot day. The words spoken in shot 572 of the film are noted
    here. The shooting script continues with the Central Park scene (film shots
    572–573).

61. A scene similar to this, but with music from the credit sequence and Noemí accompanying Sergio, appears in the shooting script much later, following the film scene in which Noemí shows him photos of her baptism in the river.

62. In the shooting script this series of shots is preceded by one in which Sergio is seen staring out the window at the city.

63. The trial scene (shots 627–647), including the dialogue and the reading of the documents, was developed later, except for Sergio's thoughts (shots 636–639), which appear in the shooting script. Almost all the dialogue was improvised during the shooting of the film.

64. In the shooting script this scene—reading the newspaper—is located at the beginning, after the breakfast (shot 58) and immediately before the tape recorder scene (shots 71–85). In its place the following scene appears:

Sergio's Apartment

Sergio is looking out the window.

The city as seen from the window.

Sergio is lying on the bed. A book has fallen out of his hand and he's sweating. He wakes up suddenly and looks at the room as if he's never seen it before.

The room. The camera passes over objects and walls.

A professional photo of Sergio as a child with his parents.

Sergio breathes uneasily. He closes his eyes.

65. In the shooting script the scene continues this way:

Sergio's Apartment

Close shot of Noemí. Her eyes are lowered while he looks at the photos. Then she lifts her eyes and looks again into the camera. She may be afraid but she maintains the challenge. The camera moves toward her. Sergio's hand enters and caresses the nape of her neck.

Then the Prado street dance appears (like the one in the credit sequence of the film but here in the presence of Sergio and Noemí). Then the close shot of Noemí ending the baptism photo scene is repeated.

Various shots of Sergio and Noemí kissing (as in shots 669–674 of the film) follow.

66. The shots of Sergio on the sofa (here and 675) do not appear in the shooting script.

67. After this scene the shooting script continues as follows:

They undress each other slowly.

They fall on the bed.

Fade out. The screen remains black for a few seconds.

(Radio noises while stations are changed, arriving at a station from the United States with sensual music.) Fade in.

The radio on the night table. Pan of the two lying together.

They move slowly and finally look at one another.
NOEMÍ'S VOICE: Don't laugh, but many nights I dreamed we lived to-
gether. . . . I thought I'd never have anything more than that: dreaming
that I hugged you and you were inside me.
*They look at each other a long time. He is on top of her. She lifts her head
and kisses him. (The song on the radio is interrupted and we begin to hear
Kennedy's speech.)*
*After the speech starts he wants nothing to do with her. He looks at the
radio. She looks at him, understanding nothing.*
NOEMÍ: Who is it?
SERGIO: It's Kennedy, I think. (*He continues to listen to the speech dur-
ing the rest of the dialogue.*)
She tries to go on, but he is paralyzed. After a while she interrogates him.
NOEMÍ: What's he saying?
SERGIO: I don't know. . . . He says there are Russian missiles in Cuba.
NOEMÍ: Missiles?
SERGIO: Atomic missiles. He says he's got proof, photographs. . . . He
says . . . I guess the Yankees, the Marines will invade. . . . They'll bomb
Havana first. . . . It's incredible. . . . It can't be.
*She lets go of his arm and keeps staring at him. She's worried. Most of all
she's afraid for him.*
He leans back against her and looks at the ceiling.
(Sound fades out.)
The room's ceiling. Sound of a car driving by.
SERGIO'S VOICE: One can imagine a shot, a knife wound, a grenade
explosion. . . . But I can't imagine the city destroyed, vaporized by an
atomic bomb . . .
Sergio's Apartment
It is daytime. Sergio is alone in his study writing in his diary.
SERGIO'S VOICE: I'm writing for no reason. Nothing means anything. I
feel asphyxiated. People move around and talk as if the war were a game.

The scene continues with shots 691–695 of the film.
68. The shooting script continues:
Archive Shots: *An atomic explosion with manniquins that look human.*
(A window bangs loudly, with the sound exaggerated.)
Sergio's Apartment
*Night: Sergio is dozing and he wakes up startled. He goes to the banging
window and looks at it. He looks outside. He takes his head in his heads,
as if he were in the middle of a nightmare.*
Then films of Fidel Castro on television appear, as in shots 705–715 of the
film. It includes a shot at the beginning of Sergio watching television,
which is left out of the film.
69. This shot does not appear in the shooting script. The following shots, until

704, are continued in the shooting script, with some modifications, after Fidel's T.V. speech.

70. Everything from this point on, until the end, appears in the shooting script as follows:

Sergio walking down the street.

SERGIO'S VOICE: Everything could just blow up. . . . Nothing's happening . . . and anything is possible.

Various freely associated shots reflecting Sergio's state of mind:

> *A bomb exploding.*
> *Letters on a billboard: ". . . OR DEATH."*
> *Hiroshima.*
> *Faces in the afternoon.*
> *Mexican skeletons on his work table.*
> *Sign: "MORTAL DANGER."*
> *Faces.*

(Suddenly there is a violent sound of tanks.)
Street
Night: CU *of Sergio frightened. He is out on the street and has just discovered a convoy of armaments. The convoy moves along the sea front avenue.*
(The sound of tanks slowly fades away.)
SERGIO'S VOICE: What's all this for? . . . What for? I don't want to come to such an end. I prefer remaining underdeveloped.
Trucks hauling cannons.
Cannons.
A semi-truck with a dark canvas covering something very big.
Sergio's Apartment
Night.   Sergio's watch.   (Sounds of ticking.)

Photos: *Photos of Missile Crisis taken from magazines:*
Soviet ships.
U-2 planes
Missile emplacements.
Public figures associated with the crisis.

SERGIO'S VOICE: What if everything started right now? That's okay, what can I do? . . . I'm not going to try to escape through a crack in the wall like a cockroach. Besides, there aren't any cracks anymore. There's no use in protesting. We're all in this thing together. I'll die the same as everyone else.
Sergio's Apartment
Nighttime. Sergio cannot sleep; he tosses and turns. He gets absorbed in hitting a thumbnail against a tooth.

SERGIO'S VOICE: This island is a trap. We're very small and too poor. This dignity doesn't come cheap. I don't want to think. I don't want to know anything. Nothing.

He goes to the medicine chest and looks into it. He takes out a bottle of pills. He pours one into his hand. Then he keeps pouring the pills into his hand until the bottle is empty. (All this action is shot from a great distance: it's seen at the bottom of the screen, through the small crack of the half-open doorway.)

SERGIO'S VOICE: What can people like me do here? What can people like me do anywhere in the world?

Street

Dawn. The street.
Militiawomen.
People. Posters.
Artillery deployed.
A change of guard or "dry-run" maneuvers.

Thus, there is a significant change in the film version; instead of ending in a suicide it opts for an open ending. The shots of tanks in the city at night (shots 727–28, 732, 735, 741) were not taken for this film. They had been taken for a film report that was never edited and were discovered by chance when the film was in the editing stage. Many other parts of this final sequence were improvised during filming.

Contexts

Source

Edmundo Desnoes's novel
Memorias del Subdesarrollo
(Memories of Underdevelopment)
was published in Cuba in 1962 and
subsequently translated into English
by the author and published by New
American Library under the title
Inconsolable Memories in 1967. During the interim, Desnoes had worked
on the film adaptation of the novel
with Tomás Gutiérrez Alea and the
translated novel includes some transformations of the original text that
were based on the film. Among the
major scenes present in the film and
in *Inconsolable Memories* but absent
from the original Spanish version are
Sergio and Pablo's conversation in the
automobile, the scene at Hemingway's home, the tape-recorded
arguments between Sergio and Laura,
Sergio's erotic fantasies about Noemí,
and the speeches by Kennedy and
Castro.

Desnoes was born in Havana in
1930 and was educated there and in
the United States. During the 1950s
Desnoes lived abroad, first in Venezuela and then in New York, where he
wrote for the magazine *Visión*. He returned to Cuba in 1960 to work for
the Cuban national book publishing
company and for the Revolutionary
Orientation Commission. He has written novels, short stories, poems, and
essays and his work has been translated into several languages. He
presently lives in New York City.

Inconsolable Memories

All those who loved me and kept bothering me right up to the last minute have left now. My first impulse after I kissed my dumb old lady (Laura would not even give me a goodbye smile, much less shake my empty hand) was to beat it away from the building, but then I decided to go up to the observation deck and watch all right down to the end. The plane lumbered out onto the airstrip and soon disappeared silently off into the sky.

My old lady's cheek was damp and over-powdered; when my old man hugged me, his bulky blue overcoat fell onto the granite floor. He spent the rest of the time we were together dusting if off nervously. I think Laura was half sorry she'd walked out on me. Up in the States she'll have to go to work, yes, until some other shit decides to marry her (she's still good-looking and a nice piece) and support her the way I used to. I never had any doubts about her loving me. In her skin-deep fashion. She couldn't give me any more than she did. She didn't have any more. She'll remember me, I'm sure, just as long as she's having a hard time. As soon as somebody takes on her problems (and she doesn't have many) she'll naturally stop thinking back to the time we were together. All Laura wants is comfort and a touch of romanticism. I've been the horse's ass: working to support her as if she had been born in New York or Paris (and bourgeois, as they say here these days) and not on this underdeveloped island. Whatever meager talent I had went down the drain of all those years wasted in keeping her amused, taking trips to civilized countries, trying to make her refined, making all kinds of efforts to avoid getting caught up in the vicious circle of recriminations and the "I love you, honey, sweetie" of reconciliation. I got her to dress like a model and not a whore and to read French and American novels. . . . So what! That wasn't what I wanted. She's a little animal and I'm a horse's ass. A deluxe little animal.

I'm glad I'm alone in the apartment; no family and hardly any friends left in Cuba. I'm not going to move, leave. Pablo is the last close friend I have left here, and he says he's getting papers ready to beat it. I'm glad because it was all a big farce: I wasn't interested in my wife's taste in clothes, and I don't love my parents very much, and being the Simmons representative here in Cuba (I wasn't born to make or sell furniture) left me cold, and all my friends managed to do was bore me stiff.

Don't feel like writing any more: in all honesty I feel miserable, forlorn in my new freedom-loneliness.

Don't feel like doing anything. I'm sitting here over my typewriter because so much sleep has given me a headache. Hung over from sleep. For years now I've been telling myself that if I had the time I'd sit down and finish that book of short stories I'd started and keep a diary to find out whether I've got anything else in me or whether I'm just plain superficial. Self-deception never ends. And all we can do is write down the life or the lie we really are. Now I feel like going back to bed. Yes, I think I will.

How can I explain the way I feel today? It's as if I were crumbling inside; as if loneliness were digging at me with a scoop. Never notice any change when I look down at my arm or up at my face in the mirror; it's all happening somewhere inside. Words are no good. Feel so sick I'd rather keep quiet. Today I feel like going out into the street. Walk around Havana; see things moving, different scenery, people. Laura? Let's face it, I don't give a damn about Laura or anybody. Even the typewriter keys I'm pounding have nothing to do with me, they don't understand, they're dumb. Jesus, I feel lousy!

I've just cut my toenails. It's revolting how self-centered I've become. No, I am, I have always been. Wasted almost half an hour pruning my square horny nails, holding my deformed toes tight in my hands. And they didn't make me sick, even though just to look at a foot (even if it's part of the most ethereal-looking female) makes me want to puke. And still my own feet don't turn my stomach. Even though they spend the whole day trapped inside a pair of shoes, sweating in the darkness of my stretch socks. And we walk with our feet. On the ground. A foot is all that's needed to show us how close we are to, no, how we really *are* animals. Maybe the arch is the only attractive part. Some women have very enticing curved arches. Flatfeet are like barnacles. Twisted stiff toes are the ugliest thing about our whole body. We ought to cut them off. Even if we lose our balance. Would we fall flat on our faces if our toes were neatly amputated?

It's nice to move: move our limbs, our body, our eyes, our memories, our senses. . . . I spent more than three hours walking up and down Havana; watching people strutting about, jabbering, getting into buses, screaming, smiling, drinking demitasses of black coffee—I felt that my worries were meaningless.

Then I began to watch the women. Looking them over as they passed on the street. What is really extraordinary about Cuban women is that they always look you in the eyes; they never avoid being touched by your eyes or touching you with theirs. That never happened to me in Europe or in the States. People there tend to mind their own business. I've spent hours trying to look into women's eyes in New York and Paris, but without much success. They look at you as if you were the red light that will change before they cross a street. Italian women may look at you a little more intensely. But they never hold onto one of your glances the way women here do.

I went into a bookstore on Galiano, next to the América theater, to browse around. I saw a cinnamon-skinned mulatto girl; she had spindly legs but a surprisingly beautiful face. She was looking me over more carefully than the records she was thumbing through. I played it cool, but inside I began to grow restless.

Then she turned around and left. I didn't have a chance to say anything to her; she hadn't said a word. But it left me with the urge to keep up the silly furtive game somewhere else and see what happened.

I needed a pocket comb. Mine had broken when I sat down in the bus. I had both halves in my pocket, next to my handkerchief. I can remember it very clearly because a few times I was going to pull it out and comb my ruffled hair, but I was ashamed to use the stump of a comb. I asked at several tobacco counters and they said "all gone, *no hay,* sorry." I went into the old five-and-ten and no luck either, "*se acabaron,* just ran out of them." We need so damned many things to keep our stupid lives going.

For the past few weeks there hasn't been a soft drink to be had anywhere. I never thought that the manufacture of soft drinks could be paralyzed just because there was no cork for the caps. That's what they say. That shitty cork I used to scrape off when I was a boy and then I'd flatten out the tin with a hammer, open two holes with a nail, and with a piece of thread make myself a disk that would spin and spin and was quite sharp. Once I almost lost a finger playing with it. Never, not then or ever after, could I have imagined how many insignificant things are necessary to keep a country running smoothly. Now you can see everything inside out, all the hidden entrails of the system. We're living suspended over an abyss; there are an almost infinite number of details that have to be controlled so that everything can flow naturally; it's overwhelming. The worst punishment they could give me would be to draw up, find out one way or another, a list of everything we have to buy from the Communist bloc now that the United States has slammed the door on us. The Revolutionary Government doesn't know what kind of mess it's got itself into.

I didn't find a comb downtown. It was only a good excuse to go back and forth across Havana. I kept on thinking that I could choose the girl I wanted at random. I looked at them and I felt that they noticed I was alone, available, handsome, intelligent, and that I had enough money to avoid a sordid relationship. I'm still naïve and underdeveloped at heart! I was fooling myself, no one noticed a thing. Females looked at me the way they always have; it was all my imagination. I had deceived myself once more. No one could notice that I was alone, that my wife had left me; sad and all fucked up and looking for female company along the streets.

Since El Encanto, the big department store, burned down, the city hasn't been the same. Havana today looks like a town in the interior, Pinar del Río, Artemisa, or Matanzas. It no longer looks like the Paris of the Caribbean, as tourists and whores used to call it. Now it looks more like the capital of a banana republic in Central America, one of those dead, underdeveloped cities like Tegucigalpa or San Salvador or Managua. It's not just because they destroyed El Encanto and the stores have very little left to offer, hardly any consumer goods of quality. It's the rabble; the people you meet on the streets now are humble, poorly dressed, they buy anything—even if they don't need it. They have some money in their pockets now and they spend it on anything; they'd pay, I swear, twenty pesos for a chamber pot if they saw one displayed in a window. You can see that they never had anything to their names. All the women look like maids and the men like laborers. Not all of them, almost all of them.

I jumped into bed to read Eddy's novel as soon as I got home. I found it in La Epoca. I won't give any opinion until I finish it.

I had originally intended to type the date each time I sat down to write something. Just came back up from looking for today's newspaper downstairs; I couldn't find it, maybe the maid threw it away. To tell the truth, dating each entry is stupid, makes no sense. Today for me is the same as any other day that went by or is still to come. *Feeling tomorrow just like I feel today . . . I hate to see that evening sun go down.*

I've just crossed out every single date. If anything changes it will be obvious from what I put down. I don't have to sleep at night and in the morning I don't have to get up and go to work. Time is a whim. All the silly conventions that we take for granted without even asking if they're worth respecting or not!

Yesterday I finally stayed home all day. Noemí didn't show up. It's weird walking through the empty rooms, the house is turning into a cavern. I feel protected and at the same time abandoned between its walls. It's an echo chamber when the buses and the cars go by down in the street outside, especially the air brakes when the buses stop at the corner; it's like a groan, a sigh from the engine. That's a stupid idea. Machines never complain or do anything remotely like it. All in my head. I'm on the fourth floor but I feel as if I were underground. Sometimes I think it's the way the apartment is built, other times that it's me. In the living room (it's a duplex) I feel as if I'd fallen into a well.

Every day now I make myself breakfast like a robot. Coffee, condensed milk, two slices of toast. This morning I was surprised by the sonorous belch I let out when I finished sipping my cup of *café con leche* as I looked out the window at the red roofs of Vedado and the ocean. I'm turning into an animal. Since no one else is in the apartment, I let myself go. I remember my father farting and belching on the porch every Sunday. I'm glad I don't have to visit my parents every Sunday!

I can't let it happen again. Even if there isn't anyone else in the apartment I have to be civilized. I would be exceedingly ashamed if anyone had heard that belch of a sated beast. An old man who has already lost control of his own body.

She left almost everything in the dresser, as if she were still living here with me. Still I don't know what to do, whether to throw it all out or just leave it there: I'm not sure whether it's exciting or soothing. I opened the long narrow drawer and stood there for a while, amazed, looking at all that shit without touching a thing. Can't understand how she didn't collect all her things before she went away, or passed them on to a friend, or just gave them away to the maid. Anything except leaving her stuff there as if she were still sprawled on the bed this very minute reading *Reflections in a Golden Eye,* the book she left on the night table.

I would have thrown it all out. Makes me restless leaving traces behind me, a trail, any object that other people, even my wife, could use to judge me, destroy me. (I only want to leave behind the order I've given my things. I, as Montaigne said, know more about myself than anyone else.) Laura didn't see it that way. I counted eighteen different lipsticks. And she said there was nothing left in Havana these days! That's not counting the ones she took with her. Some of them are almost all used up but others are brand new. I started to turn one of them in and out, in and out; I don't think there's anything more obscene than a lipstick. The names of the shades are really exotic: Black Magic, Café Espresso, Mango Sherbet, Pink Champagne, Aqua Rosa, Pastel Red, Chianti. . . . The same tones with only slight differences. The truth is I never really appreciated how much the pink of her lips would change according to the time of day and her dress. I missed that. Once in a while I did notice, but usually I was blind. Never again; I've never got around to enjoying the taste of lipstick the way I did when I was an adolescent and kissed a girl or Gloria, my first steady date. I think the texture and the taste of lipstick excited me more than anything else. When I got home late at night, back in my room, it almost brought on an erection again when I saw the red marks on my handkerchief. Laura didn't take all the Chinese jewelry she used to bring home each time she went shopping lately. Said it was the only new thing she found downtown. They wouldn't have allowed her to take out all her jewelry anyway, so she even left one of her pearl necklaces, the only piece of jewelry I convinced her she should wear regularly. I think I taught her how to appreciate the simplicity of pearls. What a damned fool!

I fingered a pair of stockings she had left behind and listened in rapture to the way the synthetic fibers rustled just as her legs would rub together occasionally as she walked. Then I took a hairpin and started to poke it into my ears, first to clean out the wax and then just scratching, twisting it around, until I saw my stupid face in the dresser mirror. My eyes were turned up, white, like a mystic in a trance or a lover.

I'm glad she left her things behind abandoned casually in the drawers, and her clothes and shoes scattered about the closet. It's almost as if I still had her here with me. She was actually made out of all those things she owned and wore. The objects that she used and was surrounded by were as much a part of Laura as her own body. Objects are less ungrateful than people. She also left a cheap Chanel No. 5. Never liked it. Laura was the sum of all those things. With everything she had left kicking around the apartment I could even make love to her again.

The only thing that burns me up is that she left the Roman coin behind. She had me fooled there: she never did like it. Yes, it's true, the first time I showed her the green, moldy, eroded coin, she grinned, I don't know whether out of surprise or loathing. Now I know it was out of pure loathing. When I had it mounted, right there in Rome, we even went to pick it up together at a jewelry shop on the Via Veneto. And I put it on for her while she held her soft ticklish hair away from her secret neck. What was it that damned Catholic fanatic had told me? *La sensualità provocata dalla donna . . . una delle prime cause della putrefazione e morte dell'anima.* Something along those lines.

The silhouette of a Roman goddess on one side, you can still make out the pleats of her robe, and on the other the profile of an emperor. Never bothered to find out what period the coin belonged to or how much it was really worth. I paid a handful of lire. . . . Just liked it; when I handled it I would start thinking about the thousands of people who must have used that coin and were dead now. I almost saw a Roman lackey buying eels at the market.

That really upset me, to see that she'd left the Roman coin behind. I most decidedly prefer objects to people. That's why I don't feel alone in the house: the chairs, the books, the bed, the clean sheets, the refrigerator, the tub with hot and cold water, sugar, coffee, the paintings, and all the stuff scattered about the apartment—they all keep me company.

I saw Pablo. He's as mean as that short sentence. I saw Pablo. What exasperates me no end is how uncomfortable I feel with almost everybody. People seem more stupid every day, and I haven't become a bit more intelligent. For almost five years we knocked around together; thinking of it makes me sick. Eugenia, his wife, hardly ever said a word, she would only stare at people and things; I liked her. The four of us went everywhere together: twice a week to the movies, Friday night to any old nightclub and Saturday and Sunday we'd spend on the beach. Not being bored was all that mattered. I can see it now, I wasted my time miserably.

Maybe it was because Pablo enjoyed morbid pictures, like *Rashomon, La Neige est sale, Suddenly Last Summer*—and because he was especially gifted at pinpointing the weaknesses of others. Mainly for that. Our weekends at the beach were spent sprawled on the sand exchanging remarks about the bodies that happened to pass by. I'll never forget what he said one day when Anita Mendoza sauntered by without even noticing us. "Can you imagine, Anita, that fleshy marvel, has her stomach full of black beans? I just saw her having lunch on the terrace." Now every time I see an attractive female I can't avoid looking down furtively at her softly rounded stomach and wondering: "What did you eat today?"

It was, even though it sounds like a joke, a deadly blow to my romantic vision of love, even carnal love. If instead of black beans (always thick and diabolical) it had been mutton, truffled quails, pheasant, salmon, cheese soufflé, I don't know, even apple pie or strawberry Jell-O, any other dish except black beans, it wouldn't have destroyed my *Weltanschauung*.

A good bowl of black beans, even if they still have to be civilized, is always a tasty treat. It's like everything else around us: it's sunk in underdevelopment. Even our feelings are underdeveloped: joy and sorrow are primitive and direct here, they haven't been elaborated and worked on by culture. The revolution is the only complicated thing that has hit Cubans over the head. But many years will have to pass before we catch up with modern industrialized countries.

For me it's already too late. Rimbaud has less right than I to exclaim: *Il m'est bien évident que j'ai toujours été race inférieure. Je ne puis comprendre la révolte. Ma race ne se souleva jamais que pour piller: tels les loups à la bête qu'ils n'ont pas tuée.*

Enough bullshit!

Pablo is leaving. He's a perfect moron. Now I can see it crystal clear; every time he opens his mouth, it never fails, it's to let out some asinine remark. He used to make fun of our society crowd to amuse himself and not to destroy them. That's the only thing I have to thank the revolution for: they really fucked up all the damned half-wits who hoarded everything here! I can't say "governed" because they didn't have the foggiest idea of what a ruling class is all about. They never even took the trouble to find out. I think I once heard Mestre say he'd read a very interesting book: *Revolt of the Masses;* he'd read Ortega y Gasset in a paperback, I don't object to that, but in an English translation, that was going a bit too far! It wasn't a joke, I would have been amused by that; he said it seriously.

Cuban society women dressed like whores. At least among the people that has a certain charm: women with loud dresses tightly accentuating all their curves and protuberances; but among the bourgeoisie it was pitiful to see those women dressed up like that and topping it off with jewelry. Not even the mistress of a Jewish shopkeeper on New York's Delancey Street looked as cheap.

Now I remember that obnoxious doctor, the offspring of an old patrician family, already degenerated (his great-grandfather had fought in the 1868 War of Independence), whom we met in Paris. Made fun of French medicine, insisted Cuban medicine was much more advanced because it had the latest iron lung and the most streamlined scalpel manufactured in the United States. He had no idea of all the experience and research and thought that was accumulated in the best French hospitals, even if they lacked the last word in perfumed anesthetic. They're great diagnosticians. Laura immediately sided with the bastard; she said: "Everybody in Paris stinks and the bathrooms are older than Methuselah." I turned to Laura disconcerted (I really admired her shallowness) and then told the degenerate doctor that he knew less about medicine than what a driver knows about his car engine. He used to wash his hands twice: once before lunch and again after coffee. I'm sure he did it on purpose, to impress Laura.

I can't think of the Cuban bourgeoisie without foaming at the mouth. I hate them with tenderness. Feel sorry for them: for what they could have been and what they wasted out of plain stupidity. For a time I tried to convince them to go into politics, throw out all those professional politicos and tin soldiers, find out what was happening in the rest of the world. I insisted that they had to modernize the country: put an end to all those thatched huts and all the Cuban rhythm and primitive gaiety and force everybody to study mathematics. Nothing. All wasted. And I've gone down with them. Alone here now.

Pablo is one of them, part of the same litter. He thinks the government is going to fall because they no longer import cars with long fins. He's so dumb he insists everybody here is against the government. Pablo has a tendency to project his feelings, to think he is the measure of all things: if Pablo is dissatisfied, everybody else must also be dissatisfied, because he is the Cuban people; others don't exist, they're only the reflection of his moods. And all that after the Bay of Pigs disaster! Spends most of his time commenting on the discontent of the people. That farmers now refuse to work on the *granjas*. He has no idea of what a modern State is all about. The power and resources at its disposal. Now, whether you like it or not, we have a real State on the island!

Pablo sees a line in front of a store and smiles. What a shit! Smiles like a saint before the scintillating image of God. Says the only thing Cubans won't stand for is a food shortage. With the hunger they've endured ever since the Spanish conquistadores landed! Tired Indians dying like flies as they looked for gold in the rivers, black slaves cutting cane twenty hours a day on a glass of brown sugar and water, the concentration camps during the War of Independence. . . . The depression of the thirties—twenty eggs for a peseta and there wasn't a poor Cuban who had a peseta. I'm all screwed up because I've looked into things more than is good for my own health; don't know why the hell I read so much. That's why I'm here all paralyzed.

Pablo is so deluded he's even thinking now about what kind of business he intends opening when he comes back. That is, after the good old *yanquis* have bumped off all the Communists and given the island back to the decent people. Oh, Pablo, Pablo, Pablo! I gave him Wilson's *To the Finland Station* so he would at least have an idea about the development of social ideas, about socialism, from the French Revolution to the Russian Revolution. I'm sure he didn't even open the book when he got home. I'll rest when he finally leaves next month.

They're all deluded, one way or the other. If they're against the government, it's because they're convinced it'll be easy to recover their comfortable ignorance; if they're for the revolution, it's because they expect to pull this country out of its backwardness.

Just lit a cigarette. I've been smoking for over twenty years now and I still don't know whether I enjoy burning tobacco or not. *That's the story of my life.* Yes, it's all right after a meal, takes away the sticky taste of the food. Other times the stream of smoke, the cool biting taste, watching how something is consumed, can pull me out of a rut. Made up my mind to smoke only when I really feel the urge and never light a cigarette just because I'm bored. Eddy was right about that. Don't want to run away from the hole I carry inside. Want to feel alone and see how deep I can go into it, see if I can get to the bottom of my emptiness. I can't stand it sometimes and I practically crumble into my own body! I've already crushed out the cigarette in the bronze ashtray.

Traps everywhere. Now I've developed a new and irritating vice: lying in wait for Noemí's visits. Three times a week she comes to clean the apartment. During the three hours she's in the apartment I'm a different person. I do everything for her sake, fully conscious that she's listening and can see me. I can hear her right now cleaning downstairs in the living room. I'm pounding the typewriter so she won't find out what I really am: a bum. That's why I also started to smoke: I'm sure she heard me strike the match and can smell the tobacco. The presence of another person can change your life completely. And turn your entire existence into a pose, the act you put on for others so they'll appreciate you. My life has just been that up to now they all disappeared and left me alone.

I'm fidgety because I have desires for Noemí. She just went by and smiled through the door. I want to have her and I don't dare. Maybe she'll turn me down. That could be bothersome; would force me to fire her, not see her again, hire someone else to clean the apartment and take my clothes to the laundry and pick up my monthly rations. Life is made up of insatiable yearnings and banalities. What would Noemí think if she looked over my shoulder and saw the crap I'm writing now!

I've tried to appear charming in her eyes. The other day she arrived and I invited her to join me for a cup of *café con leche*. She immediately accepted and sat down at the table with me. I was really surprised. Could have been hungry or flirting. I'm still undecided why she did it. Noemí was born in Matanzas and is a Protestant. For over a year she's been doing the cleaning here and I never noticed her almond-shaped eyes; when they're open her lids disappear completely. You can't see the fleshy rim of the lids when she looks straight at you, it's as if they'd slit her eyes open with a neat gash. When she said she was a Protestant, I asked her (couldn't think of anything else): "Why?" "I don't know," she answered, and I decided not to pursue the idea any further, might think I was making fun of her. But I did ask her if she'd been baptized in the Yumurí river. She went into all the details leading up to the ceremony, even described the gown she was wearing. I saw myself carrying her in my arms and plunging her into the water and then looking at the wet gown clinging to her shapely body. I could carry her easily; she's light, gives the impression that her bones are full of air like a bird's. If she took better care of herself (didn't wave her hair into those repulsive little curls) and dressed better, she'd be quite attractive. Has the body of a *Vogue* or *Harper's Bazaar* model. She's thin, but has tasty chunks of flesh in all the right places.

Now she's in the bedroom; I'm sure she's thinking about me while she's making my bed. I feel like rushing into the room and grabbing hold of her, without saying a word, just embracing her, to see what happens.

I don't dare.

Noemí. Isn't that a name out of the Bible? I have to look it up.

And if she doesn't turn me down? Would mean getting involved again. She would start demanding stupid things right away, would come to live here with me and make my life unbearable. I don't want any responsibilities. I'm much better off empty. Possessing her would be much easier than getting rid of Noemí. I inevitably try to change women into the image I have of them, and that takes up time. Would leave me exhausted for writing and thinking. I can't keep falling into the same old vicious ruts. Rather go out and have intercourse with a whore.

I went to the movies to get away from flesh-and-blood people and I almost bumped into some nasty buzzing friends of Laura's. They disappeared into the orchestra and didn't see me. I went up to the balcony so as not to stumble onto them in the dark, although I always sit in the fourth or fifth row, up close to the screen. I like to have the images surround me and engulf me. That's why television bothers me so much: furniture, my body, everything in the room is too large, seems much more real and important than the blurred images on the set, makes me feel like an awkward giant. I can't forget myself when I watch television.

I hoped I could live in the movies without any involvements, without feeling the oozing sticky drool of my fellow men. Saw *Hiroshima, Mon Amour* for the second time. I already suffered through two films from the "friendly countries," which is what the "satellite nations" of just a few years ago are called now. It's fabulous how everything changes and no one goes mad! I can't swallow another one of those pictures. They depress me terribly; they smell so old, like the mothballs in my Aunt Angelina's closet; besides, the plots all seem so remote and sordid that I feel even more alone than I really am.

Hiroshima, Mon Amour is a depth charge; I can't remember anything like it since *Rashomon,* the picture that completely changed my sense of reality. The mingling of love and destruction was soothing and sad. I had to control myself so as not to turn my head away when I saw the roasted victims paralyzed by the nuclear blast. (I read even today, more than fifteen years later, that people who were only showered on by radioactivity in Hiroshima and Nagasaki are still getting sick and dying.) I never felt that there was anything beyond the body; I think we're closer to a piece of machinery than to an incarnate soul, an electronic machine, a machine nonetheless; that's why the mutilated bodies struck me so. Our body is all we have with which to desire and hate others and to understand. The reviews were full of stupid remarks! Even Eddy wrote something in *Lunes de Revolución* when it opened.

Emmanuelle Riva seems capable of almost anything without getting scandalized. Green, ripe, and rotten all at the same time. She said something that stuck in my head: *"J'ai désiré avoir une inconsolable mémoire."* I suspect civilization is just that: knowing how to relate things, not forgetting anything. That's why civilization is impossible here: Cubans easily forget the past: they live too much in the present.

I went to see the picture again because I had missed some snatches of dialogue. There were two or three things I didn't get right (even my French is deteriorating) and when I tried to read the subtitles the letters all looked broken and worm-eaten. I asked the guy on my right if he could read them and he answered: "Perfectly." I spent the rest of the picture trying to decipher the subtitles. I'm going blind. Toward the end I had the courage to ask the guy at my left (he was involved elsewhere) because I wanted to be sure. "Quite well, I can see the letters quite well," and he put his arm back around her bare shoulders.

The oculist told me I was nearsighted. I went to have a pair of glasses made so I could see clearly from a distance. I've got to pick them up next week. People said there were no frames left in Havana but I found a very somber pair, black, at an optician's on San Rafael.

I'm growing old. It's devastating to see how your body crumbles from so much use, slips away out from under you. Now I'm obsessed with doing some exercise. Got too much of a paunch. Besides, it keeps me busy. Every afternoon I do push-ups and knee-bends and exercises to tighten the belly muscles; that way my guts won't pop out. Looked at myself in the mirror and discovered with surprise that I was beginning to look like my father: I've got the same kind of stomach. I was revolted to discover that my back, like his, sank in just above my ass. That really depressed me. When I sit down two inner tubes of fat encircle my waist.

If I still believed in or could even create an illusion about the counterrevolution, it's all over now, it's gone to hell. Nothing in their heads, no dignity, no backbone; the middle class here is like a meringue on the door of a school, as they say, yes, a meringue on the door of the revolution.

Even when they hit upon a weak spot in the revolution, they foul the whole thing up, they don't know how to focus on the situation and they invariably end up jabbering a lot of shit. The only intelligent thing Pablo ever had to say would end up degenerating into a discussion about stupid food. All counterrevolutionaries turn into an endless intestine: obsessed by food. I'm sure that Pablo would love to carry some juicy filet mignons in his pockets as a sign of affluence. "Every single word the Americans say about Communism is absolutely true," he said to me as we drove around comfortably in his Rambler, "I have proof of it now"; the smell of the leather upholstery, the chrome dashboard with all kinds of round and square indicators and numbers and needles made me feel nauseous. All the time I drove around with Pablo I felt like puking, throwing up all my family, my business; the mediocrity of my whole class had been rammed into my stomach.

"It's true what they say on the 'Voice of America,' what the *yanquis* say is true, there's no freedom, you're being followed all the time, the economy is kaput, no food or anything. Don't be foolish, I'm anything but fat. It's a question of my constitution, that's how I'm built. Besides, you don't have any idea of the troubles I go through. You don't know how I have to scheme to eat well, to nourish myself. Yes, it's true, real hunger you don't see, I'll grant you that. But it's not a matter of eating, it's what you eat. Eat, anybody can eat. Everybody used to eat in Cuba before. What's important is eating right, a balanced diet, you've got to have plenty of proteins, plenty of meat. All those people you see around are suffering from anemia. That guy right there, the one walking along the sidewalk, the fat one, yes, that one, I'm sure he's got anemia. I'll bet you anything he's got anemia." I couldn't take Pablo, all the time I was trying to distract myself by looking out the window at the people and the trees and the buildings going by. Told him I never heard of or ever saw a fat man in a Nazi concentration camp, that if he kept carrying on that way he'd end up completely off his rocker. "If I stay I'll go off my rocker for sure. I've got to leave. No, they haven't ever arrested me. No one's bothered me so far. I know how to take care of myself. But anything can happen . . . you can get arrested here for no reason at all. Sometimes I'm sitting quietly at home and I start thinking that they're coming, they'll knock on the door and arrest me in the middle of the night. I always expect the worst from these people in the government now. This is the end of Cuba."

Pablo is everything I don't want to be. Was I like that before, was I the same as he once? I guess it's possible. The spitting image. When we drove into the gas station I felt relieved. The smell of gasoline always pleases me, cleans me out, even intoxicates me a bit. I got over my nausea. Pablo started complaining because they'd forgotten to check the air in the tires and wipe the windshield. I was glad; the revolution, even though it's destroying me, is my revenge against the stupidity of the Cuban bourgeoisie, against my own moronic life. I swear to God, I was pleased as hell when the attendant gave him a dirty look, ignored him. "Please, check the oil," Pablo begged. "We're out of oil. . . . If you want, I'll check it anyhow. . . ." "Forget it," he answered and I smiled. It's the truth, I'm a traitor, a pariah.

"Did you notice the kind of service you get around here? It's obvious, every-thing is all fucked up. Not even the workers are satisfied with the revolution. Not even this poor slob is on the side of the revolution. What do you think of that?" I ignored him too, didn't answer a word. I was content to see him suffer. "If I could, I'd smash this car into pieces once and for all, run it into a tree, push it over a cliff. You want to know why I don't? You're dumb. It's in the inventory. They check everything you own before they let you leave the country, as soon as you apply. If I wreck the car they won't let me out of this trap. I've even had to have it repaired and painted. I wouldn't risk permission to leave for anything in the world. I had a fender all dented and I had it banged out and fixed. I'm not going to let them frame me on account of a smashed fender, not on your life. I won't give them that pleasure. I'm leaving them a new car, a brand-new car, as if it had just come out of the factory in Detroit. They're not going to see another new car around here for a long time. Cubans love American cars! I want to see what they're going to do now. Cubans can't stand a revolution without American cars. I'm telling you. I know my people."

Everything he said was the opposite of what I feel now. Since they national-ized my car along with the furniture store, I'm much more serene. No longer having to worry about filling the tank all the time, changing the oil now and then, parking in the right place. I always used to forget where I'd parked the car. It had become an obsession lately. I even had nightmares about not finding the car and walking all over Havana looking for the damn thing. No rest for the weary. I want to unload my problems, get them off my back. The revolution has taken quite a load off my back. A car is a pain in the ass. I'd rather abandon a car to rot in the streets before I'd kill myself trying to find spare parts in the government *consolidado,* standing in line, buying on the black market. . . . Nothing that's too complicated is worth doing. It's revolting how Pablo and all the counter-revolutionaries are obsessed with food. I'm satisfied with a cup of coffee with milk, and a slice of toast; if things start breaking down, fine, let them crumble to pieces. Ruins are soothing. I'm not going to worry about it.

"Look, if I wanted to, I could fix Laura's car, it's down in the garage, it needs ball bearings for the gears. . . . I wouldn't waste my time trying to locate the spare parts. I'd rather take the bus or a taxi," I explained to humiliate him, to make him feel ashamed of his stinginess; no dice. He didn't even sense the allusion. He began to complain again right away, couldn't get a sealed unit for the fender, he needed a new headlight to turn it into perfect shape before he left.

"They were easy to get before. You just had to whistle and a hundred sealed units would rain on you from all sides. I never would have thought that we'd run out of them too, that we'd run out of headlights. Wherever I go, 'no, we haven't got any, no, we haven't got any,' besides, they say it with such relish. They're not bourgeois, as the revolution claims, they're workers and they're against this whole mess. No one goes along with this."

"How stupid can you get? Then how come they're in power even in spite of mighty Superman, in spite of the United States," I said, conscious of defending the revolution without really wanting to, against my better judgment, just to irritate Pablo. "And the people at all those mass meetings and in the organiza-tions, and all those voluntary militiamen everywhere."

"It's all a lie," he said and I could see he was quite mad; we're all quite mad. Everybody believes what he wants to believe, even if reality keeps proving the exact opposite to you every minute. Then I offered Pablo a headlight from Lau-ra's car. Let them cannibalize the whole thing, tear it apart piece by piece. We immediately drove over to my place and went down into the garage to see it. It had no tires (I'd sold them to a neighbor for next to nothing), mounted on four sawhorses. When I leaned into the car to open the hood, my knee on the front seat, I got a slight whiff of Laura's perfume. No, it wasn't her perfume, it was her stinking smell. I told Pablo to hurry up, that I didn't like to look at her car. He didn't take just one, but both sealed units. Now Laura's car hasn't even got headlights.

I've reconstructed this whole conversation in detail to muster up enough courage to hate Pablo, to get him out of my system. I can understand that Pablo is not Pablo, but my own life. I can still maintain a certain lucid awareness; I know what's going on, but I can't avoid it. He and Laura and everybody else.

The body can be very grateful. In less than a week of exercises, I can already feel my muscles tightening. My stomach sticks out less. Don't know if this is really happening or if it's only my imagination.

Got the glasses: I wear them with mixed feelings. As if I had grown a wart on my face or they'd thrown me into a fishbowl; it's just as if I'm in a hard shell when I put them on. It's stupid of me. I can see, it's true, with greater precision. Before, everything was blurred, with fuzzy edges, like impressionist paintings, and now I can see everything with the transparent accuracy of an Ingres. Don't know which picture I like better. It's difficult, having to choose all the time!

She was wearing a wide skirt, a little above her knees, sandals, and a loose blouse with orange polka dots. I was heading toward Ember's restaurant. For some time now I had had a craving to eat Italian food to my heart's content, but I'd never got around to it, didn't want to go to the restaurant alone, can't enjoy my food, feel a bit like an animal when I eat in silence without talking to anyone, chewing my food and watching other people talking at their tables. That's why when I eat out alone I'd always rather sit at the counter, like horses drinking at a trough. But Ember's has no counter.

"What nice knees!" I said and she turned around to look at me. When I got in front of the restaurant, I saw her raising her tanned leg and looking carefully at her left knee.

Then she crossed the street and stopped in front of the entrance to the Habana Libre hotel.

"You're crazy," she told me two or three times as I tried to get her out of her shell. Finally she said: "I'm waiting for someone, I have an appointment here with a man for a job at the I.C.A.I.C." (the Cuban Institute of Cinematographic Art and Industry). That was music to my ears. Right away I thought that's not true, it won't be hard to convince her to have dinner with me. If she goes for the movies she must be romantic and fanciful. I told her simply that I didn't want to eat alone: "I can't digest well if I have no one to talk to." She told me "you're crazy" again, but when I told her "come on, why don't you join me, let's go," she came along.

Before we went into the restaurant she asked what time it was. I got the feeling she was getting ready to run away and added thirty minutes to my watch. "It's too late already, I'm pretty sure he's not coming, he stood me up," and she walked into Ember's by my side.

She refused to eat anything, told me she couldn't because she was getting shots for her nerves. I must have looked incredulous, because she immediately put out her arm toward me. I held it softly by the wrist and saw three or four pinpoints around her vein. One of the little dots was surrounded by a purple bruise. And yet, I had the most tender and soft part of her arm turned toward me on the white tablecloth.

She stared at me with her large honey-colored eyes and I noticed that her cheeks were pudgy. It was almost imperceptible but it gave her a childlike air; I could still see the little girl playing with a doll in her. I imagined her parents and all the ridiculous aspects of our daily lives that destroy the spell of any romantic situation. A woman can only be young, otherwise she's not a woman; a little girl or an old lady is removed from the femininity we seek.

I found a woman again when I asked her why she wanted to be an actress. "I'm tired of being myself," she told me, changing the careful outline of her lips, "that way I can be *other* girls without having people like you think I am crazy. I'd like to be able to split my personality." I didn't expect it; I was dumbfounded. Right away I thought she was repeating something she'd heard, read in some psychology book.

"But all those characters in the theater and in the movies are like broken records," I told her, "an actress just memorizes and repeats mechanically the same words and gestures over and over again." She paid no attention, just as if I had told her something stupid or worthless. She didn't give a damn what I thought about acting.

When we were leaving the restaurant, she told me she felt like walking; I began to lead the way. After a block I took her hand and held it and she said: "Don't think you'll get anywhere with me." I felt like cursing her and sending her away. Then I saw that she was actually frightened.

"Have you got enough clothes?" I asked and she blushed. "I don't mean on you, at home?" "No." Then I told her about how Laura had left and was a *noventa millas,* a "ninety-miler"; I insisted there were many things in the apartment that would be sure to fit her, shoes and dresses. Didn't answer me. "Laura is . . . or was, more or less your size."

I pointed out my building and she got more nervous. "You're married," she said, and I had to keep myself from laughing: "No, I'm already divorced." "What will the neighbors say?" I quieted her by explaining that there was hardly ever anyone in the elevator, the whole building had only five apartments, one on each floor. She begged me to go up alone first.

I was a bit frightened that she wouldn't come. She didn't appear for a while. I waited, trying to visualize the apartment as she would see it when she walked in. Elena wasn't to blame: a couple had come into the building after I had gone up.

She stood against the closed door.

"Take your shoes off," I told her and started the radio going, "make yourself at home." I went into the kitchen to make some coffee. When I came out she'd taken off her shoes and her bra. She kissed me first and I found out she was naked under her dress, but she refused to give in completely. I didn't insist because I could see she was very nervous. She began to repeat "I'm leaving" every two or three minutes, and explain how her mother trusted her completely, "that's why she lets me go out alone"; and she also kept on repeating "if my mother could only see me now." I didn't want to force my way in and we went up to the bedroom to look at Laura's shoes and dresses.

Today Elena walked in wearing one of Laura's dresses. Made me feel somehow like a real monster, depraved. Then I decided it wasn't that important, nothing was: giving her those clothes was no sacrilege. She needed them and it was sexually stimulating to see her masquerading as Laura.

Elena lives in the old Cerro district, her family must be very poor. Middle-class parents would never leave her so free. Petty bourgeois morality. To classify people as proletariat and bourgeoisie is ridiculous, feels as if I were dehumanizing individuals, tuning them into abstract ciphers, judging them as if I were a politician. It's the damned influence of the revolution: I've even got to watch my own thoughts!

Anything like venerating the stuff that Laura left behind would be stupid fetishism.

The dress was a little tight on Elena, because she's slightly fuller than Laura, but not much. I think it's a French dress, we bought it in Paris; delicate sentimental roses all over a white background. Roses, makes no difference whether they're real or just printed on a dress, are always revoltingly sentimental. Natural roses make me feel foolishly tender.

We struggled for a while on the couch before the dress split a seam on the side. We went upstairs to get Laura's sewing basket. Elena took the dress off and she didn't finish sewing it up until after we had made violent love. "If you'd insisted the other day," she said biting a nail, "I would have let you in."

Then she broke into tears. Said she felt guilty, that she shouldn't have gone to bed with me: "You've disgraced me." I began to worry when she was still covered with tears and sobbing and drooling at one o'clock in the morning. My mouth was already dry from talking and trying to play the whole thing down, convince her that it wasn't that important. . . . Her attitude, though, made a deep impression on me.

Elena has just left. Today, after last night, she came back at eleven. I'd gone back to bed after breakfast; I thought about changing the sheets, but didn't feel like getting up: a sweet and sour smell, left by Elena, rose up every time I turned over in bed.

She walked in singing with a nasal voice: *"Antes de que tus labios me confesaran que me querías,"* and she snapped her fingers, *"ya lo sabía, ya lo sabía."* * It all goes beyond my understanding. I found out she didn't even remember how much she had suffered and cried the night before. She was very

---

* "Before your lips confessed that you loved me . . I knew it, I knew it all along."

frisky and she offered to fix lunch and help me clean up the house. I told her Noemí was coming the next morning and let her know it would be better if she didn't drop by tomorrow.

What baffles me most about people is their great incapacity to maintain a feeling, an idea, without scattering themselves. Elena proved to have no continuity at all. She's pure alteration, as Ortega y Gasset would say. What she felt yesterday has nothing to do with her present mood. She can't relate things. Another sign of underdevelopment: an inability to relate things, to accumulate experience and to develop. That's why I was so impressed when they said in *Hiroshima: "J'ai désiré avoir une inconsolable mémoire."*

I expected more from Elena. She let me down. I thought she would be much more tangled up and interesting. There's no way to stop it; always trying to live like a European. I'm deluded and underdeveloped: and, what's even worse, I know it. It's almost impossible to find a woman here who has been worked on by experience and culture. The environment is too poor, too soft, demands too little from the individual. Whatever talent Cubans might have is wasted as they try to adapt to the present, to this very instant. Wasted on appearances. People are not consistent, they're satisfied with so little. Drop projects when they're still half-finished, interrupt their own feelings, fail to follow things through to their final consequences. Cubans can't endure suffering too long without laughing. The sun, the tropics, irresponsibility. . . . Is Fidel that way too? It doesn't seem so, but . . . I don't want to fall into a trap again, fool myself. At best I can be a witness. A spectator.

"Do you like *feeling?*" Elena asked me using the English word. I brought up last night's tragedy and she said, "Who remembers that? Tell me, what do you think of the new rhythm, *feeling?*" Couldn't help myself: told her that to forget things like that was a sign of insanity. "What's wrong is that you have no *feeling.*" I had to laugh so as not to keep on with my nonsense. *"No tienes porqué criticar mi modo de vivir,"** she began to sing, stretching out the words and lowering her head. I closed her mouth with a kiss.

Elena has become a habit: I'm getting used to having a woman beside me all the time. In life you come to expect the repetition of anything that has given you pleasure: that's where the trap lies. You suffer when you can't have it, and when you do have it, the fear of losing it is awful.

---

* "You've got no right to criticize the way I live."

I went to the airport with Pablo. Tried to recall Laura's departure and think about my parents; see if I still felt anything. Pablo kept telling me over and over: "I hope to see you soon." What for? I already know the States: but what's happening here is a mystery to me. Though sometimes it scares me out of my wits to see everything I knew so well crumbling. Besides, this is the last chance I'll have of going into myself. When they called Pablo into the passengers' fishbowl I left. Said goodbye by waving a hand. He yelled something next to the glass partition, but I couldn't make it out. We exchanged absurd gestures. I couldn't hear him and he couldn't understand me.

The other day I went to Wifredo Lam's exhibit. Two couples were walking through, they looked like civil servants (mentioned the MINCIN or the MINREX or the MINED, can't remember which); they stopped in front of a certain painting and laughed hesitantly. A stupid giggle. I felt like shutting up the women by pointing out the sexual violence of Lam's symbols and mocking the ignorance of men. Naturally, I didn't do a thing. Later on a group of Russians walked in, more women then men, and discussed each painting; they would go up close to a canvas, lean back, study each detail. They were square, fat, but at the end of the last century Americans must have produced the same effect that Russians do now. A little coarse, clods of earth. Europe made fun of Americans up to a hundred years ago, considered them savages (even the Spaniards constantly referred to the "sausage-makers from Chicago" during the Spanish-American War), and today they've imposed their way of life upon the world.

I ran into a group of Russians again at Hemingway's house; no, he's dead, it's a museum now. We had scarcely been there five minutes when a penetrating whiff, a hunk of life entered and started gesticulating: "*Compañera,* please, *pozhaluista.* Right there, just a minute, please, photography." I looked him over carefully, at once attracted and repelled; he was blond, with an enormous face, like a buttock, with this small black camera hanging down over his blue plaid shirt. He moved his hands toward Elena insistently, as if trying to stop something, asking her to keep the same immobility of those hunting trophies hanging along the living-room walls. He kept pointing at a spot just under the paralyzed head of an antelope with glassy eyes and corkscrew horns.
While Elena shamelessly placed one leg in front of the other and extended her arm casually along the back of a pink armchair upholstered with an English hunting scene, two men and a woman, three more acid and penetrating whiffs, placed themselves behind the photographer and changed the angle of the black camera in front of his face.
Always the same. Emissaries of the great world power down visiting their colonies. The same fucking tourists. Humbler men than most Americans, true, and without any holdings in Cuba—but deep down their attitude is very much alike. Besides, what they can't take away in dollars they get out of us in propa-

ganda. It would really be sad if we ever discovered that they're right. That's all they're good for, underdeveloped countries, good for fulfilling our instinctive drives, killing wild animals, fishing and basking in the sun. Enjoying living by your senses. All those Russians were sunburned, tanned. They also looked at Elena as "a beautiful Cuban señorita."

"You're giving them a terribly old-fashioned pose," I told her, plunging head-first into the game, "open your legs arrogantly, put them wide apart, like a boy, and stretch your arms out stiff, as if you were about to run away from the hunter." "Shut up . . ." she cried at me smiling; the slut was enjoying her role as a savage and exotic underdeveloped beast. The frozen antelope, Elena frozen— and then she smiled again. The Soviets, as they now call the Russians here, smiled gratefully, candidly, with smiles that glittered here and there with gold teeth. *"Spasibo, compañera, spasibo,* thank you very much. *Krasivinka,* very pretty. *Spasibo."*

"This one here is called an impala, it's highly appreciated in Africa, a very rare animal, because of the elegant beauty of its spiral horns," the mulatto guide explained with religious monotony. "Its long neck is also an attribute of its beauty. Hemingway was especially fond of this piece, it is a hard animal to track down; when Hemingway saw it he hesitated before firing, he couldn't get himself to shoot, he was bewitched by its extraordinary grace and beauty and elegance. He was really fond of this hunting trophy."

I moved away from the revolting litany and saw the empty bottles of whiskey, Spanish wine, and cognac on a table next to an empty armchair, and I lifted up a whiskey bottle with a few amber drops at the bottom.

We leaned out the window between the impala head and a poster announcing a bullfight. The four Russians walked by the window and the group gathered before the ceiba tree, its solid trunk almost as impressive as their barrel-like bodies, one next to the other for a snapshot; the men folded their arms over blue and green plaid shirts and one yellow, soiled transparent shirt.

They're desperate to catch up with the United States and become the Americans of the future, they admire Hemingway more than they admire Fidel, I bet you anything they have more respect for Hemingway than for Fidel. "They're ugly," Elena remarked watching them idly. "Even so they'll rule the world someday very soon." "I don't care," and Elena began to sing. *"Sombras nada más, entre tu amor y mi amor. . . ."* * "Come on, let's move along."

When they moved to the back living room Elena took her shoes off and walked on the lion's skin spread on the floor. Immediately I thought of all the women who had visited Hemingway in that same house: Ava Gardner, Ingrid Bergman, Marlene Dietrich. And they probably walked barefoot on the dead lion's skin too. Ava Gardner has huge feet, almost all American females have huge feet, that used to bother me when I was an adolescent, when I would use pinup girls for

* "Nothing but shadows between your love and my love."

masturbation. That's our underdeveloped lot, beating our meat while we look at the ravishing female stars of the world. I'm sure the only contact that thousands of Bolivians, Venezuelans, Mexicans, and Argentinians have had with a White Goddess is through a picture of Marlene Dietrich and her dazzling legs, insured for something like a million dollars, or Ava Gardner's.

It was a sad blow to discover that Elena hadn't the foggiest idea of what was going on in my head. She slipped back into her shoes and rudely sliced a semicircle in the air with her stiff index finger, and terminated the cheap gesture with a slap on her thigh: "So here is where Mr. Way used to live? Nothing much to brag about, books and dead animals. Big deal. It looks just like the house the Americans had down at the sugar mill in Oriente, the Prestons."

It was true. It looked just like the house of any old American sugar mill manager, exactly the same atmosphere. I hadn't thought of it before. If Elena wanted to, she could develop. . . . She's got good natural intelligence. Yes, it was the standard furniture you saw in most middle-class American houses, even the living-room set upholstered in one of those conventional English hunting scenes, the glass table with the booze on wheels, the magazine rack, the table lamps with huge shades, even the corny bullfight posters. "The same furniture and the same American smell." I asked her what an American smell was like. "I don't know, don't bother me. It's the smell of nylon, toothpaste, lipstick, deodorant, detergent, and stuff like that. Americans have a peculiar smell and Russians stink."

She just can't concentrate, she doesn't worry long enough about anything. Nothing seeps into her little head. When she says startling things like that, they simply flow out spontaneously. I thought she had lived all her life here in Havana. Had no idea she'd been in Oriente, knew the big American sugar mills there. She'd never told me anything. "I hardly remember it anymore. That awful bawling out they gave us, my cousin and me." I had to insist, she didn't want to talk. "I don't know, the door was open. A door just like the one over there, a screen door, we were delivering the clean laundry, the door was open and I don't know how it was, but we ended up walking into a room where the American lady was lying in bed half naked cutting her toenails, her face all white, full of cream, cold cream. . . . She insulted us." I insisted again. "I don't know, I couldn't understand a word, she began to scream in English. I couldn't look her in the face, I was paralyzed, I was staring at her black panties trimmed with lace. Like the ones you gave me that used to belong to your wife. . . . Let's not talk about that, I didn't do anything. I'd rather not talk about it." I asked her how old she was then. "Ten or twelve, I don't know, makes no difference. My father was out of work, couldn't make ends meet, they threw him out of the bus company and they sent me over to my aunt's. My aunt was a washerwoman. I don't want to talk about it. I'm all choked up. Things like that make me choke. That's why I don't like to remember anything, I'd rather dream things up. . . ."

Hemingway's room really impressed me. Something about it and everything in

it revealed a deep disregard for life. People waste and throw away and act gener-
ously when they have everything in abundance. Everything was thrown around,
scattered; and yet they had placed it all in a conscious disorder, they had immo-
bilized the house the same as Hemingway's existence. Everything was stiff. It
seemed rigid. But the furniture was placed any old way; memories of all sorts on
the table: a Nazi swastika, torn off an enemy soldier during the Second World
War, one of his victims, probably off a rotten corpse; a round photograph of him
when he was young; an old pair of glasses with a delicate wire frame; fishing
hooks camouflaged as insects; coins from other countries; scraps of paper filled
with notes; a ridiculous gilded Sputnik.

What really impressed me was the austerity, the aura, the monastic air of the
room, his room. The Juan Gris guitarist was missing behind the bed and instead
there was a pale rectangle, cleaner, on the spot where the oil painting had hung
for so many years. I smiled to myself, I was an intruder there, a body snatcher, I
had read about all those things in some article, in a book, I had seen him there
photographed in *Life:* Hemingway in shorts, seated on his bed, in front of the
cold Juan Gris on the wall, and all surrounded by elastic cats.

"Why is it here?" Elena cried, stopping in front of the typewriter on top of a
Webster's dictionary on the bookcase by the bed. "Where did you want him to
put it?" I answered with irritation. "On the table there. Yours is always there on
the table." "Hemingway wrote standing up" was all I managed to say, moved
and ashamed. "Why did he write standing up?" "I don't know. Maybe he had
piles." Had I read that too?

There was silence for a while and then Elena began to touch the keys, lightly,
one by one, the keys of the typewriter. Suddenly the guide walked in, I thought
he was going to scold Elena severely but no, instead he began to speak softly, in a
voice full of respect, eloquence, and submissiveness: "Every morning Hemingway got up very early, he was in the habit of getting up early and working right
there where you're standing now, señorita, stripped to the waist and barefoot, he
liked to feel the cold Spanish tiles or he would stand on that small kudu skin
there."

"Where did you come from?" Elena asked him, frowning, her nostrils twitch-
ing. "I didn't see you walk in." The mulatto, his round face suddenly even
rounder, seemed caught between shame and pride. "Did I scare you? I'm sorry if
I did . . . I was with the Russians up till now. . . . Didn't you see me? I walked
in through the door, stealthily, 'like a panther,' Hemingway used to say. You
want to know something? When he would be writing, I was the only person who
could come into the room; he'd stand right there. He used to let me come in
because I never made any noise when I walked, I wore these same tennis
shoes . . ."

He leaned his shins against the bed, all dressed in white, his starched pants
whiter than the sheets. Then I remembered, his name was René Alcázar, no,
Villarreal, and Hemingway had brought him up since he was a child, had found

him playing in the streets of the village, San Francisco de Paula, below the *finca*. You could see Hemingway had molded him according to his needs, twisted him into shape, the faithful servant. The colonizer and Gunga Din. Anyhow, Hemingway must have had a powerful personality to push around, he must have been hard to live with, unbearable.

"He used to work up till around eleven o'clock, more or less, then he would go for a swim in the pool. He always liked to swim after work and before lunch. Here, in this bookcase, we have the different editions of his novels in every language in the world. Look here, closer, this is the Russian edition; when Mr. Mikoyan was here, he brought him these books and this small souvenir . . . it's a Sputnik. Hemingway's works have been translated into every single language of the world. This is the Japanese edition of *A Farewell to Arms* . . ."

I also noticed there were the complete works of Mark Twain and remembered he had written in *Green Hills of Africa* that all American literature had come from a book called *Huckleberry Finn,* especially from the first hundred pages that I had once read with stupid and naïve care; Elena kept walking up and down the room, she didn't seem at all interested in what Villarreal was saying, and much less in Mark Twain or the Japanese translation of *A Farewell to Arms.*

"Take a look at these shoes!" Elena cried, holding an enormous moccasin in her hands. "He wore a ten and a half," our guide contributed immediately. I had the impression of seeing Hemingway for the first time, his flesh-and-blood image, walking in those shoes, strutting inside those dark brown moccasins with wrinkled dirty leather. I had never seen him in person and now I was seeing him for the first time, enormous and solid and casual and dead. "He wore a ten and a half," Villarreal repeated and rubbed his fingertips along the dusty leather, leaving clean stripes on the shoe.

"Americans have huge feet. I've always noticed it, even the most beautiful women," I explained pedantically to break the spell, and Elena said, "In a man it's nice," and she put the shoe back on the floor. "I have beautiful feet, don't you think?" "Your toes look like big-headed dwarfs," I lied, and Elena walked into the bathroom mumbling, "You're so funny! Come here, take a look at these books, he even used to read in the bathroom," and she pointed out a small bookcase set up beside the white porcelain bowl.

"Yes, Hemingway was in the habit of reading in the bathroom for a while every day. . . . See that bottle there? That's a lizard. One of the house cats found him in the garden once and grabbed him and sank his teeth into his neck, and whirled him around in the air. Hemingway saw it and tried to save him. The lizard tried to defend himself with his tail, he was brave, but he couldn't manage. Papa rescued him and tried to save his life, he said the lizard had put up a good fight, but it was no use. He brought him in here and took care of him, cured his wounds and fed him here, but it was no use. A week later he died. Hemingway put him in formaldehyde then."

I was suddenly irritated with the idolatry of the guide, his silly anecdotes were always too revealing and touching. Papa sat in that bathroom and he shitted like everybody else, and not without some difficulty, it seems. "Houdini," I pulled out the book, "he's got a book on Houdini here. Houdini used to swallow files and swords and then vomit them. . . ."

"Every day he weighed himself and wrote his weight down there on the frame of the door. Papa wrote very small numbers, you see? He had a delicate but virile handwriting. He always tried to keep his weight down to around two hundred and ten pounds, he took special care of his physical health. He would say that to write you have to be in good shape, healthy, that any sickness, any physical ailments interfered with your work. He always watched his weight."

"You think I should gain or lose weight?" Elena asked me. "You're all right the way you are, maybe a little fat, but you're all right the way you are. I was looking at you yesterday, though, you have a lump of fat in your right thigh, if you don't watch out you'll end up with cellulitis. Don't you know what that is? Comes out especially on your thighs, on the rest of your body too, they get full of lumps of fat, haven't you noticed that a lot of women have thighs that look padded, upholstered like furniture and walls . . ." "Stop it," she complained. "I think you want to destroy me, everybody tells me I'm quite thin and you say I'm getting fat. . . . I'll weigh myself right now. I don't believe I've reached a hundred and twenty." She stepped on the flat blue scale while I tried to explain that people here were very primitive and associated fat with beauty; she chuckled, stepped down, took her shoes off and got on again, adjusting her thin feet to the black rubber matting while she watched the needle with knitted brows: "See, see, a hundred and seventeen pounds. I'm gorgeous. Succulent, as you say."

"You're really impudent," I remarked while the guide kept insisting: "Please, don't you want to see the rest of the house . . . I want to show you the rest of the house."

We went back into the living room and saw a smiling Russian with his shoe in the lion's mouth, between the yellow dead fangs of the M-G-M beast. The guide pulled out a batch of photographs from a wide drawer and put them on a low table by the sofa. "These are from the Spanish Civil War. Hemingway was a war correspondent in the Spanish Civil War. These are pictures by Robert Capa." A group gathered around, pressing against the table. I looked for the physical corpulence of Hemingway but he wasn't in any of the pictures, I didn't see him. His wife had probably taken those away. Mismatched uniforms, berets, dust, and old-fashioned machine guns, toys today, and long rifles, a man running through a field, his face bathed in blood, falling, dying, flinging away his black rifle with an outstretched arm, his wide pants flopping in the wind and the indifferent grass, with ammunition or leather pouches or grenades around his waist, as if they were seeds to sow the field with, a farmer killed while sowing seeds, an Asturian *dinamitero*.

Elena pulled away from the table almost immediately, either because she didn't understand war or simply because the Russians, without deodorant, were smelling to high heaven. When we crossed over to the dining room I found her in front of the magazine rack, glancing through an old *Harper's Bazaar*. I peeped over her shoulder and saw Suzy Parker, thin, endless, in a green bikini, lying on the sand, her flaming red hair loose, her lips half opened and a dying wave rolling up to her ribs. Elena leaned her head over a little to inspect an ad for a soft blue slip and she saw me: "You know something, if I had a slip like this one, it's really beautiful, I'd go out into the street without a dress on, I'd wear it instead of a dress. It's nicer than any of the rationed dresses you get here." I pressed my thumb down her backbone and she arched, smiled, and went on looking through the fashion magazine.

The table was set for nobody. On the glass surface the dishes and forks and empty glasses, napkins with a huge H, and a floral arrangement of tiny insignificant pink and white flowers in the center. "The table was always set exactly as you see it now, those were Miss Mary's favorite flowers," the guide said; no one could stop him now. "Every day the same." "But nobody is going to eat here now," I said, but he kept on talking. He sounded like a wound-up toy. "He had two fried eggs for breakfast, well-done, because he didn't like the running white of the egg. Papa liked them well-done with a slice of toast, without butter. He used to sit facing that wall, right here. He always sat facing the Miró painting, the painting of a Catalonian farm, a painting Hemingway bought when he was young in Paris for three hundred dollars . . ." I asked about the painting, there was nothing on the wall. "That painting and several others, Miss Mary took them away, after Hemingway died, she came over and took them away; but she also promised Fidel she would send first-rate reproductions as soon as possible so that the house would be kept exactly the same as when Hemingway lived here. She promised to send reproductions where you would hardly notice any difference, identical, even the same size, to be put back there."

"But it's not the same," I murmured. "Reproductions are worthless and these paintings were worth millions of dollars. It's not the same." I don't know if he heard me, but he didn't answer. "The bullfight posters are the original ones, aren't they?" I shouted at him and he answered, still sitting on a cloud, "Yes, those are. They haven't been touched." Yes, those were original reproductions. That's all we deserve, copies, we're nothing but a bad copy of the powerful and civilized countries, a caricature, a cheap reproduction.

He went through the house again and I had the feeling that everything was varnished. I saw everything just as if I were looking at a set of jewels behind glass in a museum, with the certainty that no woman would ever show them off. How corny can I get! I have mixed feelings. I feel love and hate toward Hemingway; I admire him and at the same time he humiliates me. The same as my people, it's the same feeling I have when I think of Fidel, of the revolution. Permanently split; I can't even agree with a part of myself.

"This tower Miss Mary had built," the guide said outside while we were climbing up the spiral stairway, our hands on the rusty iron, first brushing against some twisted branches of yellow and purple bougainvillea and up on top our eyes were opposite the high arched branches of a royal palm, up there were some boots, covered by a yellowish film; the heads of wild animals, a buffalo and a tiger, on the floor against the wall.

"He worked here only the first day, when Miss Mary gave him the key, it was a present, a birthday present. After that he never came up here to work, didn't like it. He always worked in his room . . ."

While he went into the details of Papa's boring house habits, I stood staring at a bald mangy spot on the tiger's head and I thought that Cuba never really meant a fucking thing to Hemingway. Boots to hunt in Africa, American furniture, Spanish photographs, books and magazines in English, bullfight posters. Nowhere in the whole house was there anything Cuban, not even an Afro-Cuban witchcraft conversation piece or a painting. Nothing. Cuba, for Hemingway, was just a place where he could take refuge, live quietly with his wife, receive his friends, write in English, fish in the Gulf Stream. Cubans, *we*, meant very little to him.

Through the arches of palm leaves, far away, white, yellow, blurred houses and buildings surrounding the Havana harbor, and several chimneys, some of them giving off dirty smoke that blurred the distant houses, even more, the entire landscape.

When we went down to see the now empty pool, I was already completely groggy and yet I kept on listening to the guide because he was speaking in such a soothing monotonous voice: "Here all the pets are buried." And he bowed his head; the trees around the pool shaded the simple small graves of rough cement. "Here we buried Black Dog, his favorite dog; he always followed Hemingway everywhere, kept him company writing, drinking, even right here in the pool, playing in the shade while he swam. Black Dog didn't like to swim in the pool, he preferred to wait under the trees."

Elena approached running. I had been watching her all the time now, and as she stepped into the shade, two huge ovals of yellow light, filtering through the branches, hit on her left cheek and on her breast: "What's that?" "It's the grave of Black Dog." "A dog." The stains from the sun dropped down her hips to her ankles. "A dog." She walked away under the sun, distractedly, went around the pool. I saw her bump into two Russians and the three of them, "Sorry, *compañera;* I beg your pardon! sorry, *compañera.*"

"Black Dog was killed by the soldiers. . . . No, before the revolution, Batista's soldiers came around here one night searching for a group of revolutionaries and searching for arms, and Black Dog barked and barked and wouldn't let them in, and they killed him with the butt of a rifle. From that day on Hemingway began to feel bad in this house and here in Cuba. He needed a lot of tranquillity to write."

It's all over, the servants and the Americans here in Cuba, and we're also through.

"Help, 'elp, 'elp!" Elena screamed from the bottom of the pool. "Help, help; get me out of here, 'ere." I don't know how she fell into the pool, how she ever got in there. I looked down at her from the edge of the pool, Elena standing in the slanted bottom, at the deepest level of the pool. I hadn't seen her go down, I was bothered. "What happened to you? What are you doing there?" "Nothing, 'ing. I can't get out, out." "Did you hurt yourself?" "I don't know, 'ow. Get me out of here, 'ere; come on, on, hurry, hurry, don't stand there, 'ere. I'm going to cry, cry."

I'd rather not see her again. I'm falling in love with Elena, and I don't like it. Laura all over again. I'm in love, the tips of my fingers are almost certain, they're so sensitive; I feel like screaming. I remember in full detail everything we've done together lately. Elena has become an obsession and it can't go on. . . . Every single time I recall something about Elena I feel sexually excited; I feel soft inside now when I write her name, Elena, and when I remember her. I'm letting myself out again and I'm going to get hurt. Even the style of this diary is changing, I can sense it: I'm moving out of my shell, toward the outside, toward people. Inside I'm safer. It's a temptation I must reject. I've got to break up this relationship. I'm too old and she's a child. She only wants to get something out of me, have a good time. She'll betray me the same as Laura. She has a different world from mine in her head. She can't see me.

Reality seems to be slipping through my fingers. In the street I hear things I no longer understand. *"A nivel, emular, tracatrán, quemado, bajar un electrodo, mazacote, pillar, enfermedad, parquear la tiñosa, sarampionado, está traqueteado . . ."* * I can only understand these expressions vaguely. Sometimes they appear in the newspapers, but only certain ones; others I just overhear in conversations. The revolution has introduced a new vocabulary. Words I don't use but hear, as if they were Mexican or Venezuelan expressions, or Argentinisms, my own language, but in a foreign country.

If I keep on being so isolated from everything that's going on around me, the day will come when I won't understand a thing.

Up to now, I had always kept myself up-to-date on what was happening in the world. No longer possible. I subscribed to about ten different foreign magazines;

---

* *A nivel:* at a given level; denotes hierarchy (neighborhood level, national level). *Emular:* emulate; a social incentive created as a substitute for capitalist competition. *Tracatrán:* applied to individuals who carry out orders implacably; in the onomatopoeic grinding sound of the word lies part of its effectiveness. *Quemado:* burnt; a person destroyed, usually after a nervous breakdown, by too much activity or too many responsibilities. *Bajar un electrodo:* send down an electrode; an order sent down from a higher administrative level. *Mazacote:* fat, lumpy; applied to women with protuberant shapes. *Pillar:* to watch out, discover, see through. *Enfermedad:* sickness; applied to people, usually young, who dress casually and behave cool and detached. *Parquear la tiñosa:* park the buzzard; leave an unsolved problem in someone else's hands. *Sarampionado:* measled; a person intoxicated with too much Marxist-Leninist theory, a dogmatic revolutionary. *Está traqueteado:* he is banged around; applied to anyone who has stood up under pressure and survived.

received catalogs from several publishing houses, and also took trips every year to the United States or Europe. . . . Every time I read a French novel I was aware of our social and psychological backwardness. Every new American product that appeared on the market made me conscious of our scientific, technical, and industrial inconsequence. . . . We were a sweatshop, a country of parasites. Now I have no frame of reference with which to judge things, no information: I receive no books nor do I see new products from the capitalist world. Everything is dammed up here, stagnant, and newspapers only carry political slogans.

With the present violent historical acceleration—each new generation of knowledge occurs every ten years—the day is close when everything I know will be completely obsolete (for all the good it did me!) and I will still be alive.

"Close your mouth, please," I begged Elena time and again yesterday. When she leaves her mouth partly open, aping Marilyn Monroe's sensuality, she looks feebleminded. Keeps doing it all the time, especially when she pretends to be looking at me tenderly. Makes me feel unreal, an actor on stage.

Finished reading Eddy's novel. It's so naïve, I don't know what to think. Writing such stuff after psychoanalysis, concentration camps, and nuclear energy is really pathetic. He must have done it to get a place under the Socialist Sun. He must know better! The plot is simply puerile: an uprooted Cuban (with existentialist frosting), after a frustrating affair with a mulatto maid and rejecting a wealthy American heiress, decides to integrate himself into Cuban life here. Nobody ever becomes integrated; man is, always will be, uprooted, alienated.

The novel is full of typical exotic characters—half-breed, Batista soldier, native witch doctor, son of wealthy sugar planter—and colorful situations for the modern folklore taste. It's all very primitive and earthy. You can see he's tried to please the anonymous mediocre reader. All those characters taken from the popular theater have to disappear: they're typical characters of an infrahuman world. As long as those characters continue to exist in Cuba, we won't have any serious literature or any psychological depth. Men and women will live like marionettes, cardboard silhouettes.

At the very end, hold on now!—the existentialist intellectual seems determined to join the rebels in the Sierra Maestra. Eddy wants people to read his novel and exclaim with conviction: "Yes, that's the way things were in Cuba before the revolution." To say what other people already think they know, you don't have to write a novel. You have to show people *what man is capable of feeling and doing*. He must be fishing for official approval. The artist, the true artist (you know that, Eddy), will always be an enemy of the State. In that he too longs for Communism.

Eddy is one of the writers announced in a discussion on the contemporary novel at the public library. Read it in the papers this morning; Tuesday, if I remember right. I'll try to make it: want to see what he has to say. What can he say about the novel that hasn't already been said? Alejo Carpentier is on the panel too. Not bad as a chronicler of our Latin American barbarism; he's managed to extract from underdevelopment the turbulent landscape and the absurd history of the New World. Not interested. I'm tired of being an Antillean. Having nothing to do with the *"real maravilloso"*; not interested in the jungle, or in his novels about the grotesque repercussions of the French Revolution in the Caribbean. A few other so-called writers are also going to show off with Eddy.

The phone just rang. I let it ring; counted up to twenty-four buzzes. Must be Elena. My heart beats "like the cracker he eats," that's what the little girl next door used to say every time she saw me. Thirty years ago. *"Veinte años no es nada y febril la mirada te busca y te nombra, vivir . . ."** My head is full of stupid lyrics like that tango. Can't coordinate my thoughts; I'm afraid Elena will knock at the door soon. I'm fond of her, doesn't resemble the stupid gum-chew-

---

* "Twenty years is nothing, and I search for you feverishly and I call you, to live . . ."

ing teen-agers of my adolescence (am I getting senile?), but I refuse to get involved. It's too complicated. My life would become too complicated.

She might have called from the store on the corner. It's quite possible. Maybe coming up in the elevator this very minute. Better keep quiet. Won't type another single word.

Can't understand how he lets himself be used. It's all a farce. Looked just like a judge sitting up there on the dais. I don't think he even saw me from up there. When he got back, I think it was toward the end of 1960, he tried to see me several times, but I avoided him. The day he phoned, I myself told him I wasn't home. He even wrote an article against that New York magazine for Spics, *Visión,* where he'd worked for over four years. If it was such a reactionary magazine, he shouldn't have stayed there in the first place. He resigned when the magazine started its attacks against the revolution. That's what he said. What a farce! He came back because he was a nobody in New York: to show off in underdevelopment. We saw each other twice in one of the bookstores in the old section of Havana and I didn't return his nod and his smile.

The conference table still had the moldy gold coat of arms of the Republic. I doubt if he saw me from his Olympus. He pulled out a cigar from his inside coat pocket—that suit he wore, a blue Prince of Wales model, I'm sure he bought it in the Empire State—and lit that rolled-up tobacco leaf like a veteran smoker, a real pro . . . I can almost see it again. We were sitting over a glass of mango juice discussing the matter, many years ago, in the Terraza restaurant. Told me smoking was a sign of weakness, a cowardly habit, that people smoked to run away from their emptiness, to amuse themselves, not to feel the loneliness that's gnawing at them. I was smoking two packs of Pall Malls a day then. What a phony! He carefully turned the cigar around in his mouth while Carpentier was speaking (the only one who doesn't need the revolution to show off!). I'm sure Eddy felt very important, seated at a solid mahogany table way up over our heads.

There was a time when I had respected Eddy because he did everything I never dared do because of fear. He was a striving, starving young artist, living in a huge old broken-down house being encroached upon by an untended patio. Lam left it to him whenever he went to Paris. He didn't work and all he did was write and paint and read, while I spent the day selling furniture and making enough money to live comfortably. Eddy accused me of being timorous because I wouldn't get rid of my business and sit down to write. He was sort of an anarchist then: said everything was *mierda,* shit. Once you were young and pure, Eddy, and look at yourself now, Edmundo Desnoes!

I pictured myself up on the dais for a moment. It would be amusing in a way. Everybody is mad for attention in one way or the other. Maybe that's why I write so much now that I'm alone. But it's a dangerous trap. If I could move about as Lao-tzu suggested: "To have accomplished merit and acquired fame, then retire—this is the Tao of Heaven. . . . The sage is cautious, like one crossing a stream in winter." Lao-tzu's *wei wu wei* is the answer: "act without acting," without getting involved. But it's difficult to be and at the same time not to participate. Acting without being tied up and chained to the future. I'd rather be insignificant. I'm afraid of getting to enjoy appearances the way Eddy does; that would be my final undoing. I'm too lazy, I let myself be carried away. If it hadn't been for the revolution, I'd still be selling furniture and married to Laura.

We were together under the same roof, he up on the dais and I down among the audience, but there was an abyss between us. People who hold high positions, important jobs, and appear in the newspaper every day have nothing to do with me. "Napoleon never spoke to fools like myself"; I always admired Stendhal for admitting that.

No writer who has any respect for himself would give a lecture with a cigar in his hand. I can't imagine any of the writers he mentioned—Kafka, Joyce, Proust—giving a lecture in the Biblioteca Nacional. Not even Hemingway, and he was only a second-rate artist.

He should have stuck to his ideals. Continue being what he was when I knew him. People grow old and vile. Never thought he was an opportunist. I find it difficult to accept and, nevertheless, yesterday I saw him seated up on a dais smoking a cigar and pontificating about literature.

I'm a dead man among the living under socialism.

I'm going to send him my unpublished stories. While I'm still alive, I have to do something. Just reread them. "Believe It or Not!" is the way I saw things then, but I don't like it. All literary problems, as Henry James said, are problems of execution. Or something along those lines. Wrote this story in '53. Had little time and less ability, didn't live in an environment of sufficient literary density. I'll try to rewrite it without changing it too much. That will keep me busy and amused or, better still, fooled.

He'll remember me when he reads it. Eddy was the one who took me to meet old man Pereira when he was still a journalist and not yet a writer as now. Think I wrote about him quite fairly.

The stories only suggest what could have been done if I had systematically dedicated my time to writing. I'll go over them carefully. Send them to him anyway.

(This diary, yes, is being written under pressure, it's me or the revolution.)

This morning I woke up to the sound of music. I had set the radio-clock for eight in the morning; was planning to go and pick up my monthly paycheck at the Reforma Urbana. I pulled out of sleep gradually, listening to some sickeningly sweet semiclassical music to dream by, slowly stretching my legs, feeling pleasure and at the same time pain in my still sleeping muscles. Other times, when they're giving news or political indoctrination, I wake up sharply; I sit up in bed with a start and see my tousled and bloated head in the dressing-table mirror, with my hair caked on my temples and bleary, gummy eyes.

When I read in Montaigne that his father had hired a musician to wake him up each morning with a sweet air, I felt overwhelmed with yearning. I always suffer my worst attacks of anguish when I wake up each day.

The idea of opening my eyes each morning with a musician in front of me scratching on the strings of a violin was not a very pleasant image either. Belonged to another time and age. The presence of a stranger would intensify my sense of guilt; the violinist would look on me in bed as if I were a parasite or a slave driver. . . .

The fact is I'm thinking exactly as if I were in the past. Before the revolution, any eccentric with dough could have hired a violinist to wake him up each morning, but not any longer. I still can't see myself living inside a revolution, still fail to see that everything has changed: even my daydreams. I can't be, I no longer am the same. My possibilities have been reduced to a minimum. I can't travel, choose the car I want to buy or the magazine I would like to read. There's no longer bourgeois variety for the happy few, only flat socialist equality for all. There's no future for me: the future is worked out by the State. The future of a bourgeois—that's what I am, because it's true, I'm living in "the First Socialist Country of the Americas"—has been reduced to zero. The only refuge left to me is in the mind, and the revolution has even broken into this hideout like a bull in a china shop. They've eliminated bourgeois freedom in order to plan the workers' future. There's even a weird morbid pleasure in knowing that people like me are slowly becoming extinct!

I exist thanks to the generosity of the government: every month I get four hundred and thirty-eight pesos from the Reforma Urbana. I still have money coming to me for another thirteen years. No, twelve, eleven; over two years have gone by since they grabbed my apartment house. And they said this government wouldn't last another month! I won't worry about the future. We might all blow up before then. The nuclear mushroom is watching me with a smile! How the hell do I know!

Radio and the revolution have put an end to everything Montaigne (listening to a violinist at his bedside every morning) stood for. If I hired a violinist to wake me up each morning they would execute me. Put me to sleep for keeps in front of the *paredón!**

* Execution wall.

I start getting ideas, musing, making things up, and I always end up in a big tangle.

I should avoid writing anything. Really mean it. Even this stuff I've just typed is binding. Hell, I can't stand it anymore! And still I go on. Someday I'll get tired. . . .

Haven't got much hope of seeing my stories published here. Eddy won't consider them, not seriously. I'll try to smuggle them out of the country, though it is quite possible that they won't even publish them abroad. They won't publish them here because I'm a *gusano*† and abroad because I'm an underdeveloped writer.

I'm all fucked up. Anyhow, I intend to keep on rewriting them. And even try to write a few new ones.

At least I'll die without remorse: I tried to do something with my life. It's my last illusion, all the revolution has left me, the last hope I've got, the reason I have for still respecting myself, for keeping alive. . . . Even though I'm afraid it's all a big inflated bubble, another illusion I've sold myself; probably my short stories are as underdeveloped as any minstrel's rural folk songs. Well, as long as I keep on writing I can fool myself, live in a lie. It's getting harder every day. Feel like taking a crap.

Hell. An unbearable heat was beating down this morning when I left the house. I decided to walk all the way to the bank on Galiano. It's the only chance I have to see what's going on around me. I began walking in a zigzag.

Happened to go by the high iron fence and gate of Francisco de la Cuesta's house. When we were boys we used to get together after school, La Salle is just around the corner; if we saw each other twice after graduation it was too much. (Now his house is an embassy, Vietnam or Korea, I think; saw two sallow hyena-smiling Asians come out of the house and get into an Oldsmobile with diplomatic license plates.) I can't remember exactly what games we fought over. He had two huge rooms to himself just for playing; we'd sprawl on the cool design of green leaves, opaque, and ocher branches, dead, on the tile floor. In the garage they always kept a black Rolls-Royce, shining, old, without any tires, mounted on two sawhorses. Where has Francisco gone to? Does he recall what games we fought over? I try to remember, but it's no use.

La Salle is now a school without brothers and full of poor students on government scholarships who wear gray shirts instead of the blue shirts with side collars I had to wear for so many years. Still remember the day I told the brother my name was French, the same as Saint Jean Baptiste de la Salle, and there in front of all the other boys (can't forget it) he said no and I insisted, yes, and he repeated no. His arms were crossed on his chest. His cassock stank of dampness and chalk! His arms were crossed and he kept pinching the hollow on his upper lip. He always did that, even in chapel. Brother Fernando, he was called. And

† Worm, counterrevolutionary.

not Mexican or Spanish, like most of them, but a Cuban. I insisted that my surname, Malabre, was French, that my father's family had come from Haiti during the revolution . . . when the Haitian slaves began to burn everything and kill their exotic white masters. Didn't believe me. I told him about the coffee plantations they had developed in Oriente province . . . nothing doing. I felt like shouting, insulting him, knocking the bastard down with a heavy sock on the jaw. But I discovered I couldn't do it. He was stronger; he couldn't be wrong. The brothers are always right when you're in school. I was about twelve or thirteen years old. I understood then for the first time in all its pristine clarity the true relationship between justice and power.

After that humiliating experience I decided to become first in my class. Up till then I'd been a mediocre student. Went and studied like mad and for over a month I got the highest grades and was first in the class. Then the whole thing bored me and I dropped boisterously down to the bottom of the class. It was a lot more fun there. The mixture of hate and admiration generated by the damned one of the class was much more rewarding. I made an alliance with the class mischief-maker: Alejandro. One hot summer day we each made ourselves a fan out of the cardboard from a pad and we drew two naked women on them with our pencils: with long legs and aggressive, erect breasts; just the profile, it was much easier to draw. The brother of the class caught us at it. We were kicked out of school for two weeks.

The following year I met Trolo. His parents were Hungarian. They lived in a wooden house near Twenty-sixth Avenue. He studied violin and his sister piano. Armando made fun of me because I read Salgari novels, so he lent me the biography of Napoleon by Emil Ludwig. His father had a workshop and built all kinds of car and truck mufflers, somewhere on Belascoaín. His mother used to make overwhelming sweets: layers and layers of butter and cake, thin layers, and pastry filled with chocolate cream and almonds. I didn't like his sister, she was covered with freckles and she always seemed about to crumble into dust; she wore starched dresses and never played with the boys.

In Armando's house for the first time in my life I heard ideas in a conversation. An overwhelming discovery for a child who had only heard stupid remarks in his own home: "It's been terribly hot and muggy today." "Eat your steak now, it's nice and tender. It's a sin to throw away all that food." "Aunt Hilda has been operated on, her gall bladder, you know. I'm worried, she doesn't look at all well." "This month business has picked up, got two new solid contracts . . ." Armando's father was a freethinker. Each week he gave his son a peso to visit a brothel. Armando was three years older than I; took me for the first time to Colón, the red-light district. Took me to a repulsive fat whore and asked her to be nice to me, that I was his friend. He used to fuck that cow every week to save himself fifty centavos. She undressed before I had time to unbutton my shirt and wallowed into the middle of the bed like a hog. I sat naked for a while on a corner of the bed, untying my laces. Not my type. She was lying in the hollow of the mattress and I rolled down to her side. She pawed me without any success.

Nothing. Told her I had also been at it the night before and now I didn't feel very much like it. She didn't believe a word, and I offered her the half peso anyhow, all flushed. She insulted me, but grabbed the money. Armando also bawled me out, said that I'd made him look like a fool.

I knew I couldn't leave things like that, remembered they say "get back on if a horse throws you." Told Armando, now I would choose the whore *I* liked. Finally found a slim brunette with very long hair, she smelled of soap and cheap perfume that aroused me, and I told her I loved her and felt her tender and fragile in my arms. I went back the following week to the same house on Crespo and didn't see her; the matron told me the girl was sick. Not there. Told me I could have my pick, any of the other girls. I left shaking my head. . . . Felt empty and very sad, but I found another whore that same afternoon. One who refused to take off her bra because—so she said—she was still nursing her baby. Now I can understand that the woman was only a victim: but at that time I felt cheated.

During my senior year Brother León, he looked just like a porcupine, gave us a detailed lecture on the horrors of venereal diseases: sores, twisted and rotten bones, unbearable pains, deformed children. . . . For almost a month I stopped visiting the brothels in downtown Colón. Desire washed away and blurred the advice.

My original intention had been to walk in zigzag, but I ended up unconsciously looking for the streets of my adolescence. Starting with La Salle, my feet took over; things themselves were opaque, I only saw my memories.

On the corner of Avenue G and Thirteenth Street there used to be a nun's school, French Dominicans. Laura had studied there. I remember how she would invariably point it out every time we drove up the avenue and I glanced up at the Virgin in the niche; a blue Virgin, I think, stepping on a snake. Now there is a sign on the edge of the roof:

LENIN WORKERS TRAINING CENTER

I was close to Hanna's house. I walked by the corner (there, leaning against a damp brick fence, I had waited for her many times) where I had read, looking at a poplar combed by electric cables,

"La ahogada del cielo" :

Tejida mariposa, vestidura
colgada de los árboles,
ahogada en cielo, derivada
entre rachas y lluvias, sola, sola, compacta,
con ropa y cabellera hecha jirones
y centros corroídos por el aire. *

* Woven butterfly, raiment/hanging from the trees,/drowned in sky, drifting/through gusts and rain, alone, alone, dense,/with tattered clothes and hair/and centers corroded by the air. (Pablo Neruda.)

Hanna's kisses tasted of scentless petals, damp flesh. She was white and blond, and when I looked into her eyes my knees grew weak. Every afternoon I would go to pick her up at the crowded entrance of St. George School and then I walked her home. In summer tiny beads of perspiration dotted her chin.

Her father was in the diamond business. Always dressed in blue serge even in August. Her mother was young, much younger than her husband, and efficient; I still can see her arms against a slim waistline and generous hips (how much more attractive she would be if her arms were not so short, her elbows so bony and wrinkled).

It's a painful effort to remember these things because they fill me up so that I almost choke. Each memory is a mixture of honey and shit; the will to survive and sadness, success and my defeat.

Hanna left Cuba for New York and I ran after her. Was then in my first year at law school; left before the end of the term, didn't even wait for the exams. It was my only act of rebellion! In all my life. Spent the thousand pesos my father had given me the year before, when I had graduated, on the trip.

I arrived in New York sick: Hanna and her mother took care of me, put me up in their apartment. . . . Her mother treated me as if I were her own son (I never showed her any gratitude). They called a doctor; I had a fever and diarrhea that filled me with shame. For the first and last time in my life I let somebody stick a thermometer into my rectum.

Still convalescent, I moved into a broken-down hotel just a block away from Hanna. Each morning she would come by to pick me up at the room. We spent three months together: walking through the streets; visiting museums, going to the movies, the stores; whole afternoons in Central Park and evenings on Riverside Drive, and long hours romping naked in my bed. The only thing that annoyed me was having to walk to the bathroom on the carpet. I missed our cool tile floors every time I got out of bed.

We agreed to get married—we didn't believe in ceremonies, but decided it would be convenient and I have always preferred comfort to truth—when I returned from Cuba after arranging all my affairs there. I would find a job in New York and become a writer; Hanna even promised in her romantic delirium to go to work until I became famous. The first thing we would do was buy an old jalopy and travel across the country and see everything, all the way to the West Coast. (Lord, how phony and corny and I don't know what it sounds like to me now!) Always told her that I, instead of hating Hitler like most Europeans, had to be grateful. Thanks to Hitler, I had met her: if he hadn't made up his mind to incinerate every single Jew in sight I wouldn't have ever met her. Hanna would never have landed in Cuba.

I wish I could remember it all better.

We'd got back to Havana. I found that my father had already bought me the furniture store. I didn't even oppose him violently. Merely mumbled. I'm a perfect shit! I agreed to get myself into the store every day and stay behind the two huge glass windows, both opening on San Rafael, but I left my parents' house. It was my meaningless, pathetic independence.

In the beginning, before I met Emma, I often had nothing to do at night, and it was then that I wrote my first story, "Jack and the Conductor," already obsessed with underdevelopment.

It still isn't adequately written, but if I continue crossing out things it won't stand up even as a vignette. Besides, it's something that really happened; I was in the bus. When they asked if anyone knew English I just sat there quietly without saying a word. I didn't want to help out the American or the conductor either. Didn't want to intervene, wanted to see how everything would turn out without my participation. Expected to see the scene explode into a rough fight and end up in the police station. I was the only one in the bus who understood what was actually happening, the only one; I understood both what the Cuban and what the American were saying. I honestly enjoyed the whole situation. For the first time I felt a bit like God watching men destroy themselves without coming to their rescue, leaving them at the mercy of their own free will. God, like every creator, is a scoundrel!

Spent the next two years working like mad. Sold myself on the idea that in a couple of years I could save enough money so I wouldn't go back with empty hands. Eddy was leaving for New York around then, insisted I leave with him, that the store was a trap. I didn't listen to him.

A few months later I started living with Emma, the brunette (she remotely resembled Greta Garbo) who sold records across the street from the store. It was all so much more comfortable that way. Emma was thirty-four and had just divorced "her one and only love," an old lawyer fifteen years her senior. He had almost driven her mad with jealousy. Used to squeeze her breasts fiercely whenever they made love trying to deform them, so that no one else would ever see them again the way he had, forced her to walk, when she was wearing high heels, through the middle of the cobblestone streets of Manzanillo. When Emma got divorced she didn't go back to her family: her father, a stubborn Spaniard, had thrown her out of the house when she decided to marry "her one and only love." Then she came to Havana. We lived in my apartment, just around the corner from the store . . . and two years went by.

I returned to New York with the excuse of a business trip and instead of shopping around for new furniture designs, I looked up Hanna. Had not written to her for six months. It was raining when I went to pick her up at the apartment house. She was still living on West End Avenue. Told me she could only spare a minute, have a cup of coffee with me, was very busy; had a date. She was having an affair with a real writer, he had already published several articles in some lousy little literary mag. I had filled her with the passion for literature so she could betray me with a crummy slob! We went for coffee: my hands were trembling, I tore open the sugar envelopes and covered the counter with white grains that crunched under my elbows. I left her—didn't want to leave her—under the marquee of her apartment house. (I was wearing glasses at the time; yes, I remember now, had a slight case of astigmatism, very slight, but wore glasses for the novelty, not as now when I really need them.) She was as desirable as ever: plastic surgery had removed the only flaw on her face: a slightly hooked nose. I told her, watching how the city lights reflected the drops of rain on my glasses, that "they looked like diamonds." "You'll never change," she said. Still don't know what she meant by that.

From New York I went directly to Europe; in Germany I found ruins all over and the ovens of Buchenwald made me feel still more shattered.

Later on, already married to Laura, I found out with glee, yes, with real satisfaction (an old buxom schoolmate from St. George told me; they must write each other platitudes, though it shows an admirable loyalty on Hanna's part) that she had got divorced. I'm glad she wasn't happy either.

I got back from seeing Hanna for the last time and from the monstrosities of Germany completely capsized. A despicable period followed then; probably the most aggressive and dynamic of my entire life. I took refuge in business. I tried, above everything else, to succeed, to erase my failure, to forget my cowardice. I pulled myself together with what was left of my will power: the business, naturally, prospered; prospered, I think, because (basically) I didn't give a damn whether I went bankrupt or made a fortune. Now again I want to pull myself together, even if it means having to defile myself.

"Yodor" belongs to that period, maybe my best story too, although I hardly did anything; that's why. I'd bought myself a tape recorder and once in a while I picked up conversations without letting people on to it.

All I did was leave just the answers and the explanations Torres gave me and I eliminated my own participation. It's a bit too long, like most conversations; I'll probably have to cut a third of it when I retype it.

It took place in my office. The day Torres brought along the album with the complete story of Yodor. Don't know why he did it; probably suspected I was about to can him. Like a true dreamer, he wanted to soften me up, influence my decision. I was really impressed—it seemed like some kind of symbol of life in Cuba—with this robot he had put together all by himself, but I concealed it, told him nothing, wasn't letting myself feel pity for anyone. I had to put him out in the street; he wasn't producing what I had expected. That's how I managed to build up the furniture business. I hired Torres because I thought he'd be a good designer, but it didn't work out. I had to get rid of him.

This month I went over to the bank comfortably seated in a cab. Worried though: I always anticipate that they're going to stop paying me. At the bank I hardly had to wait. Only seven or eight decrepit bodies waiting in line. Made me feel like a social parasite. Not exactly: a sharp knife never to be used. No one my age queued up there to collect. Shriveled old men full of white hair on moles that they probably had overlooked shaving that morning, and blind old ladies with their money tied up in grimy handkerchiefs. Some were waiting to get their pensions. Didn't see a single familiar face; months ago I would still meet some neighborhood cronies, old acquaintances who always brought up business matters or dames. The last time I saw Lorenzo, the record-shop owner, he told me: "Now they say that I, after grinding my whole life away working like hell, am a thief, an exploiter!" He no longer knew what year he was living in, he even asked me how Emma was. Where could she be? Maybe she had also left the country. Or became a rabid revolutionary in revenge, because I, a rich bourgeois proprietor, had abandoned her. Why should she remember me, I wasn't so hot as a lover; I'm really a big shit! And yet, she might remember me more than Hanna or Laura, even though I rejected her (not because of her class origin, but because she was old; ten years older, almost my mother).

I slipped the money into my pocket and walked over to Parque Central. I was so bored I sat for one of those photographs that turn yellow from one day to another. My face is getting bigger every day, I feel it growing, but actually I'm getting bald.

I took a bus home. It was full when I got on; I sweated like a damned coolie (read the other day that monkeys don't perspire; horses, by the way, do); it bothered me to feel the wet shirt sticking to my back and people bumping into my body all the time. I felt like a slimy slug, about to leave a silvery trace behind.

For the first time since they took it away I missed the car. When they nationalized the store they also kept the car because I had it down in the books as business property. The car had isolated me from my fellow men. It was really pleasant then to drive home along the Malecón, watching the sun set in a twilight that was an apotheosis; listening to a song on the radio, even a ridiculous tango like "Uno":

Uno va arrastrándose entre espinas
y en su afán de dar su amor,
lucha y se destroza hasta entender
que uno se ha quedado sin corazón.
Precio de un castigo que uno entrega
por un beso que no llega
o un amor que lo engañó,
vacío ya de amar y de llorar
tanta traición. *

I wouldn't like to *"tener el corazón, el corazón que di."* * With the years I've forgotten the poems I once knew by heart. To quote Neruda, I had to look it up in

---

* Crawling through thorns/eager to love,/we fight and destroy ourselves until/there is not a heart left./A price you must pay/for a kiss that never arrives/or a love that fails,/empty already of love and tears/for so much betrayal.
* "Have the heart, the heart I gave away."

the *Tercera residencia*. The lyrics of any old song, however, would burp up at random. Like that tango. I can associate almost anything with a song: a place, a person, a mood, an idea. Popular songs are heavily loaded with memories and sensations and tastes and odors.

Thirty-nine years and I'm already old. I don't feel any wiser, as an Oriental philosopher would expect, not even riper. A dried-up mango, bagasse. . . . Maybe it has something to do with the tropics. Everything ripens and rots easily here. Nothing endures like the taste of cod liver oil. A regular habitué of the Havana brothels when I was thirteen. At fifteen I thought I was a genius. At twenty-two, the owner of a sophisticated furniture store. My life is like a monstrous, spongy, tropical vegetable. Enormous leaves and no fruit.

Got a letter from Laura. She's working as a cashier in a cafeteria on Fifty-seventh Street. I'm sure now she'll find a "good catch," as her old lady said. Writes me that she's lonely, that even though we may never make up, *"aunque me pase la vida llorando, tan sólo llorando, no vuelvo contigo . . . ,"** I ought to leave Cuba before "it's too late." She'll soon find someone to keep her company, even if he doesn't love her.

I kept the letter hidden in the back of a drawer for more than a week before daring to open and read it. . . . Haven't answered it either. Damn it, how it hurts!

Discovered several envelopes full of pictures in the bottom drawer of the dressing table and started looking through the stacks. Also found the album Laura had bought at El Encanto in which to paste up the best ones. Only two pages have pictures. The rest are empty. Black pages, nothing on them.

I emptied out all the envelopes on the floor and I sprawled between the door and the bed to study them. The first images that caught my eyes were Laura everywhere: in the Piazza San Marco, feeding the stupid pigeons; posing at the beach, arms in a triangle behind that beautiful head; in New York, on Fifth Avenue, with the stiff mannequins of Bergdorf Goodman in the window behind. But the photograph that really seduced my eyes was Laura in full color, in front of a cabana at the Havana Riviera pool, barefoot, standing on tiptoes, silk shirt and slacks in soft pastel colors; behind her, the door with pink shutters—but the picture was faded, Laura had turned purple. Her face, smile and all, had the violet red tint of putrid meat. In another one we were both with the Simmons executive from Chicago; he had invited us to the pool. . . .

I found myself as a child with my mother, my head leaning against her ticklish hair, cut *à la garçon,* and my little shoulder leaning against her soft breasts. My old lady was wearing a necklace, a single string of pearls, and her lips seemed darkly painted. I had the same big mouth, drawn out (Emma once told me it looked like a cunt) over the enormous jaw, and frightened eyes. Eyes always

---

* Even if I have to spend the rest of my life crying, only crying, I won't go back to you . . ."

frightened in all the pictures. Even in the one where, dressed like a Mexican *charro,* not yet ten, smiling, I was aiming a pistol at the camera.

The ones taken the day the furniture store was inaugurated are real poems. I'm standing there, all dressed in white, with a pair of scissors in my hand, about to cut the ribbon; next to me, the priest with his embroidered gown and the aspergillum, also about to sprinkle holy water through the whole store (even got back into the workshop). And then the regular shit-eaters of the entourage and the señoritas who were premiering the dress that a poor Luyanó seamstress had just finished that very morning. We drank Spanish cider. I look at myself now in those pictures and I can't recognize myself. Looks as if I were on top of the world riding the crest of the wave, and, actually, I never felt so completely lost. Seems I could only smile then.

I'm especially fond of three pictures. We were strolling through Riverside Park in New York. Laura was furious when I climbed into a huge wire basket full of crumpled empty cigarette packs, newspapers, sticky candy or ice cream wrappers and wax containers and even contraceptives. I adjusted my tie and asked Eddy to take our picture with my arm around Laura. First she refused, but finally she behaved and agreed to be photographed: I inside, with all the garbage, she at my side, outside, my arm around her shoulder but her chin up in the air like a snubbed actress.

Another one was taken in that stinking Xochimilco lake in Mexico; I even have two of those Mexican blankets on, sarapes, and the look of a *bandolero,* with a frightfully wry face. I'm the only one in the picture who looks like a desperado. Snapped on a vacation trip we took as complete tourists, a month of incredible stupidity. We even flew to Acapulco and saw that pitiful Indian who dives from way up on that steep rock and drops into the transparent water!

And finally the one I had had taken alone the other day on a path in the Parque Central. The street photographer asked me if I wanted it for my passport and I said yes. It was easier than finding an adequate pose. Then he placed a black oilcloth behind me, dangling and all full of cracks and fissures, isolating me from the rest of the scenery, and he snapped the shutter. My face is full of shadows, but I'm not grinning as in all those other photographs taken under the diarrhea of our tropical sun. My mouth is still large, drawn, though slightly curved down (now it most resembles the withered sex of Villon's *la belle Hëaulmiere:* before *ce sadinet assis sur grosses fermes cuisses, dedens son petit jardinet* and now *du sadinet, fy!*), a frightened look, but with heavy dark circles under the eyes. I think a certain dignity shows through.

I think the tape recorder is already completely broken, or at least severely damaged. I'm not going to bother having it repaired—both the tape recorder and my Laura are broken, damaged. It wasn't her feet and shoes and heels, they only twisted a spool, dented the sides—it even kept on recording. I heard that tape so many times, stopped the recorder so often and went over and over so many passages, that I think a resistor conked out or something. The voices come and go, but anyhow I managed to transcribe the whole conversation. From playing the tape and listening to Laura so many times I've come to deal with it as something impersonal, detached from my intimate experience. Often it's as if I heard another couple arguing. I watched myself carefully, and now I understand that Laura was right, I'm cruel, mentally cruel. She wasn't what I wanted her to be, and so I twisted her arm. I couldn't change her. Why should I? It was an act of sadism to torture her with the tape recorder, there was nothing funny about starting it and forcing her into an argument, into making a fool of herself . . . an argument that ended up as painful to me as it was for her. Just as painful. She was really serious about leaving. I'm a heel, for the first time in my life I'm doing the right thing by living alone. Fewer people can hurt you when you're alone and at the same time you have less opportunity to mess up other people's lives.

I prepared for it all carefully, with malice aforethought, but the thing backfired. Laura was reading in bed when I started the tape recorder, I was afraid she'd hear the hum of the motor and the winding spool:

"What are you doing?"

"Can't you see, reading. . ."

"No, I meant to ask you *what* you were reading?"

"Something totally modern and banal. *The Best of Everything, Lo mejor de todo* you could call it in Spanish, or *Lo mejor del mundo*. I'm a good translator, don't you think?"

"Yes, they made a picture out of that book, with Louis Jourdan and that famous model. Who was the old harpy? Joan Crawford, now I remember, about career women . . ."

"That's what I want to be, a career woman, I'm tired of being a rich, frivolous kept woman. We're married, but I feel as if I were your mistress. I want to be a woman efficient in business and passionate in love. . . . You can't live elegantly here, for that kind of life you have to be in New York. . . ."

"Your complexion deserves the best, do you think your complexion deserves the best in the world, as the ad says?"

"Why not? Let me read. . . . What are you doing, sitting there looking at me that way? You know I can't read or do anything when you stop and stare at me that way, analyzing me as if I were a strange bug. . . ."

"Why don't we talk for a while?"

"What's come over you," she said in English. "What's bugging you?"

"A bug. What's bugging you? You seem to be mentioning bugs for everything. . . ."

"What do you want me to talk about? Cuba is a country full of bugs, of dirty people, uncouth, rabble. . . . This is a place that sets you back, as you say . . ."

"What do *you* think?"

"What a pleasant surprise. I never thought I would ever hear you worried about what I thought about anything! Really, *what's come over you?*"

"You're practicing your English quite a bit lately . . . I suspect you're anxious to leave."

"But this is going a bit too far, it was you, you yourself who got me a special English teacher . . . for traveling, so I could read novels in English, and now you're criticizing me. I don't get it. Never have figured you out."

"Don't be corny."

"So what? I'm corny, you want to make something of it?"

"Go on, keep it up, you know that's the way I like you, when you're true to your humble origin, part of the rabble, that always arouses me sexually, when you're trapped between elegance and vulgarity, between the wooden slippers of tenement houses and your new sophistication. . . ."

"I've been watching you all this time and I find you uglier every day, what have you done with yourself? Your appearance, I don't know, you no longer . . . you're just less desirable."

"It's all because I don't have Yardley cream for my hair anymore, no more imperialist after-shave lotion either, you know those things really help a man. . . ."

"That's it. We need a trip abroad."

"It's just the opposite with you. I find you more attractive every day."

"But I'm getting older, I'm already . . ."

"Makes no difference, beauty is something artificial, and every day you became more artificial. I dislike natural beauties, beauties who owe everything to youth, I like women like you, created artificially by education, good food, exercise, expensive clothes, makeup. . . . Thanks to that, you stop being a cheap *cubanita* and become a devastating attractive female. . . ."

"You're getting on my nerves, I can't stand you. I never know when you're serious or making fun of me."

"Both."

"Well, you better go make fun of your mother's wrinkled teats . . ."

"Ha, ha, ha!"

"Drop dead, you mother-fucker."

"That's always a good one."

"If you don't want me to keep on talking like this, you'll have to get me out of here, right now; I can't stand living here another minute. . . . I'm not even going to get into bed with you again. I can't stand making love to you without air conditioning, the monster is still out of order. . . . I can't stand it when you start perspiring and you get all sticky, you sweat a lot, you're a sweating horse . . ."

"You want to know something, every single word you've said is being recorded. . . ."

"I don't believe it, you're out of your mind, you son of a bitch, you can't do that to me. . . ."

"See for yourself, it's all being faithfully recorded, every word is right there on that tape you see whirling around on the recorder. Don't look so hard, it's right there before your eyes, down there, on the floor. . . ."

"You're a fucking bastard, I'll never forgive you, never, you're a monster, a beast, I'm going to destroy . . ."

"Don't do that, don't do that . . . be care . . . don't be afraid, go ahead, hit it harder . . . shoes . . ."

"What do you want, you want me to kick your brains out instead?"

"Much rather. . . ."

"I'm not going to give you the pleasure. You and I are through, it's all over. I don't want you near me, I don't want to ever see you again. Ever. I don't need you anymore, I'm not interested in having you come along with me. Not for love or money. I know how to take care of myself. I'm going away alone, alone. You hear me!"

"Grrrrssshrru . . ."

"Stop banging the recorder. . . ."

"I feel like it. Are you going to stop me? When I leave, you won't play with your stupid toy again. I'm sure you'll waste no time in getting yourself another woman so you can torture her the same way you've tortured me. . . . At least you won't be able to record the voice of a whore on this machine, all the women left in Cuba now are whores . . . there are only whores left. You can keep your toy and go right on recording. I really don't give a damn."

"You're going to leave me all alone?"

"I am. . . . Besides, I'm tired of having you treat me as if I were some laboratory rat for your whims and schemes. I've got to live my own life, I'm already getting old, I've got no time to lose, I'll be thirty-five soon. I'm going away, you'll never hear from me again. I don't need you any longer. It's all over between us, I'm through with you."

"You're leaving me now because things are getting tough, you once said you'd love me for the rest of your life."

"I'm leaving you, I'm leaving you . . ."

"You said you'd wait for me, that we'd leave together or not at all."

"That was yesterday."

"So you're leaving me?"

"I'm leaving you and I'm leaving alone."

The guy handled me with kid gloves, addressed me as "señor": "Look, I hope I'm not bothering you," "it's a very delicate matter, you must understand, very delicate," "my sister was a señorita, a virgin," "put yourself in my place": but he looked sinister with those wide pants loose as sails, with huge pleats that drooped below his hips.

I put on a grave mask of astonishment. Looked at him and couldn't understand why he hadn't slugged me yet. That was what I was afraid of. My apparent serenity had nothing to do with the gruesome ideas that kept on buzzing in my brain.

Elena, he claimed, was a virgin before she met me and now my obligation was to marry her. As soon as possible. I agreed, in order to get rid of him. As long as we were talking and reasoning things out, the advantage was on my side. I was simply terrified. No, I had not violated his sister, I insisted. Then demanded to speak to Elena: I played it sentimental, told him first that Elena had to repeat it all to my face. "You've disgraced her," the guy insisted, "you've disgraced her."

All because I refused to open the door for a week. Elena phoned, knocked violently at the door: I didn't answer or open it. Women are vipers when they feel rejected. I had made up my mind to deny it all up to the bitter end. I wanted her to accuse me, insult me to my face—and then flatly deny that I even laid hands on her. Naturally, I wanted nothing to do with the police; was willing to marry Elena if she asked me to, if she carried things too far. I'd much rather have her family—must be an infinite tribe—beat me alive a thousand times instead of rotting away in a jail.

The vicious brother right then and there wanted to go get Elena, but I insisted it would be better later on, at night. He accepted. Not to oblige me: it was his lunch hour, and he was due back at work. Said something about "absenteeism" and the goals of the revolution.

If I could close my eyes and only listen he sounded very cordial, but he was a malevolent sight if you looked him over carefully.

We agreed to meet at El Carmelo: told him I ate there every night. Didn't want him to come here again. Couldn't endure seeing him again in the apartment, plunged in the well of my living room. Besides, El Carmelo was a good place to give him an inferiority complex; an air-conditioned atmosphere and what is left of the middle class, that would certainly make him uncomfortable, I thought; he'd feel embarrassed.

I was willing to marry Elena. Much better than going to jail for corrupting minors. I felt miserable, corralled; there were moments when I felt like telling him to go fuck himself, but fear sobered me up.

When I sat down to eat alone in El Carmelo, while I waited, I discovered I'd made a stupid mistake. If the expensive environment humiliated them, they would also humiliate me with their presence. It didn't make any difference: I was willing to let them destroy me. I was sure, though, that she hadn't been a virgin. That hadn't been my privilege. And her mother cried about the blood she'd discovered on her daughter's panties. Let's not jump ahead.

For over a month I haven't been able to write a word. Just recalling certain scenes is enough to give me insomnia; I can smell sweat and bad breath again and the peculiar stink of certain prisoners. An ambiguous terror takes over with the mere thought of it.

Elena insisted that I had "disgraced" her. To believe here in this tropical island that sex is a disgrace! I didn't bat an eye. Played the victim: I gave in. Would marry Elena. "It has to be right away," that fiend of a brother of hers yelled. I said: "What about the papers I have to have for the ceremony? Things like that have changed, you know, since the revolution" (hadn't told him yet I was still married to Laura). Elena said without facing me, refusing to look into my eyes, that I had fooled her, that it had happened because I had promised her, that it was really the first time, that never before; she was all flushed. But as long as she could insult me she kept pouring it out. Even brought up her crying hysterically after we had made love. Eyes from other tables in the restaurant were fixed on us.

We left to meet her parents, they were waiting at a nearby corner. On Línea, seated on a bench, in front of the white parish church. After school I used to sit right there with Pablo. Everything has changed! That depressed me even more. They wanted to destroy me—and yet they were pitiful.

"My daughter, my beautiful daughter, we've always taken care of her as if she were made out of glass!" her mother cried. "Fragile." The father barely spoke; every now and then he came over and shoved me or held onto my shirt, that was all he managed to accomplish. Her mother insisted that the night of the crime her baby had returned home with "blood on her little panties." I was scared, felt sorry for Elena and for her parents and for her simple brother; was depressed, couldn't stop thinking of prison walls and bars. "We pampered her, she had all a girl her age could ask for, we didn't mind any sacrifice, you see, she's always been a very sick and nervous child." In less than a minute the mother would change her tack, put on another record and start insulting me: "Degenerate, son of a bitch, what you've done to my daughter has no name . . ." And she would rub her face as if she wanted to erase her features.

Her fiendish brother, as he'd been promising all along, called a patrol car and we all ended up at the police station. Don't even know what precinct it was; somewhere near the ominous Príncipe hill. A step away from the penitentiary gates. They made depositions while her mother cried noisily and her father shook me by the shirt. Her brother took over: he made all the charges, wanted to throw the whole book at me, talked his head off, demanded I marry Elena right then and there. I heard the typewriter bell sounding like a pistol shot at the end of every line. Every time the carriage came to the end of the line that damned bell clanged. I agreed wholeheartedly to everything. My mouth was dry.

Right there in the station they threw me into a cell with six or seven other jailbirds. I shriveled up. Didn't look into any of those faces. Had no idea of how I should behave. "If they push me around what can I do? Can't scream. If I squeal they'll beat the shit out of me." I stared at the dirty scabby walls. One of the guys, hairy, with small eyes sunken into his face, shifted over to my side and asked: "What you here for?" Told him the truth; toughened my voice, used as few words as possible; offered him a cigarette. When they saw the red pack they all jumped on me. Left me with an empty crumpled pack of Pall Malls. "You're a Cuban," another one told me. "Yes, I am," I said, "born here"; he didn't believe me. I didn't insist: told a stupid lie. "My mother is a foreigner, that's why, she's French, but my father, he's Cuban. I've lived abroad a lot, you know. Ten years away from Cuba." Made it all up. I could listen to myself as if it were someone else talking in jail, and I felt miserable. I made up a whole story so as not to disillusion the sagacity of a pilferer.

I felt naked, exposed to a way of thinking and acting that was totally foreign to me. First time I was ever locked up. I promised myself to avoid any squabble and always answer with rough gestures. I wallowed on the floor; that way they wouldn't notice so much the difference between my imported clothes and all those faded pants and shirts, probably bought in cheap stores on Monte. If they saw me so prim and proper they might get strange ideas and then I'd be the one raped instead of Elena.

There was also a deaf-and-dumb creature in the cell. He groaned whenever he tried to say something; you couldn't make out what he wanted to say from his weird gesticulations. Desperate eyes; he looked enraptured. Someone said they'd brought him in for slapping female behinds. Wasn't the first time. He was a thin consumptive guy. Had anxious dog eyes, a bit moist and as mute as his throat.

I felt ready for suicide. Never again would I . . . I can't talk about it.

Early next morning they came and released one of my cellmates, the tallest in the group; he'd been singing way into the early hours of the morning "*miénteme más, que me hace tu maldad feliz . . .*"* Think it's the only time in my life I've felt envy. Wanted to run out of the cell and away from the station house. I was exhausted from so many strange bodies and faces surrounding me, watching me there, making up lies about me. I couldn't relax. Sweat and urine and dampness and shit and bad breath. Everything sticky and uncomfortable. I was desperate for privacy, even loneliness. Just to be able to walk freely along any street—like the guy they took away—seemed to me the utmost happiness possible. To walk unhampered through the streets, breathing freely, watching other people go by; just to wander around seemed to be all the happiness a man could ever desire in this world.

Then they took away the rest of my comrades of the night before, cleaned out the cell of all humanity, and left me alone. They were transferring them up the hill to the Príncipe penitentiary. Into the filthy cells. A little later they would lead me into court. I felt relieved to be all alone. The floor was filthy here too, the walls damp and scabby; there was nothing soft in the cell and even so I felt fine. People make me desperate. I can't stand being close to anyone for too long. There's nothing as revolting as men all bunched together. That's why, locked up in our houses, we dream of walking alone along the shore of a deserted island. A man alone is something really formidable, but a lot of men all together is depressing.

I could live happily ever after in a cell like that of the Count of Monte Cristo.

---

* "Lie to me more, your evil makes me happy . . . ".

Anyone could. The nightmare is having to bear hundreds of other prisoners and hungry eyes and desires. Other people's desires and hungry looks. That's our constipated age: you can find masses even in a prison ward.

Made up my mind not to marry Elena. Haven't the faintest idea where the hell I got enough energy to reject the trap they had set for me. And I don't believe in acts of pity. Suddenly I preferred a prison ward to deceit. I didn't want to marry Elena and I was willing to face all the consequences. They'd gone too far, harassed me too much: you can't do that to a man. Even if her mother dies of sorrow and her father continues pulling me by the shirt until his arms drop off. Her brother can beat me up. I wasn't willing, simply couldn't, fall into another trap. This is my last chance. I was in a cell, loathing myself, but I didn't want to marry Elena; decided it when I found myself alone. If I'd continued being crowded into a corner of the cell, I would have got married just to avoid the constant presence of so many strange comrades.

They walked me over to the *audiencia,* behind the Plaza de la Revolución and the statue of José Martí, always huge and motionless in its marble.

I claimed that the girl had not been a virgin.

Her mother was still disconsolate, all tears; her father and her brother were unable to explain the case. It was pitiful. They referred to me as the "deceased," probably having read it once in an obituary. Got all mixed up trying to use legal jargon. The fiendish brother said I had "profaned her stealthily." I was the only one able to speak coherently. Don't know how, but I explained things clearly, the whole truth. That was my undoing. Immediately the judge addressed me as if I, resorting to my educated ability and diabolical intelligence, had deceived a poor girl—deceived "the people," everything now is "the people." He dealt with me as if I were a despicable murderer.

Cuba has been turned upside down; or downside up; it's possible. Everything has changed. Before, I would have been a respectable citizen and they disgracefully guilty. Now I was the downtrodden one. They, with their poverty, their incoherence, even carrying over into the revolution the prejudices about marriage and virginity they had inherited from the bourgeoisie, were respectable citizens. I was guilty of my education.

I requested that they put Elena through a medical examination to determine if I had violated her or not.

Then Elena's insanity made its appearance. Her mother insisted that Elena was crazy. That's what she said, crazy. That ended up turning me into a soulless monster. I had already known that Elena wasn't quite normal. But who isn't abnormal today!

There was that bit about having a split personality that she had brought up at the restaurant the day we met.

Her mother insisted that they belonged to a "decent family," that "my poor baby is not well . . . she needs special care . . . this man is a cruel, degenerate monster, only someone sexually perverted . . ."

I testified I had no knowledge that the girl was unbalanced, that I had met her by accident in the street and no neurosis is obvious at first sight, that when we were together she enjoyed full mental faculties, that no one could determine. . . . The judge ordered me to be quiet.

A few minutes before the doctor felt her up, someone had mentioned that she had spent several months in the country teaching during the illiteracy campaign. Elena was also an *alfa-betizadora,* and later had received a government scholarship to study at the new art school. I saw myself irretrievably lost. Locked up. I held my breath. The judge took note.

The outcome:

"Considering: The accused, particulars stated elsewhere, seems, from the legal charges of the present case, to have taken a minor, Elena Josefa Dorado of name, to his private apartment under false pretenses and there enjoyed her virginity, regardless of the fact that said party was not in full possession of her mental faculties.

"Considering: The forensic doctors of this court, after examining Elena Josefa on these premises, have declared that, by her physical condition, pilose system, and dental evolution, she appears to be not under sixteen and not over seventeen years of age. Extensive examination was made of her genital organs, and it was determined thereby that the hymen, or virginal membrane, had been totally ruptured and for some time now. Her mental state, judging from the pertinent examination and thorough questioning of this court, is that of a person in adequate use of her mental faculties.

"Considering: After checking her penal background, it was discovered that on the twenty-third day of August last, Elena Josefa was arrested in the lobby of the Habana Libre, suspected of practicing prostitution among foreign visitors at the hotel. Therefore, we advise and recommend her temporary confinement in a proper institution and prompt and specialized psychiatric treatment.

"Considering: No factual evidence exists to constitute a case of rape or violation, foreseen and sanctioned by Article 482-A-B-2 of the Civil Defense Penal Code, and, from these proceedings, no criminal evidence has been proved against the accused.

"Therefore. After consulting Article 384 and other pertinent clauses of the Law of Criminal Judgment and Procedure and Statute 109 of 1899, the accused is herewith declared judged and, though still subject to any new development of the present case, his immediate liberty is decreed . . ."

I haven't seen Elena again or her brother, or her mother and father. I hope they haven't confined her. I am guilty: they're right. There is something, an ethic, something, that leaves me in a very dubious light. I've seen too much to be innocent. They have too much darkness in their heads ever to be guilty.

Women have always cut me in two: they've given me the greatest pleasures of my life and got me into the worst trouble. From the very beginning. All psychological stories about childhood, drooling with sentimentality and insight, are suspect. We must be much more critical about our childhood if we want to mature enough not to give a damn when we disappear from this clinging earth. "Rogelia" is that kind of maudlin story. It's about my first sign of weakness when faced with underdeveloped femininity. Not cruel enough. My mother was a sophisticated bitch and Rogelia was just plain stupid and ignorant. Their clash had something to do, I can see that now, with what the Marxists call "class struggle." My first experience with the basic source of my yearning and my satisfaction and my astonishment. I can only feel totally comfortable with a book, looking at a painting, at the movies: but all that is a lie. A woman is a book, a picture, and a painting, but flesh-and-blood real.

That's what screws up everything: man's nature is bicephalous, can't do anything noble without hurting someone, can't be vicious without benefiting someone. All good is also harmful, and everything harmful is beneficial at the same time. Something like that.

I went to bed after lunch and right away the book dropped out of my hands. . . . I suddenly woke up bottomless. Couldn't hold on to anything; the objects in the room, hard and cold, had no relation whatsoever to me.

Lasted only for a few seconds, but it was the strongest attack of anguish . . . no, not anguish, the deepest rupture that I've ever felt between my consciousness and the rest of the world. I can't explain it, get it straight; words betray me, turn everything flat and insignificant.

We have this terror, deeply rooted in our consciousness, of being annihilated, of losing contact with the assurance of knowing that "my name is so-and-so," afraid to let go of the pleasure and even the pain of all we have and know . . . I've got to find out if there is anything beyond that abyss, beyond the perplexity and helplessness and total bewilderment that inundated me. If there is anything going on once the mind has stopped stuffing us with ideas, desires, and emotions. It's a silence that first appears as terror, terror in the face of emptiness-silence; and I couldn't go on.

Every time my old lady writes me from the States she slips a stick of chewing gum and a Gillette Blue Blade into the letter. She knows I don't chew gum and that I've always used an electric razor. I can hardly make out my old man's handwriting. They're mad. I never have much to say, so I answer them with a postcard. So I won't have to invent news. Just write that I'm all right and that's about all.

I've only asked them to send me magazines and books, but nothing doing.

They go and send me canned hams and cereals and Nescafé and cartons of cigarettes. Disaster. We never manage to communicate.

I've got the tip of my tongue irritated from constantly poking it into a cavity I've discovered in one of my molars. Once in a while it throbs like hell. This very afternoon I'm going to the dentist. I'm going because losing the tooth frightens me more than that vicious drill.

Feel somewhat alleviated even though the dentist discovered three other cavities. It's all right now. The first obstacle has been overcome, and the most difficult thing in the world is to begin something . . . and to know when to end it. Now it depends on the dentist. The next appointment is on Friday. From the moment I sat in the chair I began to protest—"ah, ah, ah"—at the mere thought that he might touch a sensitive nerve with the bit. It reminds me of that thorny iron ball attached to a club in the Middle Ages and used in physical combat; with the only difference that men tried to avoid the blows then and today we have to submit voluntarily to the dentist's torture.

Fear is always the same. I was watching myself. Fear developed in the first place because I didn't want to accept the reality of the dentist, I wanted to run away; when I managed to convince myself that it was inevitable, I felt relieved, tranquil. You suffer when you don't want to suffer. If I could only overcome my fear of other people and of my own death with the same ease with which I dissolved the fear of the drill, I'd be another man.

Tomorrow I'm planning to drop by the pool at the Habana Riviera. I understand they now rent the cabanas to anyone with five pesos in his pocket. I'll bask in the sun, see if it sucks out my brains.

It's two o'clock in the morning and I can't sleep. Don't even dare lean back in the chair, I just move my shoulders slightly and feel as if they were pricking me with a thousand needles. My skin is burning. And it even rained in the afternoon.

While I was basking in the sun I watched the other bathers. Most of us are exhibitionists. The athletic type usually parades around with the cruel refinement of a horror movie. They come on stage walking around slowly, with the elegant gait of a panther and the halting swing of a gorilla. They laugh, wave effusively at two or three friends scattered around the pool. . . . The crucial moment comes when they're about the jump into the water. They stand at the very edge of the pool with tense muscles and when you expect them to dive in, they draw back. . . . They repeat this four or five times. The fascination disappears once they finally dive in headfirst: suddenly they're in the water, their faces dripping and their limbs wiggling instinctively; they know it, subconsciously, because I don't believe they can analyze their conduct. In horror films the electrifying moment also takes place a split second before the monster or the murderer appears on the screen.

Adolescents, a gang, were wrestling. Couldn't determine whether they wanted to impress the girls or just needed or wanted to paw each other.

Then I saw an itsy-bitsy figure of a woman walking up and down as if she were a luscious tropical beauty. Everybody thinks she has beauty in her, somewhere. Could be she had a lovely heel. I didn't see her that intimately.

It all turns into a spectacle, when you're not taking part and just watch the game from the outside. That's why I enjoy reading so much.

I began to study carefully the different ages women go through. There is an exquisite point, somewhere between thirty and thirty-five, when Cuban women suddenly pass from ripeness into decay and corruption. Fruits that rot overnight. It's astonishing. With the giddy speed of the sun plunging into the sea each afternoon.

It's a maddening game to stare fixedly at any part of the human body; ears, for example, or just bellies. To say nothing of the different shapes and sizes feminine asses take on here. The *S* formed by the stomach and the ass reaches a point in certain Cuban women where it becomes independent, out of proportion with the rest of the body, even having its own personality.

All in all, people give me the impression of invalid animals, defenseless, half hairless, precariously balanced on two feet. . . . I believe, got it from some surrealist, that man's intelligence and imperfection is the result of having been the premature fetus of a monkey that survived and reproduced.

Clouds began to gather and cover the sky in the afternoon. Gusts of sudden air shook the coconut trees, dragged papers into the pool, and lifted high the skirt of a gray-haired old lady. Gave me the impression of living in a fictitious world.

Lightning zigzagged and plunged into the sea, thunder bounced against the cabanas and the towering hotel. It was a hollow sound, as if they were crushing cardboard rocks in the sky.

The sounds of war must be like that, I thought, and I couldn't help seeing an invasion clamoring like thunder, splitting the island like lightning traveling through a piece of sky.

Can't get it into my head. The only possibility, for an insignificant creature like myself, is total resignation; a thought that clears my head and invariably makes me feel light and stupid.

Some guests (they seemed to be foreigners) were swimming in the pool under the rain.

Today I even enjoyed the whirling drill-bit, realized the pain wasn't so strong; if you don't put up any resistance, nothing happens and the dentist can work on the cavities much better. Pain is sweet.

For over a month I haven't touched this diary. Now I'm writing in a notebook. The flashy clatter of the typewriter gets on my nerves. Brings back memories of the police station.

I spent hours looking out the window, not exactly hours, just minutes, yet minutes today are the hours of our grandparents who started to measure time. If I'm not mistaken, my grandparents, both of them, spent their honeymoon at the Trotcha hotel. From here you can see it clearly and, when I stare down at it, I'm conscious of never having met them: have only seen my grandparents in faded sepia photographs. And I try to imagine the American officers also enjoying the hotel while they occupied the island after the Spanish-American War. In those days Vedado must have been a wilderness, bushes and trees and mud. It's really impressive to see this old, genteel, broken-down building in contrast with the Riviera hotel, built during the last years of Batista, inaugurated with fanfare, the "Steve Allen Show" even came down for the opening, while the rebels were about to shoot their way down out of the hills and put an end to the party. It was a windy night and it was winter. The party is over. The Trotcha is dry wood, one of its bodies, the rest is thick solid colonial masonry and red-curved shingles on the roof. Two stories high, while the Riviera is over twenty of reinforced concrete, almost without any windows, and air conditioning in each room. Two different periods and both fucked up.

There is a tiny sailboat just off shore; small because it's alone on the grayish blue sheet of water. Clothes hung out to dry are fluttering on some of the roof-tops. All so boring that I don't know why I'm describing it. Now I'm looking at the small Portocarrero painting of Havana hanging on the white wall: so much more attractive than the city itself. Densely colored, and the composition is much better. Havana, though, hasn't got those colors. Havana is white, yellow; it's whitewashed in pale colors, faded or dirty: green, blue, gray, pink. A motley of buildings—not just colonial balconies and thick balustrades and stained-glass doors and partitions as painted by Portocarrero. He has chosen the city that interests him and given it the colors it has in his imagination. Everybody has a different city in his head.

My Havana is the one I see here from my window. It's made up of the poplars of Vedado and crestfallen, grimy pines. The Trotcha is now a broken-down, rickety boardinghouse; I can see a woman sweeping in the wooden area, she's just pulled the shuttered door out to sweep behind it. The balcony has those wooden icicles or snowflakes seen through a microscope or those tablecloths old aunts used to embroider. But the wood is gray and dirty and worm-eaten.

On a flat roof across the street a child is playing by himself, among the nauseating traces of human beings that soil and sadden everything. He has just thrown himself down on the flat rooftop after running in circles around the clotheslines. Stopped, simply bored with running, and threw himself down. There he is, still sitting there with his legs sprawled out.

Down on the street, cars go by and people seem very small. Not a word they say can be heard up here. Not interested either. I can well imagine.

What does it all mean? Why do I waste my time describing this? I'm going up to my studio. What possible meaning can lie in those roofs, the ocean, damp clothes flapping in the air, tiny people walking by down in the street, old buildings, new buildings, children playing and grimy pines?

Noemí came by today with a bunch of pictures. Said she'd been wanting to show them to me for a long time now but "always I forget." "Maybe you were ashamed," I remarked and she blushed. They're pictures of when she was submerged and baptized. It wasn't the way I had imagined it. Nothing is. The white robe didn't cling to her body. Noemí is surrounded by other people: I had imagined her alone. Witnesses are all around and everywhere.

I looked up her name in the Bible. She is Ruth's mother-in-law. Noemí, my Naomi, should tell herself, instead of advising Ruth: "Thou shalt mark the place where he shall lie, and thou shalt go in, and uncover his feet, and lay thee down; and he will tell thee what thou shalt do."

The radio was screeching at the other end of the bed, and I couldn't turn it off without leaving Noemí's body. Was going to ask her to hug me tightly so we could roll over, so I could stretch out my arm and silence the radio—but no. I was even more reluctant to withdraw and come back after shutting off the music. The slightest awkwardness could ruin everything. The music bothered me less than the singer's voice, it gave me the uncomfortable impression that she was there in bed with us and that made me freeze so I couldn't concentrate completely on Noemí.

Everything had been natural and feverish from the moment I stopped and kissed her on the eyes; she closed her eyelids, always invisible when her eyes were open. I caught her eyelashes between my lips. That was down in the living room.

The static bothered me too, the static of the Miami station I had tuned in on by accident, wanted everything to be pleasant, avoid any quick change, pleasant as it already was for me. For more than a year I had been yearning for Noemí. Her body was light, just as I'd figured, just as if her bones were full of air like the bones of a bird. As delicate and light as the first whore I had taken in my arms. And she believed in God. I felt young again.

And I told her. "You have no idea how much I suffered every time I made up your bed," she told me. "Don't laugh at me, but many nights I've dreamt we were both living together, that this was my house too, and that was enough for me, I never thought our relationship would go beyond that, it was enough for me to dream that I had you in my arms and in my body." Her words blended in with the song: "I hate to see that evening sunn go dowwn, 'cause my baabyy has gone and left this towwn." Tried to imagine it was also Noemí's voice and not the voice of a stranger. "Feeelinng tomorrooow just like I feeel todaaay. Feeeling tomorroow just like I feel todaay. I'm going to pack myyy trooouubles . . ." Everything was right, even the song, I always hummed it out of tune to myself when I felt happy and melancholy. It was a humble song, humble like Noemí, a sad Negro song. Everything, I felt, was right.

I moved slowly, our moans too blending with the alcoholic, scratchy voice of the record. "The music bothers me because I want you all to myself," I told her with my stiff arms sunk into the mattress on both sides of her chest, my body covering her up to the waist, looking down into her face in the dim room. "You have me," she answered. In love, all the stupidities of the world sound profound. "I can't understand a word she's singing."

I remember the precise moment when they interrupted the song. Noemí had pulled up her head, with the tips of her hair, short and tousled, and blacker than the dark headboard of the bed, barely touching the pillow, and she kissed me carefully. "Aggressive conduct, if allowed to go unchecked and unchallenged, ultimately leads to war. . . ."

"Who's that talking?" Noemí asked, after I had stopped, after a while. "It's Kennedy, President Kennedy, I think. . . ." I never retain exact words but I remember these: "I have directed . . . initial steps be taken immediately . . . a strict quarantine on all offensive military equipment . . . continued and increased close surveillance of Cuba and its military buildup. . . . It shall be the policy of this nation to regard any nuclear missile launched from Cuba as an attack by the Soviet Union on the United Sates, requiring full retaliatory response upon the Soviet Union. . . . Now your leaders are no longer Cuban leaders. . . . They are puppets and agents of an international conspiracy. . . . Your lives and lands are being used as pawns by those who deny you freedom. . . ." Or something like that. And other words more terrible.

"What is he saying?" I was staring fixedly at the parchment light on the dial in the casing of the radio. "I don't know. . . . He says there are missiles in Cuba." "What are they, love?" she asked and she embraced me, but I could no longer feel anything. I was numb. "The atomic bomb?" "Yes, the atomic bomb," I answered her. "They say they have concrete evidence, photographs. He says . . . I guess the marines will land, they'll bomb Havana. I can't believe it, missiles here, in this beautiful tropical island." Noemí let go and cried: "Shit!"

We stood still for a minute looking at the ceiling. Slabs, coins, and splinters of light filtered in through various crevices in the half-closed blinds. Spears of light moved across the ceiling, and the cars, down in the street, could be heard passing louder than ever.

It's all over. Good things always come too late, when you're no longer able to enjoy them. Cheap philosophy but true. Noemí beside me and I couldn't feel anything tender, only terror. Instead of feeling my flesh alive, I felt my ribs and my lungs inflating and deflating with difficulty. We were naked in bed, defenseless, two hairless animals, without powerful muscles, invalids. Sensuality turned into sadness. I felt ridiculous, naked in the bed, sprawled on the sheets with my lungs inflating and deflating out of anguish. Her small breasts, Noemí's dark nipples next to me were shattering me.

There's no reason for me to write at all now. It's all meaningless. Nothing has happened, but I feel asphyxiated. People—I've just come back from the street— move about and talk as if war were just a game. I saw the German cities after the war. Ruins that looked like decayed teeth in Berlin and Hamburg. People shriveled up, ruined, breathing among the debris. The mutilated. Hunger and fear and the insignificance of man. No idea here of what can happen. They're mad. So serene that it's admirable. I write just to distract myself, to see if I can breathe a little better. I look at the things in the apartment and they tell me nothing.

I was alone in Germany after the war. Toward the end of '47; I had dollars and that made a god out of me. But I couldn't enjoy it, enjoy, hell! I didn't understand a thing. Twenty-four and childishly in love. Arrived running away from Hanna, felt busted, looking for an intense experience, for hell, fucked up, a Jew ready for the gas chamber. I tried to shove my memories and desires away. Who was going to get into bed with a German fräulein who was living in a half-destroyed house, with hardly enough to eat, her brother killed in the war? Everybody went through one of those corny dramas, but real, living. Everything was twisted. I haven't been able to forget the shock, it stuck in my head too intensely: I was walking along a street and I threw away my cigarette. All of a sudden three or four guys pounced on it, don't know where they came from, all of this in less than a minute. It was an American cigarette. I blushed. Even a roly-poly gentleman with a gray suit and wine-colored tie jumped in to retrieve it; he looked like the essence of respectability, a German Herr Professor—still, he threw himself down after the cigarette butt, leather briefcase and all. I'm still ashamed of having witnessed the scene. I looked up, this I remember neatly, clearly, and saw ruins: a roofless room with nothing but two scorched walls, green, the kind that have rococo garlands close to the ceiling.

If they stop those Soviet ships in the middle of the ocean, on their way over. . . . Us, nuclear bombs, here! Us, missiles. I just can't get it into my head. You can imagine a shot, being stabbed by a knife, the explosion of a grenade. I can't visualize the city of Havana destroyed, evaporated by a hydrogen bomb. They wouldn't drop a bomb here, radiation would poison the atmosphere in Florida. I feel just like one of the cows on our farm when it rained. They would stand motionless immobile in the middle of a field. Wherever the rain caught them.

What I feel, what I'm going through is meaningless when confronted by the facts. *Nada*. Everything seems out of proportion. We here, and the rest of the world. Nuclear energy and my small apartment. Everything is out of proportion. *"Los ex-ter-mi-na-re-mos,"* Fidel declared just a while ago. Most likely the Pentagon will exterminate us. But he's assumed the responsibility, whatever that is. He grabbed the bull by the horns. Ready for anything. He's mad. For a moment I felt, as he talked, that he was speaking from the only possible position we can take. We're on the summit of the world and not in the depths of underdevelopment. Now I feel stupid again, insignificant . . . I was carried away. Other people are deciding my life. And there's nothing I can do. No control over anything. If I go to bed, I might not get up again.

"Nosotros adquirimos las armas que nos dé la gana de adquirir . . . y tomamos las medidas que consideremos necesarias para neustra defensa. . . . ¿Cuáles son? Ne tenemos que decirles a los imperialistas. . . . A nuestro país no lo inspecciona nadie, porque jamás le daremos autorización a nadie, jamás renunciaremos a la prerrogativa soberana de que dentro de nuestra frontera somos nosotros los que decidimos y somos nosotros los que inspeccionamos y nada más. . . . ¡Cualquiera que intente inspeccionar a Cuba debe saber que tiene que venir en zafarrancho de combate! . . . Si hacen un bloqueo van a engrandecer a nuestra patria, porque nuestra patria sabrá resistir. . . . Nosotros somos parte de la humanidad y corremos esos riesgos, pero no nos atemorizamos. Tenemos que saber vivir en la época que nos ha tocado vivir y con la dignidad con que debemos saber vivir. ¡Todos, hombres y mujeres, jóvenes y viejos, todos somos uno en esta hora de peligro!"*

We're all one, I'll die like everybody else. This island is a trap and the revolution is tragic because we're too small to survive, to come through. Too poor and too few. It's quite an expensive dignity. The revolution is too big for us. I'd rather not think. I read every sentence Fidel said yesterday several times to try to understand, to fill my emptiness; the rhythm of each sentence stuck in my brain, the tone, and now I want to forget it all. I want to lose myself. Disappear. I don't want to know anything. I don't want to remember. I don't want to have an inconsolable memory.

---

* "We shall acquire whatever weapons we feel like acquiring . . . and we shall take the measures we consider necessary to guarantee our defenses. . . . Which ones? There is no reason why we should tell the imperialists. . . . No one is going to inspect our country. No one is going to come to inspect our country, because we grant no one the right, we will never renounce the sovereign prerogative that within our frontiers we will make all the decisions, and we are the only ones who will inspect anything and only we. . . . Anyone intending to inspect our country should be ready to come in battle array! . . . If they blockade our country they will exalt our nation, because we will resist. . . . We are part of humanity and we run the necessary risks, yet, we are not afraid. We must learn how to live in our allotted times and with the dignity with which we know how to live. Everybody, men and women, young and old, we are all one in this hour of danger!"

I went out and came back. I can't stand the house or being out in the street. Along the waterfront, the waves were splashing over the wall. An island is a trap, the revolution caught us all inside; I felt no relief watching the open water. Could see nothing, still, I would feel the battleships, the gray aircraft carriers almost brushing past my face. First they'll certainly bomb us, to soften and destroy us, but the sky was quiet, I was still alive. The safety of that very instant meant nothing, it was an instant without a future. It is the same too right now, this very moment is a moment without a future. Everything can suddenly burst into "roaring flames" and "brilliant luminosity" twenty miles high, as it says in that description of the hydrogen bomb that I just read. Nothing happens, everything is possible.

I walked and walked, and suddenly I heard a roaring sound that was growing and growing. The roar seemed to fill the city. Tanks began to appear, trucks hauling cannons behind, cannons, moving lumps, often incomprehensible, a long truck, almost endless, a dark tarpaulin covering everything, a huge shape. My legs grew weak, I was afraid, afraid they would arrest me in the middle of the night walking along the waterfront, accuse me of being a spy; I didn't even look around, I looked straight ahead, I only listened to the roar of the vehicles. It was either a missile or ethereal fuel, I saw all of us blown to bits. I felt a sharp pain on my leg, I jumped, crouched, and picked up a piece of the pavement. The steel track had torn out pieces from the asphalt avenue in the dark. I kept on walking. The final cannons went by, pointing backward at the stretch they were leaving behind with me.

Up above, the stars were lighting up insignificant dots in the now pitch-dark sky. The stars are no comfort to anyone, they ignore us from afar. They're completely indifferent. Have nothing to do with us. It's impressive how much romantic babble a revolution can destroy! You get rid of your illusions and are left with nothing, vulnerable all around.

The idea of bombings, invasion, blood, stinking corpses, mutilated, rotten, is worse than accepting nuclear destruction. Yes. I'd rather be blown up all of a sudden in a brilliant flash of light, devoured, evaporated by roaring flames than lose a leg, bleeding to death in the street. Dying at the center of a clean bomb, as Eisenhower, I think, called it first. A clean bomb. Before, I had thought it was a stupid and macabre idea invented by puritanical hypocrisy, but now I find it comforting; it's a stupendous solution, a clean death, artificial, without pain or blood; a clean bomb without much fallout.

Another long truck went by like a train with another huge amorphous mass covered by an opaque and greasy tarpaulin. I thought I saw a hand waving at me as I turned to look.

We're already a modern country, we have twentieth-century weapons, atomic bombs, we're no longer an insignificant colony, we've already rushed into history, we have the same weapons that the Russians and the Americans rattle at each other. Our power of destruction makes us an equal for a moment to the two great world powers. Still, I'm sure they'll never accept us on equal terms, they'll take our weapons away, ignore us, crush this island.

I haven't heard anything from Noemí, is she coming by tomorrow? I don't care about tomorrow. I can't love anyone, everything is paralyzed. I feel impotent to desire her. Life has ended, I must really let go of everything now: the world is opening up under my feet, it swallows me, I'll lose my body.

Last night I couldn't sleep. Today I went out into the street again. A biting north wind is blowing. The waves hit the seawall and fling themselves over the barrier, crash down on the trucks and cars, against the iron rails and the pockmarked facades. The air gets all powdery with water then. It's cold. Several watery bursts crashed down on us, scattering dark pieces of water-soaked wood onto the street.

I saw a butterfly in an open lot, and I felt suddenly like stopping, things were coming to an end in that very minute. Flying silently and yellow through the air—everything seemed suspended, dead.

Out in the street I felt worse, more vulnerable. Walking around doesn't solve anything. Everything is much more dangerous out in the street; I can't do anything. I'm a victim. I can't explain it, but seeing the butterfly was the most terrible hallucination I've had, and I don't know why.

The phone rang, it sounded like long distance, and when I picked up the receiver I heard a strange conversation. "I didn't tell her anything, she doesn't know anything. She didn't notice all the coming and going in the hospital," the man's voice said; then a woman asked: "She didn't ask you anything?" "When they started putting all those strange wooden tables in the hall, for the bodies, it was frightening, Irene, long tables with tags to tie around the ankles of the corpses, with a number or a name or something, that's what the nurses told me; when she saw the tables, she asked me about them." "What did you tell her?" "I told her it was a hurricane. The sky was gray and this north wind gave me the idea, I told her we were expecting a hurricane." "Yes, she can understand that much better, she lived through the hurricane in '26 and in '44, but never, she's never seen a war." "Neither have you." "Are you afraid?" "They'll have to kill me." "Don't you even mention it, sacred heart of Jesus, that's asking for bad luck." "There's no such thing as bad luck, I'm a revolutionary, revolutionaries don't believe in religious superstitions like that." "Anyhow, you should respect my . . ." "*¡Patria o muerte! ¡Venceremos!*" he screamed. I hung up. It was the only violent reaction I had heard during these last terrible days. People in general are very calm.

They called back, again the prolonged long-distance rings, but when I answered there was no one on the line. Might be Laura or my old man trying to get in touch with me from New York. I'm not going to answer. I don't want to talk to anybody. I have nothing to say, what could I say? I don't want to hear anything from anyone.

After clicking down the phone I went into the kitchen and took a bowl of rice out of the refrigerator, but I couldn't swallow it, the cold grains of rice stuck in my throat.

I don't know what I'm doing, I just stuck my thumb into my mouth and started tapping the nail on the edge of my teeth. Several minutes of that. My finger came out with a transparent string of saliva. I wiped my thumb off on the rough fabric of my khaki pants.

I want to put it all down. Everything I do seems weird to me. I pulled a pack of cigarettes out of my soft damp and drooling shirt, a blue-and-white pack of cigarettes, Dorados. I pulled out a cigarette and thumped the end of it on the table. The fire consumed the green match head while I watched it and almost burned my fingers. I drew in the smoke, a mouthful of hot smoke went into my lungs. I stared at the tip of ashes and the white stick leaning into the ashtray. I picked up the cigarette, exhaled the smoke over the table, over the books and my diary. A piece of tobacco dropped onto the table.

I looked down at the floor and saw a ball of lint, of hair and a spider web and dust under the bookcase.

I got into bed and put the light out: but I couldn't sleep. The missiles are there, in Pinar del Río, Santa Clara, in Oriente. . . . The island seems to be covered with missiles all over. They'll brush us away, put us out, they're going to sink this alligator island into the bottom of the Caribbean. Then the battleships will sail over us and say: "This is where Cuba used to be." And the waves, the tides, will sweep over the island that had sunk into the bottom of the sea.

The Pentagon must already have a plan to destroy us. They'll crush us with the sheer weight of their arms and men. And if the Russians fire their missiles the earth might split in two. All because of Cuba. Never have we been more important nor more miserable. Fighting the United States—we're so small—might have a touch of greatness, but I reject that fate. I would rather go on being underdeveloped. Not interested, a fate that must face death each minute is not for me. Revolutionaries are mystics of this century: willing to die for an implacable social justice. I'm a mediocre man, a modern man, a link in the chain, a worthless cockroach.

The slightest sound can be the end of the world. A car going by in the street, someone starting a motor, if they slam a door. . . . Every sound is the beginning of the end. No, can't conceive nuclear destruction, it's something completely blank to me. The unknown. Have no way of relating myself to the phenomenon. I will become hot breath. No use complaining: I live here in Cuba and will die like the rest. They've pinned me down. No way out, none, I can see myself among the ruins of Vedado, a speck of dust, a smudge. . . .

I don't want to sleep nor do I feel like staying here. Have to go downstairs and get a glass of water, eat something; not even that. If I go down into the street, it could be worse. People, just to see people. What's the use, hanging on like this?

Let go, let go.

But I don't want to die, there's always the stupid hope of breaking through, of being happy some day. Fucked up. Never learn. Now, now is all that I have.

Why? Fear of losing my shitty personality, my memories, my desires, my sensations. Mine.

This diary is useless.

Underdevelopment and civilization. Never learn.

I take myself too seriously.

Everything I say oozes out and shoves me down. Still here. Go away. Leave.

If they drop the bomb, if we survive. My head. No, I don't want it. Makes no difference. It's a lie, it does make a difference. I do care.

And what if at this very moment the bombing were to start?

Everything breaking into hell. I get more tangled up. Scream. Scream for what. Why should I put down a question mark. Periods, semicolons, letters.

Accept, accept, accept. Not even that. My head's a trap. I'm tied down. Thought. Separates me from everything. Me, me nothing. I'm still here, here, here. Everything is painful and not what it should be.

I'm going to die and that's all. All right, I accept it. I'm not going to try to sneak away through the cracks like a cockroach. There aren't any more cracks left. Cracks and holes and shelters are over.

The October Crisis is over. The Caribbean Crisis. The Missile Crisis. To name huge things is to kill them. Words are small, meager. If I had died, everything would have been over. But I'm still alive. And staying alive also means destroying any deep moment of intensity. (What damned silly words!)

Want to preserve the clean and empty vision of the days of crisis. Things around me and fear and desires choke me. It's impossible. Beyond this, I have nothing to add. Finished. Man (I) is sad, but wants to live. . . .

Go beyond words.

Aftermath: Politics and Cinema

Despite the favorable reception *Memories of Underdevelopment* received from film reviewers in the United States, it had great difficulty finding an audience because of U.S. government interference in its distribution. The documents that follow illustrate two of the most publicized examples of such interference. In 1972, a number of Cuban films intended to be shown in New York as part of a Cuban Film Festival were seized by the Treasury Department acting in behalf of a U.S. economic embargo of Cuba. The seizure prompted a strong letter of protest from many of the country's best-known film critics.

In 1974, the National Society of Film Critics conferred an award on *Memories of Underdevelopment* but Tomás Gutiérrez Alea was denied a visa to attend the ceremonies and was also denied access to the monetary award of $2,000 that the Society conferred. Again there were public protests, but the government's position did not change. The *New York Times* accounts both describe and comment on the issue; Alea responds in a letter to the Society.

Federal Agents Seize
Cuban Festival Films Here

Henry Raymont

Less than an hour before the first New York Festival of Cuban Films was to go into its second day at the Olympia Theatre yesterday afternoon, Federal agents carrying a search warrant confiscated films and propaganda material. The action forced the cancellation of six programs scheduled for yesterday and today.

After seizure of the films, Michael Myerson, international director of American Documentary Films, the California-based, nonprofit organization sponsoring the festival, said that the confiscation order would be challenged in Federal Court here tomorrow. . . .

The warrant authorizes the seizure of 25 films which, it is charged, had been brought into the United States "fraudulently, clandestinely and without required declaration of entry.". . .

The action had been expected Friday night after Treasury Department officials in Washington said that none of the films to be shown at the festival had been licensed and that their importation into the United States constituted a violation of the Trading with the Enemy Act.

From the *New York Times,* 26 March 1972, p. 62.

Film Critics' Letter

To the Editor:

On March 25, at the doors of the Olympia Theatre in New York, agents of the United States Treasury Department confiscated the Cuban film *Days of Water,* forcing the organizers of the First New York Cuban Film Festival to postpone screening some 25 films. A few days later, the Museum of Modern Art decided to cancel screening of several Cuban films after being told by the Treasury Department that legal action would follow exhibition of unlicensed work.

Whatever the legal particulars of this case, it is not the place of the United States Government to decide what Americans should or should not see, read, or hear. A law which can be used for political purposes to keep Americans from seeing the art of a foreign country is an oppressive law. We object to political regulation over what works of art may enter and be exhibited in this country. We object even more strenuously to the use of that noxious power arbitrarily. We think it either sinister or absurd when access to foreign art can be turned off and on like a tap to suit the government's current policy, when Americans are not allowed to see Cuban films only weeks after the President has been televised world-wide cheerfully applauding the Peking Ballet and after videotapes of it are broadcast across America amid choruses of official self-congratulation. At that point, an illegitimate power arbitrarily used begins to smack of outright thought control.

The blockade of Cuba by the United States has been a foolish and destructive mistake. Apart from that, the art of any foreign country, whatever its politics, ought to be freely available to Americans whenever it is practically feasible. The government ought never to have the power to interfere with that freedom.

We protest the government's current policy toward Cuban film. We urge the immediate licensing of the films in the Cuban Film Festival for exhibition throughout the country. And we urge prompt enactment of whatever changes in the law may be needed to guarantee not only freedom of expression to artists but, for the public, full freedom of access to their work.

JAY COCKS, JACK GELBER, RICHARD GILMAN,
NAT HENTOFF, STANLEY KAUFFMANN, STEPHEN KOCH,
DWIGHT MCDONALD, JONAS MEKAS, ANNETTE MICHELSON,
ANDREW SARRIS, AMOS VOGEL, WILLIAM WOLF

From the *New York Times,* 9 April 1972, sec. 2, p. 7.

U.S. Refuses Visa to Cuban Director to Get Film Award

David Binder

The State Department announced today that it had denied a request by the Cuban film director Tomás Gutiérrez Alea for an entry visa to accept the award of the National Society of Film Critics in New York Sunday.

A visa application was also turned down for Saul Yelin, director of Cuba's National Film Institute,* who had asked to accompany Mr. Gutiérrez as an interpreter.

The award of $2000 and a plaque was to honor the 45-year-old director's 1968 film, *Memories of Underdevelopment.*

Hollis Alpert, chairman of the critics group, said he was warned today by a United States Treasury official that it would be a violation of the Trading with the Enemy Act for anyone to accept the award on behalf of Mr. Gutiérrez. . . .

The official said the United States had granted visas to "well under 100 Cubans" in the last year to attend international conferences, go to the United Nations and participate in certain amateur and professional athletic events and "for humanitarian purposes."

"The denial represents a continuation of U.S. policy toward Cuba," he added.

From the *New York Times,* 17 January 1974, p. 41.
* Yelin was actually Head of Foreign Relations for the Institute. -ed.

Editorial: Celluloid Menace

The specter of Cuba as a threat to this nation's security would seem to have been largely eliminated with the dismantling of the Soviet missiles in 1962. It is therefore puzzling in the extreme why the State Department has considered it necessary or proper to deny entry visas to two Cuban film representatives who were invited to the United States in order to accept an award for artistic excellence from the National Society of Film Critics.

Permits were inexplicably denied to Tomás Gutiérrez Alea and to Saul Yelin, Director of Cuba's National Film Institute.* Mr. Gutiérrez was to collect a $2000 award for his widely acclaimed film, *Memories of Underdevelopment*. Going beyond the State Department's official inhospitality, Treasury officials warned the American film critics that anyone who might accept the award on Mr. Gutiérrez behalf would be in violation of the Trading with the Enemy Act.

The absurdity of such sanctions must be measured against the fact that the USA is now busily encouraging trade with the Communist superpowers. But the transmission of a prize for cultural achievement is treated as a subversive act. The irrationality of such behaviour is particularly disappointing in the light of recent promising signals from Cuba which followed on the heels of constructive Cuban-American agreements in the battle against aerial hijackings.

At a time when detente with the Soviet Union and the normalization of relations with Communist China are rightfully considered diplomatic triumphs, the suggestion that Cuban filmmakers might constitute a menace only exposes American officialdom to ridicule.

From the New York Times, 19 January 1974, p. 30.
* See note on previous page.

Telegram from Tomás Gutiérrez Alea

Mr. Andrew Sarris
Chairman, National Society of Film Critics
Algonquin Hotel, Oak Room,
New York, N.Y.

It is with deep regret that we are unable to attend the ceremonies at which we were to accept the award conferred by you upon the Cuban film MEMORIES OF UNDERDEVELOPMENT. We write these lines first of all to express our satisfaction with the interest the film has received and with the esteem you have displayed for it. But, above all, these lines will inform you of the explanation of our unavoidable absence at the ceremonies as well as certain other things. The reason for our failure to attend is very simple: the State Department has denied us a visa to enter your country and has not given any explanation in this regard. But that is not all: the Treasury Department has threatened your Society with judicial proceedings that could put some of your officers in prison if you grant us the award (US $2000) or even if you merely give us a plaque.

None of this is new. It should not come as a surprise to us. This superpower has subjected us to acts of aggression, to a blockade decreed against our country, and to misinformation ever since our revolutionary process began. These acts of aggression—which are to a certain extent reflected in our film—and all acts intended to interfere with any kind of contact between our people and the people of the United States have the immediate result of keeping the American people in ignorance and preventing them from getting the truth about what is happening in our country. Last year [*sic*], using the same absurd pretexts and the crudest of repressive measures, the US Treasury Department prohibited the New York showing of a group of Cuban films brought together for what was to be a Festival of Cuban Cinema. On that occasion as well, the State Department denied visas to a group of our film directors, thus preventing them from entering into a direct contact with the North American public. All of this is obviously contrary to the principles of freedom supported by the people of the United States and pro-claimed—with an insistence that is quite suspect—by the US Government. We believe that the threats which the Treasury Department has aimed at the officers of the National Society of Film Critics are ridiculous and that nothing they can do can take away the recognition that Cuban cinematography has received from your Society. We would also point out, in closing, that all these manifestations of

(Read at the Algonquin Hotel on January 20, 1974)

pompousness and arrogance on the part of the Empire toward a country that stopped being its servile colony 15 years ago also affect—in some important ways—the interests of the North American people. Among other things, they are thus forbidden to receive information which very nearby people are offering to communicate about their process of finding their own identity, becoming masters of their own destiny, and liberating all of their own creative energy.

Tomás Gutiérrez Alea

Personal Recollections of T. G. Alea

Tomás Gutiérrez Alea's recollections of the making of *Memories of Underdevelopment* and of his career as a Cuban film director are represented here. In a 1977 interview with Julianne Burton, Alea discusses *Memories* in the context of Cuban cinema, and in an essay he published in 1980 he examines the way the film manipulates reality and is itself manipulated by the expectations of a particular audience.

"Individual Fulfillment and Collective Achievement" An Interview with Tomás Gutiérrez Alea

Julianne Burton

The following interview was conducted in Spanish (and subsequently translated and edited) by CINEASTE Contributing Editor Julianne Burton in Havana in January 1977.

Q: *As I'm sure you remember, MEMORIES OF UNDERDEVELOPMENT met with great success upon its theatrical release in the U.S. in 1973. How would you evaluate U.S. film critics' response to the film?*

A: I am not fully informed of critical response to the film in the U.S., because the only thing I can base my assessment on is a file of clippings which the film's U.S. distributor, Tricontinental Film Center, has sent me. Naturally, the reviews range from good to bad to mediocre, but in general, I would say that several of them are extremely interesting. The tendency to interpret the film as a subversive act was not as manifest in the U.S. as, for example, in England. *Sight & Sound* which published an absolutely sinister article which began by comparing the film to Buñuel's VIRIDIANA—made under Franco's very nose and proceeding to blow up in his face—and ended up comparing me to Solzhenitsyn. It was obvious that the intention was to misconstrue both the film and the circumstances under which it was produced, for the actual situation had nothing in common with the version put forth in the review.

It seems to me that MEMORIES was in general much better understood and evaluated in the U.S. because people perceived the attempt to criticize a bourgeois mentality which, understandably, persists in our society despite the many changes we've gone through.

Q: *It also seems, however, that there were many critics who articulated that critique much less vociferously than what they perceived in the film as a critique of the revolution itself.*

A: Yes, of course, such a critique is also implicit in the film. But what was the nature of that critique? What I'm saying is that most of the U.S. critics were on target in that they realized that in contrast to the bourgeois mentality represented by the protagonist, the film reveals an entire people in the process of being

Excerpted from *Cinéaste* 8, no. 1 (Summer 1977):8–15, 59. The complete interview has been reprinted in *The Cinéaste Interviews*, ed. Dan Georgakas and Lenny Rubenstein (Chicago: Lake View Press, 1982) and in Burton's own *Cinema and Social Change in Latin America: Conversations with Filmmakers* (Austin: University of Texas Press, 1986).

born—with all the problems and difficulties which that involves, but with enormous vitality as well. This new world devours the protagonist in the end. That is the image we wanted to convey with the film, and judging from the reviews I read, it seems to me that U.S. critics grasped it more clearly than their counterparts in other countries.

Q: *I have shown and discussed the film with many audiences in the U.S., and one striking thing is the tremendous urgency and persistence with which they search for a shred of optimism regarding Sergio's fate. Because they identify so completely with him, they desperately want to believe that he is somehow 'saved' at the end. Surely Cuban audiences view the end of the film very differently.*

A: Yes, they do. The film had a very good response here, relatively speaking. In fact, something happened with this movie which I had never seen with either my own films or anyone else's: many people went to see MEMORIES more than once, and some returned as many as four or five times. That does not happen with many movies. It makes me think that the film hit its mark, which was, first and foremost, to communicate with the Cuban public—not with audiences from other countries. It achieved its goal in the sense that it disturbed and unsettled its audience; it forced people to think. When they return to see the film again, it means that it has kept on churning around inside them even after they leave the theater. As far as I'm concerned, this is the most important thing.

Q: *It's true that the film seems to achieve a remarkable growth in depth and coherency between the first and second viewing, and thus has a great deal to teach people about the possibilities of cinematic expression. The first time around, the film might seem a bit disconnected, but with the second viewing there is clearly nothing disconnected about it. On the contrary, all the implications and motivations of the interwoven documentary and fictional sequences begin to come clear.*

Though it is quite conventional for a feature film to be based on a novel, the particular adaptation process by which MEMORIES was generated has always struck me as somewhat unique. Would you comment on the collaboration of novelist Edmundo Desnoes on the production of the film? To what degree was he involved in the actual filmmaking process?

A: Well, obviously, the film was based on a novel which he had written and which I found to be extremely suggestive. My work with him was very good because it was an extremely creative process. We did not attempt to 'translate' the novel into cinema. For me it turned out to be much easier, but for Desnoes it perhaps demanded a much higher level of violence against his own work and against himself, because at a certain point his novel was to be betrayed, negated, transformed into something else. He was fully conscious of this and worked over his novel as if it were raw material, not like something already fully achieved which was going to be 'translated' into cinema. Because he maintained this attitude, which is, of course, the only one to have if you are going to do this kind of thing, our work together was very fruitful. He often attended our shooting sessions, and made many excellent suggestions.

The original screenplay which we worked out together kept being transformed in the actual shooting process. There are even several scenes—and this is very significant—which carry great weight in the film but were never anticipated in the original screenplay. There were also details. The telescope, for instance, which becomes a very important image, a symbol of Sergio's alienation from his environment, didn't occur to us until the first days of shooting, almost at the last moment. Or scenes like the one where Sergio is returning home and comes across a group of people marching in the opposite direction on their way to a political gathering. The scene is very significant, because Sergio is always heading in the other direction from everyone else. As an image it functions very well. The sequence was filmed almost coincidentally, and at Desnoes' suggestion, because we just happened to come across a group that was preparing for a May Day demonstration or some such celebration. It was his idea that we take advantage of that situation, and I think that it turned out very well because we were able to film it very spontaneously. We simply had the actor begin walking through that group of people. There were no extras involved, no preliminary preparations.

Q: *What about entire sequences which did not appear in the original version of the novel, like the one which takes place in the Hemingway museum? Were these developed at your initiative and only later incorporated by Desnoes in the subsequent English version of the novel?*

A: Yes, he later included these scenes in the revised version of the novel on his own initiative. The fact was that I felt the need to say other things than those included in the original novel, and thus he would write something at my request which I would later expand and rework. But I think that even the second version of the novel is quite different from the film.

In my view, the Sergio character is very complex. On one hand, he incarnates all the bourgeois ideology which has marked our people right up until the triumph of the Revolution and still has carry-overs, an ideology which even permeates the proletarian strata. In one sense Sergio represents the ideal of what every man with that particular kind of mentality would like to have been: rich, good-looking, intelligent, with access to the upper social strata and to beautiful women who are very willing to go to bed with him. That is to say, he has a set of virtues and advantages which permit spectators to identify to a certain degree with him as a character.

The film plays with this identification, trying to insure that the viewer at first identifies with the character, despite his conventionality and his commitment to bourgeois ideology.

But then what happens? As the film progresses, one begins to perceive not only the vision that Sergio has of himself but also the vision that reality gives to *us*, the people who made the film. This is the reason for the documentary

Alea filming Sergeo typing his manuscript

sequences and other kinds of confrontation situations which appear in the film. They correspond to our vision of reality and also to our critical view of the protagonist. Little by little, the character begins to destroy himself precisely because reality begins to overwhelm him, for he is unable to act. At the end of the film, the protagonist ends up like a cockroach—squashed by his fear, by his impotence, by everything.

So then what happens to the spectator? Why does it trouble him or her to such a degree that s/he feels compelled to see the film again? Because the spectators feel caught in a trap since they have identified with a character who proceeds to destroy himself and is reduced to . . . nothing. The spectators then have to reexamine themselves and all those values, consciously or unconsciously held, which have motivated them to identify with Sergio. They realize that those values are questioned by a reality which is much stronger, much more potent and vital.

I feel that it is in this sense that the film carries out an operation which is the most revolutionary, so to speak, the most dialectical with regard to the spectator. The film does not humor its audience; it does not permit them to leave the theater feeling self-satisfied. The importance of this phenomenon lies in the fact that it is the precondition for any kind of transformation.

Q: *It is interesting to observe how well the character of the film's protagonist corresponds to a whole stratum of not just Cuban, but Latin American intellec-*

tuals from the haute bourgeoisie. *What has been the response to the film among Latin American audiences?*

A: Unfortunately, it has not been widely shown, but it has enjoyed great success in the countries where it has been seen, according to the news which I've received. For example, it was shown in Chile during the Allende period, and I received very positive responses by word of mouth. Unfortunately, before the reviews could be assembled and sent to Cuba, the coup occurred and they were lost.

Q: *Speaking of the need that the audience feels to see MEMORIES more than once, in your most recent film, THE LAST SUPPER, and in other films which we've seen here in Cuba, it seems that the narrative line has become flatter, more chronological, more* linear. *Do you see this change from a more narratively fragmented and 'deconstructed' kind of filmmaking as a current tendency within Cuban cinema, or have I begun to draw conclusions from too narrow a base?*

A: It's not really a matter of identifying a tendency since it seems a little risky and potentially premature to draw such conclusions. I believe that we are guilty of having over-indulged our interest in historical topics despite their great importance at this stage in our national development. We are very much involved in reevaluating our past. All of us feel the need to clarify a whole series of historical problems because that is a way of also reaffirming our present reality. It is a genuine necessity. It has, however, led us to neglect our contemporary situation a bit. Clearly the challenge which we now confront is to develop a penetrating vision of our contemporary situation, and to make more films dealing with current problems. . . .

Q: *. . . I would like to ask how you see the evolution of the Cuban cinematic process in the last decade. What do you see as the major influences on Cuban film activity—not only in thematic and stylistic terms, but in terms of the mode of production as well, that is, the process by which Cuban filmmakers organize their filmmaking activity?*

I know, for instance, that the influence of Italian Neo-Realism in the early years was substantial, and you are in an excellent position to evaluate its impact since you studied in Italy and have subsequently witnessed the whole evolution of Cuban filmmaking first hand. Then, of course, there are other influences as well—early Soviet cinema, the French New Wave, Hollywood films, other films from Latin America. . .

A: Perhaps I won't be able to answer your question with as much depth and precision as I would like because I am not very clear about the most recent years. As a matter of fact, at this particular time I am in the process of trying to analyze and weigh the various factors influencing this situation, but I have not as yet developed a full analysis.

However, one thing is obvious. From the beginning of the Revolution, our artistic foundation was in fact essentially Italian Neo-Realism. Very obvious considerations account for this, and not only the fact that Julio [Garcia Espinosa][1] and I had studied in Italy during that period and were pretty permeated with that mode of approaching filmmaking.

I have to say that when we returned we continued to hold a very positive estimation of that experience in an historical perspective, but when it came to our evaluation of Neo-Realism as an aesthetic we were no longer so positive, because we had conclusively seen all the limitations to which it was subject. What we were looking for was something else. However, Neo-Realism was our origin, and we neither are able nor want to deny it.

Q: *Could you be more specific about the aesthetic limitations you mentioned?*

A: At the time it appeared, Neo-Realism sprung up apparently spontaneously. It reflected a very confusing reality—that of postwar Italy. To the degree that it did this accurately and honestly, it was, of course, very constructive, because it allowed the essence of that reality to be shown. It was a very transparent kind of reality, since such convulsive historical moments virtually express themselves. Because everything seems so apparent at such times, the requisite analysis turns out to be much easier. Since film is a good medium for capturing apparent realities, the Neo-Realist experience is a very constructive one. That reality perceived by the camera in and of itself conveyed a situation full of contradictions; the act of documenting that historical moment could not in fact avoid bringing them to the forefront.

In our view, as that particular reality began to evolve and to change, Neo-Realism began to lose its early driving force. It did not evolve in a parallel or proportionate way, but instead began to deteriorate, to accommodate itself to a commercialized concept of film as simply merchandise. Thus only those spectacular elements of Neo-Realism which were capable of maintaining a hold on the public continued to be exploited. We saw this very clearly.

What happened to us, then? We date the beginning of our filmmaking here from after the Revolution, since EL MEGANO is nothing more than a forerunner which, if you like, reveals our concerns but without yet integrating them. So when we began to make films in a post-revolutionary situation, that Neo-Realist mode of approaching reality was very useful to us because in that early stage we needed little more. First of all, we were not developed enough as filmmakers to posit other approaches. Secondly, our own national situation at that juncture was convulsive, very transparent, very clear. All we had to do was set up a camera in the street and we were able to capture a reality that was spectacular in and of itself, extremely absorbing, and laden with meaning. That kind of filmmaking was perfectly valid for that particular historical moment.

---

1. Julio Garcia Espinosa, founder and vice president of ICAIC since its inception, has made feature films (THE ADVENTURES OF JAUN QUIN QUIN, 1967) and feature-length documentaries (THIRD WORLD, THIRD WORLD WAR, 1970).

But our revolution also began to undergo a process of change. Though certainly not the same as that which occurred in postwar Italy, the meaning of external events began to become less obvious, less apparent, much deeper and more profound. That process forced us to adopt an analytical attitude toward the reality which surrounded us. A greater discipline, a much more exact theoretical criterion was then required of us in order to be able to properly analyze and interpret what we were living through. We, of course, retained the clear intention of projecting ourselves toward the future, of fulfilling the social function of cinema in the most effective way possible.

I'm not sure that this is really a complete answer to your question. I should add that subsequently we have had access to the entire gamut of world film production. We have obviously been influenced by the French New Wave. Naturally this produced a few flawed efforts, since the concerns of the New Wave filmmakers had in fact very little to do with our own reality and with our own approach to it.

Godard, for example, has exerted an inescapable influence. Since he is such a brilliant destroyer of the cinema, he offers many challenges. From this distance, I think that the Godard phenomenon can begin to be properly evaluated, noting his limitations as well as his successes. His intention was clearly to make the revolution in the realm of the cinema before making the revolution in reality. However, his endeavor has a very constructive force because he succeeds to a certain extent in making us see, in making us question the degree to which we might be at the rear of the revolutionary process rather than in the vanguard.

Our role is to be united with the revolutionary process. Thus our language as filmmakers has to evolve parallel with the revolution. It is important to be conscious of this, because one can accommodate oneself very easily to stereotypes, to comfortable ways of doing things. Let's face it, there is a tendency sometimes to resist change, don't you think? So that I think Godard's work has been useful to us in this sense. Besides, as long as you look at that phenomenon from within the revolution, it seems to me that you see it much more clearly. This permits you to be on guard against its limitations and false steps. What condemns godardian cinema in the last analysis is its own incommunicability. If it doesn't reach the people, it is of no use. For us, genuine communication is absolutely fundamental, so we must avoid falling into this syndrome at all costs. However, as I've been saying, to the degree that Godard provoked the destruction of an entire series of models of bourgeois cinema, his work has been very valuable.

What other influences have we felt? There's the 'marginal cinema,' with which we are only partially familiar. We have seen very little of the North American underground cinema, for example, so I am unable to evaluate it.

We are familiar, though, with the kind of alternative cinema which is being produced in several Latin American countries (Venezuela, for example): a militant cinema which aims at the poorest sectors of the country and seeks the kind of response that will spark a *toma de conciencia* about the social and political problems which those people face. It is a kind of filmmaking which I believe is valuable to an extent, a necessary kind of cinema, but one which must not forget that the cultural struggle must also be waged and won on the commercial screens. In making that kind of 'marginal' or alternative cinema, you can obviously not compete with the kind of Hollywood spectacles shown in commercial theaters, the kinds of films which attract, among others, that very section of the population which the militant filmmakers are trying to reach. It is thus also necessary to try to reach the commercial screens with a kind of cinema which is essentially different from, for example, JAWS. (Actually, I haven't yet seen JAWS, but I imagine that it is a fitting example of the Hollywood film-as-spectacle.)

Q: *Your emphasis on the importance of a commercially viable alternative cinema makes me think of the Brazilian Cinema Novo movement, because of the effort Brazilian filmmakers made throughout the 60s to ensure and expand their access to a broad national public in commercial theaters. Has the Cinema Novo movement exerted any influence on Cuban cinema?*

A: Yes, Brazilian cinema also had an impact here. It was a kind of revelation for us. Primarily, the early works of Glauber Rocha, although a great deal of Brazilian cinema has been shown in Cuba.

In fact, we see an extremely broad range of films here. Of course, our situation is very different from that of most film-producing countries. This is due to the fact that in addition to controlling production, we also control the movie screens. That is, what we see is in fact what we choose to see. This is another way to educate the public.

This process of training the public taste is very interesting. Obviously, we made a revolution here, we won, and that revolution developed and was radicalized quite rapidly; in the process we became conscious of what socialism was. All this happened very fast, at an almost dizzying pace. But during this very fervid time, the Cuban public continued to see Hollywood and Mexican films—until the time when the U.S. imposed the blockade [1961], when it was no longer possible to continue to see the new Hollywood films, though the older ones continued to be shown with great success. Mexican movies also stopped coming, even though diplomatic relations with Mexico were never severed, once the Mexican film enterprises which existed in Cuba had been nationalized by the revolutionary government.

Initially it seemed that this cutting off of the feature film supply was a disaster. Our public was thoroughly accustomed to those films. But I think it was actually a great boon for us. Traditional Mexican cinema—apart from a few exceptions and some interesting things that are currently being done—is absolutely dismal. It conditions the public to respond to the worst commercial motives and devices, just as Hollywood films do to a very large extent (I don't mean to say that every Hollywood film functions this way, but certainly the vast majority do).

So what happened when the supply was so abruptly cut off? The film-going public, despite being at that time in full support of socialism, ready in fact to give their lives in order to preserve the revolutionary system of government which was being implemented here, and unreservedly enthusiastic about the revolution, was reluctant to go to the movies to see the films which we were able to show at that time—Soviet films, Czech films, in short, what was then accessible to us—because these films represented a new kind of film language for them, one that was too alien.

There's another thing which should be noted. Because of the film shortage, we were compelled to import films rather indiscriminately, without a careful selection process to determine which films were more adaptable to the taste and needs of our people. Instead, it was necessary to bring in whatever we could because we had to fill the screens of our theaters. So, many things that were in fact quite mediocre (because mediocre films are produced everywhere) were brought in.

Subsequently, film exhibition became much more diversified. A great deal of European production was brought in. All the films imported from the socialist camp were subjected to more of a selection process. Currently, the film-going public in Cuba—well, you can see it for yourself—is massive. It's really very impressive. They have come to accept and understand other film languages, other approaches to filmmaking. I think it's very interesting that the evolution in the awareness and sophistication of our viewing public, though it was forced upon us by circumstances beyond our control, turned out to be very positive.

Q: *Have there been studies here in Cuba of audience response to various kinds of films?*

A: It's an area that we've just begun to work in. Personally, I think it is of cardinal importance. It grows out of something we were discussing before, of the necessity which all of us feel to delve deeper into the theoretical criteria with which we confront our cinematic task. As I've said, up until now these have been quite spontaneous and circumstantially imposed, but now—in our current stage of institutionalization[2]—theoretical inquiry must acquire a new level and a new dimension.

Q: *Do you think it's possible to identify specific characteristics of Cuban cinema—not so much of the production process but on the level of the films themselves?*

A: I take it that you're asking whether there is an identifiably Cuban film 'language.' Well, let's see. Since our entire initial stage was marked by improvisation and an emphasis on what was feasible, it may have been somewhat slow in its utilization of expressive resources and whatever, but it certainly manifested itself in a very fresh and direct way. It has continued to consolidate a certain style which seems to mark each of us equally. This has been to our advantage. At this stage, the idea is not to abandon that style, but rather to take advantage of it—of its popular, authentic, organic elements. I think the formation of a

---

2. 1977 has in fact been named the Year of Institutionalization. The First Party Congress, the inauguration of popular elections throughout the island, the founding of the Ministry of Culture, are but a few examples of the breadth and importance of this current stage of consolidation.

certain style, a tendency or direction which marks us all is inevitable. But still there is a certain dispersion as well; many different styles and concepts continue to exist. We're still in a period of quest.

When it comes to trying to generalize as to the nature of this style, it is clear that our Neo-Realist foundation has not totally disappeared. Despite all of its ideological and political limitations, despite our own evolution which has gone in a different direction, one thing is sure and continues to condition us: our film production must of necessity be inexpensive. We do not have the means to undertake super-productions. So the kind of cinema which adapts itself to our interests, fortunately, is a kind of light, agile cinema, one that is very directly founded upon our own reality. We have never lost sight of this. In fact, I think that the best of our cinema, the most fully realized works, are achieved through a very direct link with our particular circumstances. You must have seen this in DE CIERTA MANERA, for example. The film seems a bit careless, a little awkward, almost as if it had been let loose on its own, but it also succeeds in penetrating our reality to an uncommon degree, producing an impact which is somehow charged with poetry. I think that it is there above all that our reality is shaped. . . .

Q: *With regard to your future plans, will assisting in the development of younger directors be your primary activity?*

A: In fact my intention is to keep alternating between making films myself and assisting developing filmmakers. This year I plan to make another film. I'm already so involved in the undertaking that I have to give this project priority when it comes to deciding how I will allocate my time. My second priority will be to continue working with that group of younger directors.

What I am also extremely interested in is to continue developing a level of theoretical activity. This is one of the things that most concerns us, because now, at this particular stage, we realize that we must dedicate much more attention to theoretical work, to formulating our concerns on a much more profound level. We have to analyze all that we have done in order to plan for the future with a greater awareness instead of leaving everything to spontaneous solutions, which is more or less what we have been doing up to now.

I should clarify that our work was never totally improvised; there have always been theoretical investigations, but never with the degree of discipline or insistence which we should now be able to achieve. It is not that this work is just beginning now. In fact it began some time ago, but these theoretical inquiries have to continue to expand. I think that now we will see increasing emphasis on this kind of work.

This is not likely to produce immediate results, but I'm committed to it even though I know it's a long-term process. I'd like to define more clearly all that we have done here at ICAIC. I've begun to work on the question of the relationship between the film as spectacle and the audience. Specifically, what are the different levels of relation between film as pure spectacle and a cinema of ideas?

Clearly, these are not mutually exclusive poles, but rather both kinds of filmmaking must be employed simultaneously because each fulfills an important social function. I'm interested in how audience response is produced and in the uses to which this knowledge can be put. My aim would be to achieve an even greater effectiveness in the socially-committed, revolutionary propositions which can be made through film.

Q: *As a final area of discussion, I'd like to ask what you see as the personal advantages of the kind of state-owned film production system that currently exists in Cuba, in contrast to the Hollywood system, for example, or to conditions in Italy when you studied filmmaking there in the early 50s.*

A: I imagine that this is a very difficult thing for the majority of people in a nonsocialist country to understand, because they're clearly marked by bourgeois ideology, and they find the idea of giving up certain limited bourgeois freedoms to be a very painful one because they are unable to conceive of freedom in any other terms. For me, their point of view has very grave limitations.

To the extent that we are part of our revolutionary process, to the extent that we believe in it and (to ground the discussion in our specific situation here in Cuba) to the extent that we realize that for the first time we are in control of what we're doing, of our own actions, we are exercising a much greater freedom than that which can be exercised in any country where conflict between different classes continues to exist. For a social system based on unequal exercise of power and influence *always* works in favor of the most powerful, who sometimes grant some scraps of apparent freedom to those whose lives they dominate. However these always turn out to be more illusory than real.

In contrast, the freedom that we feel here—I'm sorry if this sounds a little abstract, but it's hard to express—derives from that fact that we are very aware of working together toward a common goal. We feel united around an idea and involved in implementing it together.

I'm not sure whether I've succeeded in conveying to you the full measure of our feelings and point of view. This freedom which we feel in working together is a completely different experience from the purely individual creative freedom so precious to people in capitalist society.

We too have to undergo certain contradictions. We discover things which we feel we have to fight against. But it is on another level. For example, the struggle against bureaucratization is one which we know we will win. It is not that despairing fight that reduces you to a state of frustration. On the contrary, we here have to be optimists. Not because anyone requires us to be, but because our real-life situation imposes that optimism on us in indicating to us that we are on the right track.

A state-owned, centralized production system like the one that we have is very different from what an 'independent' private company, for instance, might be. I put 'independent' in quotation marks because under such a system one is always dependent to some extent on those in power. When you attempt to free yourself from that dependence, you are reduced either to impotence or to total incommunication. So you see that there is really no means of comparison.

Q: *I remember in 1973 when there was all the commotion about the U.S. State Department's refusal to allow you to attend the National Society of Film Critics' awards ceremonies where you were to receive a special award for MEMORIES OF UNDERDEVELOPMENT. I think it was in the speech that Andrew Sarris gave as president of the organization where he lamented that you had not been allowed to make another film here in Cuba subsequent to MEMORIES. Even though the assertion was false—you had already made A CUBAN STRUGGLE AGAINST THE DEMONS—it is typical of strong desire abroad to view you as a prisoner of the Cuban regime. Their idea is that you are a great director who should be putting out a film a year. If you are not, it must be because you are not allowed to.*

A: That was in fact the most unfortunate statement to be found in all the articles which I read, because it is evident that the man had a personal stake in giving his own interpretation, despite the fact that it had no connection with the actual situation. His lack of information was such that one suspects a kind of tendentious ignorance, if such a thing is possible. It's hard to know in such cases where ignorance leaves off and stupidity or malice begins.

The fact is that I have been dedicating a lot of my time to the kind of work which I was describing to you before—the process of acting as advisor for other *companeros*—which I view as being just as important as my own personal achievement as a director. For someone like Andrew Sarris it must be extremely difficult to understand, but I have to say that for me what I might achieve as an individual director is no more important than what the whole group of us here at ICAIC achieves together. I have no desire to stand out more than the others simply in order to fulfill my own creative needs at the expense of my fellow filmmakers. Individual fulfillment is not everything. In a situation like ours, the collective achievement is just as important as the personal one. This assertion does not grow out of any attempt to appear more generous, less egotistical, but rather from my firm belief in what we as a group are doing.

In order to be completely realistic, in order to avoid appearing saintly, like some extraterrestial being removed from all personal interest, I would like to state that in order for me to fulfill my individual creative needs as a director, I need for there to be a Cuban cinema. In order to find my own personal fulfillment, I need the existence of the entire Cuban film movement as well. Otherwise, it's impossible. Without such a movement, my work might appear as a kind of 'accident' within a given artistic tendency. Under such circumstances, one might enjoy some degree of importance, but without ever achieving the level of self-realization to which you really aspire. This is not measured by the level of recognition you might achieve, but rather by the knowledge that you are giving all you can and that the environment you work in guarantees you that possibility.

Memories of *Memories*

T. G. Alea

More than ten years have now passed since *Memories of Underdevelop-ment* was premiered at the Fourth Pesaro Film Festival (Italy, 1968), late the first night with a feature-length documentary about Vietnam by Joris Ivens, after a long agitated day of discussions, protests, explanations, confusion. The echoes of France's May events resonated throughout Europe, and in some places, like Italy, they were felt with renewed fury. Many intellectuals solemnly proclaimed their decision to commit suicide as a class. Few of them actually did so, but at that moment anyone could believe them because everything that was happening was unfamiliar and beautiful. Too beautiful.

The blows to the superstructure were spectacular and revelatory, and it was the turn of the film festivals. Cannes had already suffered an onslaught. Venice was also shaken by the shock wave. What would happen at Pesaro? It was clearly not a bourgeois festival. There were no stars showing themselves off, no starlets doing their number to attract the attention of the producers, no gala reception or cocktails. We were marginal to the world of prizes, the greed of the dealers, advertising, 'show business.' On the contrary, Pesaro was where the most rest-less filmmakers gathered, the 'independents' who were trying to pull cinema out of the crisis of superficiality, conformism, and commercialism; here they could make their work known, establish contacts—almost always fruitful—and par-ticipate in a real exchange of ideas. I remember the first round tables where Christian Metz, Pier Paolo Pasolini, Roland Barthes, and others argued mainly about film and linguistics, and then increasingly—bit by bit—about film and politics. There was Cinema Novo from Brazil, the New American Cinema, the underground, parallel cinema, militant cinema, revolutionary cinema. That was where we first got to know the work that bespoke the spirit of renewal abroad in the cinema of different countries. Latin American cinema also found its place at Pesaro. In short, it was a festival of the left.

Nevertheless, that year Pesaro too came under question. There was a contest between different groups to see who was furthest to the left. Everyone talked of 'manipulation,' of being 'used' by others. You had the menacing impression that the establishment was a powerful monster, all-devouring and able to assimilate any kind of rebel manifestation. At the same time, groups of fascist provocateurs appeared on the scene, ready to fish in troubled waters. And finally the 'forces of law and order' violently attacked the festival participants who had gathered *en*

Originally published in *Casa de las Americas* [Havana], No. 122 (Sept.–Oct. 1980). Included in *The Viewer's Dialectic,* translated by Julia Lesage (Havana: José Martí Publishing House, 1988). Trans-lated by Michael Chanan.

masse in the square. Tear gas, truncheons, broken heads, a headlong rush through the labyrinth of alleys, arrests. The monster was unable to swallow it all placidly. Some things just got in its way and it had to try and chew them up first. The action of the police defined the camps and promoted the temporary unity of the different progressive tendencies within a festival that would not be assimilated.

I recall all this now because more than ten years have passed—enough time for a film to age, exhaust its potential distribution, and be forgotten. Yet *Memories*, like *Lucia* by Humberto Solas (also 1968), continues to have an effect on viewers every time it's shown, and is far from being forgotten.[1] Moreover, and above all, it has for me a special meaning, for it seems to show in the most diaphanous and exemplary way the workings of those forces which are unleashed in the spectator-spectacle relationship and which stimulate the audience, as Antonio Gramsci would say, "to participate in self-criticism." On the other hand, the unexpected reception which the film has had in the United States disposes of all my former doubts about how an essentially hypocritical system can manipulate a work.[2] This encourages me to reflect on the film and suggest certain perspectives.

Manipulation has become a kind of evil spirit which may manifest itself when and where it is least expected. The constant threat that weighs on those who wish to express themselves in whatever medium and whose activity may produce certain repercussions, is translated into a healthy concern not to lose sight of the ground we tread, the values we are defending, the enemy we are fighting against. This implies that we should be very naïve if we didn't know that there are actions that, in spite of being carried out in good faith, allow the enemy's momentary appropriation of some of our weapons.

Naïve or astute, filmmakers will always be subject, to a greater or lesser degree, to having their work manipulated on behalf of interests different from those which gave rise to it; 'to a greater or lesser degree' because *some works are more manipulable than others*. It is also important to point out that those which seem to adhere most to orthodox canons, politically and ideologically, do not always turn out to be least susceptible to manipulation.

---

1. In a survey by James Monaco in the Canadian magazine *Take One*, asking a group of leading film critics across the world to select the 'best films of the decade' (1969–78), *Memories of Underdevelopment* received the highest vote among so-called Third World films ("What's the Score? The Best of the Decade," *Take One*, 6, no. 8 [July 1978]). More recently, it also figured among the ten most important Latin American films in a survey conducted at the Huelva Film Festival of 1981, and among the 150 most significant films of all time in a survey among film clubs in more than one hundred countries published by FICC (Fédération Internationale des Ciné-Clubs) in 1985.

2. The film was widely exhibited in the United States in 1973 in the so-called art circuit and various universities and institutions. It was then selected by the *New York Times* as one of the ten best films of the year, receiving a prize from the National Society of Film Critics, and another from the Young Critics Association of New York.

Memories of Underdevelopment was no exception. The year after its premiere, an article appeared in a British film magazine where one could read as follows: "Alea's implied criticism is presumably also directed against the new society, which with its inflexibility and failure to assimilate the deviant thinker is certainly no panacea for the intellectual and his existential problems."[3] Evidently the critic unabashedly identified with the character of Sergio, and along with Sergio he shared the destiny awaiting the bourgeoisie with the arrival of the Revolution. As the critic writes, "with the missile crisis of October 1962, external, political pressures finally impinge on Sergio's situation; tanks and armored convoys urgently threaten his non-alignment and reveal the impossibility of the individual solution in a Communist society."[4]

Some time later, in 1973, the film received the U.S. National Film Critics award, but the U.S. government refused to grant me a visa to attend the awards ceremony in New York. At the ceremony, after reading my telegram,[5] the president of the critics' association went on to say:

Ironically, our award was dictated more by artistic than by political considerations. Unfortunately, the politics has been thrust upon us, not only by the woefully shortsighted decision of the State Department, but also by some of the questionable political rhetoric of the film's American distributor, Tricontinental Films. I cite in particular the following sentence in a recent press release: "Mr. Gutiérrez Alea and his work are products of socialist Cuba." I would submit that *Memories of Underdevelopment* has no more been honored by us as a product of socialist Cuba than *Day for Night* has been honored as a product of capitalist France or *American Graffiti* and *Payday* as products of capitalist America. We vote for the works of individuals, and not of systems. Indeed, what has struck most of us favorably about *Memories of Underdevelopment* is its very personal and very courageous confrontation of the artist's doubts and ambivalences regarding the Cuban Revolution. Some of us had even expressed the hope that our award might assist Mr. Gutiérrez Alea's career since, to the best of our knowledge, he does not seem to have made a film in five years, *Memories of Underdevelopment* having been originally released in 1968.

If Mr. Gutiérrez Alea had been here today, he might have shed some light on conditions in Cuba for a creative artist of his caliber. He might have disabused us of any misplaced concern for his future as a filmmaker. Indeed, he could have provided a high level of educational experience for film students in the New York area. In his absence, he joins such previous victims of bureaucratic bigotries and blacklists as Charles Chaplin and Luis Buñuel,

---

3. Don Allen, "Memories of Underdevelopment," *Sight & Sound* (Autumn 1969), p. 213.
4. Ibid.
5. For the text of this telegram see *Cine Cubano* [Havana], no. 89–90; see also David Binder in the *New York Times,* 17 January 1974, and New York Times editorial, 19 January 1974.

John Garfield and Arletty, Pablo Neruda, Ezra Pound, and many, many other creative people of various political persuasions.[6]

This critic, Andrew Sarris, clearly reveals his own real weakness for every kind of ambivalence. After assuring us that the prize "was dictated more by artistic than political considerations," a little later he states that "what has struck most of us most favorably about *Memories of Underdevelopment* is its very personal and very courageous confrontation of the artist's doubts and ambivalences regarding the Cuban Revolution." What can those doubts and ambivalences correspond to if not political considerations? This seems quite clear, above all because Mr. Sarris immediately goes on to support this notion by referring to the assistance that the prize might give to the development of my career, which, as he puts it, seemed to have been truncated after *Memories of Underdevelopment*, presumably because of political problems. Aside from the fact that Mr. Sarris was misinformed (by 1973 I had already made another movie[7]), the critic's 'ambivalence' ends up with his throwing fascists and communists together in the same bag as "victims of bureaucratic bigotries and blacklists."

From such a position it is very easy to identify with a character like Sergio, to see in *Memories* a "very courageous confrontation of the artist's doubts" etc., and thus raise the flag of 'ambivalence.' All this is consistent with a whole way of thinking prevalent in the United States and a way of defending self-interests that of course are hardly those of the Revolution. The result, then, is the well-known phenomenon of 'manipulation.'

It is in the cinema that this mechanism is most objectively located, because filmmakers work with images—and sounds—which constitute material capable of providing an *illusion of reality* to a greater degree than the material of other art forms. Fragments of reality are isolated, separated from their original context, and arranged in such a way that they produce a particular significance which is sometimes quite different from their significance in other contexts. We can therefore say that cinema itself is a clear manifestation of what we could call the 'art of manipulation,' since films are the result of the filmmakers' 'manipulation' of the elements—the material—offered by reality in its broadest sense. It follows that every film can become in turn the object of manipulation, even when its formal integrity is respected—that is, when no cuts or changes are introduced in the editing (montage). Just taking a film out of its original context allows us to see other elements in it, so that it becomes charged with new meanings.

But whether it occurs in cinema with the elements of reality, or in reality with cinematic works, the success of that manipulation, its range and efficacy, depends on many complex factors and not just on the possibilities provided by the material used or the skill with which the operation is carried out. And in the last

6. Andrew Sarris, "A Tale of Two Circles (Films in Focus)," *Village Voice*, 14 February 1974.
7. In 1970 I made *A Cuban Struggle against the Demons*, which as far as public acceptance and international impact are concerned was not as successful as *Memories*.

instance, it is important to know whether the intention is to reveal, hide, or distort the profound meaning of the reality being dealt with—that is, whether manipulation is carried out on behalf of truth or of deceit.

We therefore have to keep in mind the changing significance of the cinematic spectacle, depending on the concrete circumstances in which the relationship with the public is established. Different groups of spectators may understand the content in diverse ways, according to the ideology prevalent in each group. Thus, a propaganda documentary produced in South Africa with the goal of attracting cheap labor from neighboring countries for the sugar harvest, might well be effective among certain groups dominated by the ideology emanating from such a relatively powerful country; it might even elicit some degree of admiration. Nevertheless, the consciousness of a viewer who has fundamentally broken with this ideology—an example of bourgeois ideology in one of its most brutal and retrograde manifestations—will see in the same documentary a reason to reject not only the specific intention of the film but also the world it pictures as a whole. Thus, without intending to, the film actually serves a progressive function since it becomes a testimony of denunciation against a pathetic and unjust reality.

In terms of *Memories,* the general tone of the reviews published in the United States was on the whole very positive and sometimes surprisingly perceptive.[8] Still, aside from a few attempts at conscious manipulation like the one already mentioned, there were also cases of what could be called 'unconscious manipulation,' emanating in good faith from among the more or less progressive strata in the North American intellectual world, with its abundance of 'left-liberal' positions, as Julianne Burton observed in a perceptive essay on the film and its U.S. reception.[9] We already know that in the deepest sense this term is highly ambiguous and contradictory. You cannot be a true leftist and at the same time a liberal. But there are those who bear this label, and of course it's one of the most succulent mouthfuls that the Establishment feeds itself on. It is also a mouthful that is relatively easy to digest, because the left-liberal does not want to change the system but rather to make it function according to an ideal pattern. They struggle—when and if they do—for an idea, and sometimes sacrifice themselves for a cause which they have never fully understood. Such left liberals have at times expressed themselves enthusiastically about *Memories* and this could well cause us a certain unease, because we know their praise is not necessarily calculated in terms of hidden interests, but is rather based on healthy identification with what

8. See Daniel Diaz Torres, "Cine cubano en los Estados Unidos," *Cine Cubano* [Havana], (Jan. 1971–May 1974), No. 86–87.
9. Julianne Burton comments on this phenomenon: "In a film of such structural intricacy and thematic complexity, the viewer is compelled to exercise certain perceptual priorities. These are culturally conditioned and reinforced, and tend, I believe, to generate a selective and fragmented view of the film among American audiences when the film's most outstanding achievement is its synthesis—the integration of diverse components into a unified whole." "Memories of Underdevelopment in the Land of Overdevelopment," *Cinéaste* 8, no. 1 (Summer 1977). Reprinted also in this volume.

seems to them clear proof that within the framework of the Cuban Revolution there is room for criticism and dissent. But once we get this far, we must be cautious if we are not to make mistakes. Our task is to know how to distinguish one thing from another. We must also understand that the criticism present in a film like *Memories* has nothing to do with criticism as it is understood from liberal positions of whatever type or shade; primarily, because this film is an example of militant cinema produced in a country where the Revolution is in power. This perhaps calls for a small digression.

Among our peoples, rebellion seems to be ripening throughout the continent. Few countries maintain an appearance of stability. We have just experienced Nicaragua's epic, and everything seems to indicate it will not be the only one we shall live through in the next few years. Aside from the fact that conditions the world over daily call out, ever more urgently, for essential changes, heroism is also contagious.

In Cuba the Revolution is in power. This means that the conditions of struggle have changed.

What is the significance of film in the midst of all this? Where and when does cinema become truly important as a weapon in the service of the Revolution? When is it merely a cultural contribution whose revolutionary 'efficacy' is less evident, or only long term?

The particular circumstances in each country determine the possibility of a genuinely revolutionary militant cinema. Sometimes, after considering every possible theoretical analysis, the decisive factor—the public—is not sufficiently taken into account. Cinema's militant character is circumstantial and a function of the public it is made for in two respects. First is whether the film reaches the intended audience materially, physically; second, whether it reaches them intellectually and emotionally, that is, whether it is understood by the audience and capable of mobilizing them.

It is easy to see that conditions in Cuba favor the development of a militant cinema that goes beyond a mere contribution to artistic culture. But at the same time a militant cinema within the Revolution, primarily directed at those who share these historical circumstances, is no simple proposition. Especially if we are not satisfied with traditional formulae, which tend to simplify and schematicize reality for a supposed exaltation of revolutionary values; nor if we remain unsatisfied with useless rhetoric and believe that cinema provides an active and mobilizing element, which stimulates participation in the revolutionary process. Then it is not sufficient to have a moralizing cinema based on harangue and exhortation. We need a cinema that promotes and develops a critical attitude. But how to *criticize* and at the same time *strengthen* the reality in which we are immersed? At what or at whom is this criticism which *Memories* provokes essentially directed? Let us look at the various aspects of the mechanism which a film ought to generate in its relation to the public.

The image of reality provided by *Memories of Underdevelopment* is multifaceted—like an object contemplated from different viewpoints.

A popular dance serves as a background to the credits, something like a carnival dance, with fiery music and a certain appearance of chaos and frenzy. Suddenly gunshots are heard, almost drowned out by the music. We can just make out a man shoving his way through the dancers. The persistent rhythm of the music continues. No one stops dancing, even when they see the blood-stained body of a man lying in their midst. This is almost immediately lifted by policemen and carried away through the dancing crowd. Nothing has changed. The dance goes on, and in the middle a black woman's defiant face remains fixed with an expression of subterranean violence. All of this is presented to the spectator from the most 'objective' point of view, the most detached and least engaged, that of the wide shot.

Later, toward the end of the film, we return to the same dance and the same situation, but now we see it from another perspective, so that new meanings emerge and new concerns arise: the images are the same or very similar, but the sound has nothing to do with what we heard before, which actually (realistically, as it were) corresponded to that image. Now the sound is disconnected and vague, without a definite center of gravity; it is confused, and corresponds to a frame of mind obviously dissociated from what the overall image portrays in its shocking way.

But there is also a new element in the image itself: Sergio is now in the middle of the dancing crowd. He is there and yet he is not there. That is, he is present but incapable of becoming involved in the general flow of unconcern, relaxation, unburdening joy, and violence. As much as he tries, he cannot submerge himself in 'his' people's tide. This alternate soundtrack therefore expresses the subjective tension of the protagonist and at the same time maintains our distance from the dance; it keeps us, the spectators, from being passively pulled along by the current. It is no longer the same as at the beginning. Now we feel, along with Sergio, the *distance* that separates him from the environment in which he moves, and this induces us to revise our attitude. Seeing the same scene with Sergio as a point of reference, we realize that we cannot evaluate it in the same way when we consider it from his perspective as we did when we looked at it from our own point of view, as spectators without any previous information, at the beginning of the film. Perhaps the metaphor of a man dying as the victim of violence in the midst of a popular dance that never ceases while the incident occurs, and which reveals a substratum of violence, was not sufficiently meaningful for the spectator in the film's opening moments. Now, seeing it for a second time, from another perspective, and relating it to the central character about whom we already have sufficient information to predict his tragic destiny, the metaphor is expanded. It stretches beyond its initial direct and contingent significance; it opens up and leads to considerations about the reality within which the protagonist is trapped and which he is incapable of understanding in any depth.

Then come the initial scenes at the airport showing the exodus that took place in those first years after the triumph of the Revolution. During these scenes, in which no one speaks and all that is shown is the moment of departure, we are

Filming the departure scene at the airport

constantly observing Sergio, and cannot help but see his ill-concealed mixture of relief and discomfort. When Sergio returns to the city in the bus and thinks about his relatives who have left, above all his wife, the same scenes are repeated, but now from Sergio's point of view. Only then do we see his wife's and parents' faces; only then do we listen to Sergio's cold, almost cynical voice, which contrasts with the pathetic image of his relatives. The use of a telephoto lens for these images contributes to the isolation from the general ambience of the airport in the faces conjured up by Sergio and helps us understand these images as dreamed or remembered, rather than perceived directly. You could say that first we observe the scene of departure and its effect *upon* Sergio 'objectively,' and then we see it 'subjectively' *from* Sergio's point of view.

Also near the start of the film we listen to a tape recording of an argument between Sergio and his wife Laura. It is a silly, frivolous discussion, which begins as a small provocation on his part and proceeds to assume an ever more aggressive tone. The scene accompanying the tape recording shows Sergio alone in their bedroom, amidst the chaos of departure, playing with his wife's jewelry, prolonging the mockery, until little by little the game turns into a bitter corroboration of his cynicism and loneliness.

Much later, on the night Sergio takes leave of Elena after sleeping with her for the first time, the memory of the argument with Laura comes back to him. The earlier scene is repeated and continues past the point where Sergio previously turned off the tape recorder. Sound track and image now go together as Laura falls to the floor in the course of a violent struggle, and then gets up sobbing, insulting Sergio and affirming her decision to leave the country. Once again the film presents first an _evocation_ of the action relating to Sergio's frame of mind, and later presents it again, but this time as a _representation_ with the character of 'objective' information. (No matter that the second time too the point of departure is a certain state of mind on Sergio's part, nor that Laura's image is seen through Sergio's eyes: the action is still presented with a certain degree of objectivity.)

Further on, during one of Sergio's first excursions through the city, we see among other things the faces of the people in the street _as Sergio sees them_. They are sad, exhausted, tired, unhappy faces. Sergio asks himself, "What meaning does life have for them . . . ? And for me? What meaning does it have for me . . . ? But I'm not like them." Nevertheless, Sergio's face remains frozen on the screen, showing him to be equally unhappy. (Here again we have jumped from the 'subjective' to the 'objective.') Then, at the height of the October Crisis, when Sergio once more observes people on the street, we see the faces again, but this time they reveal a state of mind in open contrast with Sergio's, who walks the streets preoccupied and afraid of the atomic disaster which threatens everybody and which he seems to feel more than the rest. In both cases the images of faces are 'objective' in that these are real faces filmed at odd moments in the street. Nevertheless, in each case these faces' meaning is quite different. If at first we get a desolate impression, it is because obviously the protagonist, with whom at first we tend to identify, projects his own emotional state onto the reality that surrounds him and brings us to see it through his eyes. This is the reality that he sees, that he chooses, not what is strictly to be called _objective reality_. Neither do the faces at the end constitute objective reality in and of themselves, but they draw us much closer to it because they negate the previous impression without totally cancelling it out. The truth lies neither in the one nor the other, nor even in the sum of the two, but rather in what the confrontation between the two sequences and the main character suggests to the spectator in the overall context of the film.

Using this multilateral perception of the object as the film's structural principle is not exactly the 'ambivalence' referred to earlier, in the sense of ambiguity or indeterminacy. It is rather the expression of contradictions whose purpose in the film is none other than to contribute to the concerns and impulses for action that we wish to awaken in the spectator. It thus becomes an incentive to stand at a distance from the images, and in this way encourages a critical attitude, that is, a 'choosing of sides.'

Thus, on the one hand, we have a vision of reality conveyed to us by the protagonist through his personal reflections and critical judgment, and on the other, he himself becomes the object of our judgment. The situation is that of a character observing reality like a detached spectator, but with sufficient critical sense so as to provoke other judgments in the viewer. The telescope on his balcony is the most direct symbol possible of Sergio's attitude toward reality: he sees everything from above and at a distance; he is capable of judging reality—from the subjective point of view, of course—but he cannot actively participate in it. This character judges everything, including himself, but his judgment is not always lucid even though it is sometimes quite shrewd. And finally, we have the vision of the 'documentary' reality, which the film offers as counterpoint to the protagonist's vision.

The inclusion of documentary images which alternate with fully fictional images allows us to broaden considerably the scope of the relations that successively engage the protagonist. But the most important thing is that the relationship between the subjective world of the protagonist and the objective world he belongs to *passes through different levels of approximation to reality*. We are dealing with the same reality which the spectator has momentarily left behind, and this alternation facilitates the spectator's return to reality filled with new concerns and a greater degree of information and even comprehension.

The documentary images in the film help locate the conflict within its social and historical framework and reach the spectator via different routes: directly, when accompanied by some commentary or reflection by the protagonist; through television or the newspaper, in the form of news—which also sometimes comes from the radio—and finally, as the significant space in which the protagonist moves physically (walking in the street against the flow of people on their way to the May Day rally; at the swimming pool of the Hotel Riviera, etc.). All those moments were filmed without prior preparation, either with a hidden camera or at least with the minimum interference possible in the normal, spontaneous course of the activity thus encountered.

Although the more or less 'documentary' images most appropriately express the objective world in which the protagonist is located, some of these images correspond to the character's own subjective world and reflect his mood, thoughts, and consciousness (the faces he observes in the street, for example). This, of course, is the best proof of Sergio's false objectivity, which is not a matter of truly *objective* images. That is, we must not be misled by the documentary images in the film—obtained through the direct filming of reality (newsreel fragments, magazine photos, newspaper articles, people in the street filmed by a hidden camera . . .)—imagining them to constitute an objective reflection of the reality in which the fictional plot occurs. These images are selected and arranged by the filmmakers and for that reason are marked by their subjectivity. They are just as tendentious as the other images in the film which have been carefully worked out before shooting begins. Even those fragments which seem to be grafted on to the film because they come from somewhere else, because they belong to another dimension which seems to have nothing to do with the film's dramatic or narrative development, even in the case of these fragments, which somehow retain their autonomy (magazine photos, fragments of newsreel . . .), once they have been incorporated into the film they can no longer be understood in isolation, but rather in close relation to the rest of the piece, in the context in which they have been repositioned.

In this way, the confrontation between the individual and society, between individual consciousness and the historical circumstances which one way or another condition it, takes place by means of two interweaving lines of development, two focal points of critique, two perspectives, two angles of vision: one reflecting the subjective viewpoint of the protagonist, the other, the 'objective' viewpoint of the filmmakers as much toward the protagonist as toward the reality surrounding him, and surrounding us.

The stimuli for criticism are thus already present within the film. What interests me now is to discover where these stimuli lead, and by what means.

The primary goal of criticism *within* the revolution ought to be to arm the spectator to fight for the revolution itself, to strengthen the principles it is based on and to accelerate its development. Here it is interesting to see how the protagonist's attitude reaches the spectator through the mechanism of identification, while at the same time this identification with a character who is constantly critical (justly or unjustly, it doesn't matter which) prevents this mechanism becoming absolute, for it helps the viewers to keep their critical sense awake and to share (or of course reject) the filmmakers' own critique of both the protagonist and the reality which includes us all.

Thus, the de-alienating effect of *Memories* provokes the spectator's identification with the protagonist. But if the film is primarily directed toward viewers who live within a revolution that already eliminated the bourgeoisie some years ago, how is it that it aims at identification with a character who clearly incarnates the very values of that class? Sergio is a bourgeois who has nothing in common with the man in the street, the worker, the peasant, the revolutionary intellectual. Yet we discover that not only the revolutionary intellectual but also the ordinary employee find reason enough to identify with him. Only in the case of the peasant is the identification weaker, more on account of linguistic differences than relative ideological distance. We should recall that the bourgeoisie was the dominant class until the triumph of the Revolution, and its ideology was therefore the dominant one until a few years ago. It is understandable that the values which marked *all* layers of society for centuries do not disappear completely overnight. This, without doubt, is one of the principle problems confronting the Revolution, which the film takes as the basis of its argument. It is therefore possible for the spectator not only to understand the protagonist, but also to some extent to share his expectations; especially if certain other peculiarly cinematic resources are brought into play, namely, those of bourgeois cinema: the protagonist is not only lucid and intelligent but also cultured, elegant, handsome, with a certain sense of humour, and with time on his hands, for he has a good income with no need to work. Furthermore, he has a luxury apartment and sleeps with beautiful women. He thus represents in good measure what every man at some moment in his life has wanted to be or to have.

This is not all. Sergio says things and makes observations about the reality in which he moves which are sometimes disconcerting and contradictory but not always to be rejected. They can become a challenge or stimulus to thought. For he is evidently a cultured person and *in this sense* above average. He undoubtedly suffers from the mediocrity which surrounds him, and in his gut rejects those traits and features of ours which made it seem as if we were a branch office of Miami. This even leads him to comprehend the deeper significance of the relationship to our tropical isle of a complex figure like Hemingway. But to this mediocrity Sergio opposes what to him is the highest expression of culture: "I have always wanted to live like a European," he laments. His contrariness and the source of his dissension lie in knowing himself to be alienated by cultural patterns foreign to his own environment, and nevertheless unable to struggle to assert himself. He is already a defeated man who reveals the cultural colonization that has victimized us throughout our history, the consequence of which, within the revolution, is located in a general sense of our underdevelopment.

With all his profound contradictions, Sergio can lead us to a conscious grasp of what underdevelopment means in economic, cultural, and ideological terms. There comes a moment when the spectator, who initially follows the protagonist and shares some of his observations and judgments on our reality, begins to feel disturbed because the figure with whom they have identified begins to drown in a sea of contradictions, doubts, and paralyzing incomprehension. Sergio cannot reach an understanding of the values underpinning the world being born around him, and he goes under. In a profound sense, it is Sergio who appears to be underdeveloped in the face of the world surrounding him, that of the Revolution.

From everything we have said thus far, it emerges that it is precisely the spectator who is the target of the criticism unleashed by *Memories*—the spectator who lives *within* the Revolution, who is part of our revolutionary reality. It is to the spectator that the film should reveal the symptoms of possible contradictions and incongruities between good revolutionary intentions—in the abstract—and a spontaneous and unconscious adherence to certain—concrete—values belonging to bourgeois ideology. And the very goal of the film is to question the survival of the values of bourgeois ideology in the midst of the revolution. As the film proceeds, the spectators should become progressively more aware, through the destruction suffered by the protagonist, of their own situation, and the inconsistency of having momentarily identified with Sergio. Thus, when the film is over, the viewers do not come out satisfied. The passions have not been discharged, but quite the contrary: they have been filled with concerns which should first lead to action upon oneself and then upon the reality in which one lives. It is therefore a question of a revolutionary act: a conscious grasp of one's own contradictions, the impulse to achieve coherence and project oneself actively on reality.

Inevitably, then, the question arises: Why did *Memories* seem to some an easy target for attempts at manipulation? Why *Memories* more than other films? We believe that every work created within the Revolution, and above all in a difficult stage of the construction of socialism like the one we are living through now, if it casts a critical eye over reality, can be used in some way by the enemy. Above all if it is a work like this in which the problems posed are not resolved with the final image on the screen but tend rather to extend beyond the movie theater, a work open to a problematic whose final development and eventual conclusion are located in the consciousness of the viewer who has been invited to reflect on them by the film. However, as we have seen, it is these traits which characterize *Memories*—notably the intention of disturbing the viewer by posing problems and contradictions to be resolved in the manner indicated—it is these features which constitute the film's vulnerability; there its greatest force and revolutionary scope can be found.

I mentioned earlier that after more than ten years the film continues to have an effect on the viewer every time it's shown. I think it will have lost its primary significance, its operative effect, and grown old, when all those vestiges of bourgeois ideology in the spectator have disappeared. It will then remain simply a testimony to a certain moment in the struggle, a difficult but also lively and hopeful moment.

I hope that the film grows old as quickly as possible.

Reviews and
Commentaries

Reviews and Commentaries

Reviews of *Memories of Underdevelopment* in the U.S. press were generally highly favorable, despite the political differences between the two countries. Even reviewers who, like Stanley Kauffmann, saw Cuba as a repressive state, acknowledged the power and subtlety of the film. Its reputation in America was especially enhanced by the perceptive and admiring comments of Vincent Canby, the principal film reviewer of the influential *New York Times*.

Some reviewers, such as Don Allen, found the film subversive of Cuba's revolutionary purposes, a reading emphatically denied by the film's creators. European reviews were more likely to judge the film within the framework of a more fully developed political ideology, while the excerpt from Fernando Pérez's article offers an example of a Cuban response to the film. Julianne Burton's lengthier assessment discusses the cinematic sophistication of the film and attempts to place it within postrevolutionary Cuban culture. Enrique Fernández takes up a more specialized but important subject, the film's complex narrative point of view.

New York Times
Vincent Canby

"**M**emories of Underdevelopment" (Memorias del Subdesarrollo, based on the novel by Edmundo Desnoes, published here in 1967 as "Inconsolable Memories") is the journal of a youngish (late 30s) upper-class Cuban intellectual who, in 1961, refuses to flee to Miami with his wife, family, and friends whom he ridicules as parasites, but who can never bring himself to be more than a jaundiced observer of the social and political revolution taking place around him. Havana, the old Havana, is wearing down—running out of lubricating oil, European style, and spare parts for practically everything—while Sergio looks on from his terrace above the city. Just as Sergio studies the anonymous faces of the people on the sidewalks below through a telescope, he remains at a distance from himself, commenting on his own inability to become involved with as much cruel purpose as he comments on the progress of the revolution, which, to him, is sadly doomed.

The film jumps backward and forward in time as Sergio recalls past love affairs and his marriage, imagines a new affair with a pretty country girl whose Baptist faith strikes him as being enormously erotic, and carries on a hilariously unsatisfactory affair with a lovely looking, would-be actress who remains steadfastly underdeveloped (mentally) in spite of his efforts to Europeanize her. Nothing in the film is really simple, however. Sympathies and loyalties are always divided. There is a visit to the museum that once was Ernest Hemingway's home, where an old Hemingway retainer acts as guide and delivers a memorized spiel that would make a Circle Line tour host sound positively sincere. "Hemingway molded [his servants] to his needs," Sergio thinks. "He must have been a dreadful man." A minute later he dumps his underdeveloped mistress without a qualm, letting her get back to Havana as best she can.

At another point, Sergio attends a roundtable discussion by Marxist writers (including author Desnoes), who push their ideas back and forth with all of the grace of midgets playing catch with blocks of cement. "Words devour words," says Sergio on the soundtrack, "and leave you in the clouds." It's left to Jack Gelber, the American playwright who wrote the introduction for Desnoes's "Inconsolable Memories," to stand up and suggest that the authors, representatives of one of the world's greatest revolutions, may also be the world's greatest asses.

It is obvious that Alea, who made the film in 1968 when he was 40, is European in his own sophistication. After receiving his law degree in Havana, he studied film direction at the Centro Sperimentale di Cinematografia in Rome. At times, "Memories of Underdevelopment" seems almost to be a companion piece

From the *New York Times,* 2 April 1972, Sec. 2, p. 5.

to Bertolucci's "Before the Revolution," with Bertolucci's incurably romantic Fabrizio grown, after the revolution, into the intellectual outsider, Sergio, played by Sergio Corrieri with the haunted, amused diffidence of the early Marcello Mastroianni. It is through this European sophistication that we see refracted, slightly bent, a uniquely Latin American revolution in the equivocal terms that are perhaps most comprehensible in this land of overdevelopment.

Within the film, Sergio is described—I think not entirely facetiously—as neither a revolutionary nor a counter-revolutionary, but as simply an observer. In a tightly controlled Marxist society (which has no room for observers), he would automatically be classified counter-revolutionary.

In an excellent, seemingly balanced piece on the Cuban cinema in the current (Spring) issue of "Film Comment," Pierre Sauvage reports that Alea's last film, "A Cuban Struggle against the Demons," has less in common with European films than with the rougher, wilder, completely committed revolutionary films of Brazil's Glauber Rocha. However, even if "Memories of Underdevelopment" is a momento of Cuban cinema during what Sauvage calls the vintage years from 1963 to 1967—"when bureaucratic supervision was limited"—it remains a lovely achievement, one of the finest Latin American films to be seen in New York (no matter how briefly) in the last 12 years. Debates about the motives that prompted its production, and about the motives that are now prompting efforts to show it here (after it's already been shown in London and Paris), must be beside the point.

The New Republic
Stanley Kauffmann

This is an extraordinarily sensitive piece of work—exactly the opposite of the gung-ho stuff one might expect from a newly organized government. Like the Hungarian film, *Love*, it's one of those complex, self-questioning films that occasionally come from police states in their periods of planned relaxation. . . .

Gutiérrez Alea has made the film with a tactful, confident skill that proves itself through reticence. The only effect that stands out in memory is the use of the hand-held camera in the opening airport scenes, to give the feeling of actuality—how nicely it slides into conventional camera use as Sergio goes home. There are a few other "real" touches, notably a symposium of Cuban writers that Sergio attends, including the author of the original novel, Desnoes, and the caustic comments of a visiting American, Jack Gelber.

But the picture rests on the vision and exploration of Sergio's character and the casting of Sergio Corrieri in the role. Corrieri's face and manner fix the delicacy, the intelligence, the faded strength, the stubborn curiosity that is needed. To put the matter in shorthand, what the film gives us is an Antonioni character in the middle of a political revolution, a man who comes out of 100 years of cultivation-as-refuge, now facing profound changes that may alter the reason for the refuge and the refuge itself. He is an anachronism who lives in quasi-fear that he may turn out *not* to be an anachronism, who has only a shaky faith in the revolution that may make him obsolescent.

Memories is memorable, primarily for the truth of Sergio's character and the tensions of his situation; but it's also noteworthy for an extrinsic fact—that Cuba made this non-caricature film about a non-revolutionary's questions. There is no alternative to this change, says the film, but will this finally change the alternatives? Out of a revolution bred on slogans comes a film without answers; thus lending some credibility to the revolution.

From *The New Republic*, 19 May 1973, p. 22.

The New Yorker

Penelope Gilliatt

C uba, 1961. The small island that every big power would like to take over. The past Havana, now running out of both the old European grace and the less old American spare parts for refrigerators, cars, radios. The new Havana, looking a little like the razed and rebuilt Warsaw, full of cheer, short of food, replete with fun and progressives. The airport: reactionaries saying good-bye to their relatives and leaving for Miami; babies crying; a man who looks rather like Paul Scofield, and whom we recognize to be the hero of the film that is starting. Not meaning to be callous, probably, he wipes the mark of his departing wife's lipstick off his face after she has kissed him goodbye. The piteousness, the concealed loneliness, the irrevocability of farewells at airports, cloaked in the stabbingly practical hospital bustle of these places. The sequence makes you wonder how people ever leave the loved.

The hero, called Sergio, is marvelously played by Sergio Corrieri. The film is the Castro Cuban "Memories of Underdevelopment," from a novel by Edmundo Desnoes called "Inconsolable Memories." It is one of the very finest, subtlest of Latin American pictures. Sergio's memories are indeed inconsolable. They have a bitter, passing sting that seems more European than anything to do with Fidel. Things inflict pain that is nearly unbearable, and then the pain almost goes. On the bus back to his apartment, where he makes a living as a landlord, the hero obviously remembers the parting with an intensity that he can barely manage, but then it makes him yawn. Everything happens to him at a distance. He has a telescope on his terrace. He almost seems to be looking at himself through a telescope, too. He is also a writer, and his prevailing sense of stasis will probably prevent him from ever being a good one. Camus's Stranger was *engagé* by comparison. In a revolutionary society, Sergio has only one role to play psychically. It is the role of witness. The pinched nature of the part he has allotted himself shows in his work (we see a fragment of it, eloquent but tinctured with complaint, rolled into his typewriter), and in his way of saying goodbye to intimates, and in his refusal of spontaneity, and in his comically self-absorbed love affairs. When he is coming away from the airport, his voice, over an image of him sitting in the bus on his way back into Havana, says chillingly about his wife, whom he has seen off to America, "She'll have to go to work there until she finds some dumb guy who'll marry her." He is glad to be on his own and away from all the people who "loved and nagged me to the last moment," as he taps on his type-

From *The New Yorker*, 26 May 1973, pp. 122–123.

writer; sometimes his writing voice has the note of Dostoevski or Goncharov being farcical.

He peers through his telescope at Havana. Everything seems the same to him, except that it has the look of a set. So what about the revolution, you can catch him thinking. No imperial eagle? "Where is the dove that Picasso was going to send?" He plays with his own birds, in a cage on the terrace. He has a moment of admitting that the country is falling behind. Havana is no longer the Paris of the Caribbean. To his mind, Cuba is an island collapsing into desuetude and neglect, caught between Russia and America, ruled by hunger, inhabited by people who seem to him to be getting more stupid. His conservative friends' crassness irritates him, until one of them suddenly says something discerning. The conservatism depicted is Freudian. It is an ethic of everyone returning to his own individuality when he wants to get away from the infection of communal misery.

Three times a week, a Baptist maid comes in to clean up the spotless bachelor apartment. Her being a Baptist strikes him as buoyantly sensual. But his self-consciousness always stops him short of real eroticism. People on a diving board make him think of defenseless and almost hairless animals absurdly managing on two legs. He has sex in the head (as the gamekeeper in "Lady Chatterley's Lover" had, for all Lawrence's railing against such a thing). What exerts power over him? Nothing public or revolutionary, certainly. Personal change? He likes an actress for enjoying being able to be someone different, though repeating the difference every evening baffles him: he feels surrounded by lives that are scratched records. Even books look dead. Why didn't he go to New York with Hannah, his German ex-girlfriend, he asks himself. She was the best thing that ever happened to him. He wished to be a writer. She believed in him. They wanted to go to New York. What was missing in him, this wonderful, tangled, risky film asks. It doesn't suggest that it might be the impulse of history. Sergio has chosen to stay, to try to merge into Castro's Cuba, and he even amusedly tries to educate a culturally "underdeveloped" girlfriend called Elena by taking her to museums and writers' conferences, but salon Socialists strike him as irredeemable asses. He agrees with New York's own left-wing writer Jack Gelber, who funnily and seriously says as much at an actual conference in Cuba.

The director, Tomás Gutiérrez Alea, was born in Havana in 1928. He studied film in Rome, and then got involved in revolutionary filmmaking in Batista's time before helping to found the famous Instituto Cubano del Arte e Industria Cinematograficos (ICAIC). This is a beautifully organized picture in its technique, with the most skillful possible use of voice-over, of newsreel footage of the Bay of Pigs, and of leaps backward and forward in time. The note is sardonic and also immensely affectionate toward effort. It is a startling combination in a film made in a revolutionary country, even such a surprising one as Cuba. The film has the lightness of a bird coasting, and a humorous gravity that makes it a piece of work without burden, extending much charity to the stoic hero's hidden distress.

Sight and Sound

Don Allen

It seems as improbable that Tomás Gutiérrez Alea's *Memories of Under-development* should have been approved for export by the Cuban authorities as that Buñuel should have made *Viridiana* under Franco's nose. Both films in their different ways undermine, or significantly question, the cultural values of the country which sanctioned them.

A man, Sergio, and his country, Cuba, are at crisis-point. The search for new values, the re-orientation and positive reconstruction of Cuban society in 1962, have repercussions on the metaphysical quest of the individual. He cannot operate indefinitely in his apolitical vacuum yet he cannot embrace the naïve, simplistic fervour of the Revolution. By a historical accident he is a peripheral adjunct of the great Communist society: he has rejected his bourgeois formation yet his lucidity, scepticism and quirky humour lead him to reject also the over-facile, ready-made alternative—unquestioning acceptance of the Castro Revolution. Neither of these stereotypes provides him with an adequate solution.

According to Edmundo Desnoes, on whose book the film is based and who collaborated with Alea on the script, Sergio's 'irony, his intelligence, are a defensive mechanism which prevents him from being involved in reality. . . . He does not assume his historical involvement,' i.e. in the creation of the post-revolutionary society. Yet Alea's direction evokes sympathy not condemnation for Sergio's plight—superseded but miraculously not annihilated by the new order. (He even expects to continue living on his rents for a further dozen years or so.) Alea's implied criticism is presumably also directed against the new society, which with its inflexibility and failure to assimilate the deviant thinker is certainly no panacea for the intellectual and his existential problems.

When Sergio bids an unemotional farewell to his wife and friends at Havana airport in 1961, his feeling of relief in the face of this exodus of 'decadent, bourgeois imperialists' matches the mood of the nation. But this resemblance is only superficial. Sergio's motives are revealed immediately afterwards back in his apartment. As the camera pans round the room his voice on the soundtrack tells us that for years he has wanted to write a diary. His inner silence and solitude as he drinks his coffee and butters his bread in the kitchen are moments charged with incipient awareness of the isolation of his condition, breaking in upon him almost with the force of a rebirth. He muses ironically about change: both himself and Havana seem the same; it is not yet the millennium. The 'Cuba libre e independiente' statue down by the harbour no longer has the imperial

From *Sight and Sound* 38, no. 4 (Autumn 1969):212–213.

eagle but 'where is the dove that Picasso was going to send?' He plays a tape of a conversation with his wife, Laura. She finds him disgusting so he sneeringly remarks that it is because he has run out of Yardley's hair cream and Colgate toothpaste. Touches of voyeurism and fetishism are revealed plus a capacity for self-mockery, whimsy and sensuality. The opening section is completed by a series of close-ups of sad faces (joyless, post-revolutionary Cuba!) and then a freezing shot of Sergio which emphasises his isolation, poised Janus-like between the old and the new culture, accepting neither and wondering: 'What is the meaning of life for them and me—but I am not like them.'

By way of brilliant contrast the next section reveals that neither is he like Pablo, who epitomises the right-wing standpoint and whose dismissal of the new Cuba as inefficient seems vindicated when the garage mechanic, who has been asked to check the oil, says they haven't got any but he can always check it anyway. In the presence of Pablo guilt flits uneasily across Sergio's mind, like a series of Oxfam poster images, as he recalls that four children die of malnutrition every minute in Latin America.

A brief episode with Noemí, the girl who does Sergio's cleaning, enables him to indulge in erotic fantasies. Elena, the next girl he picks up and then tires of, can be seen as a microcosm of the new Cuba. Her ambition to be an actress is mocked, and actors are compared to scratched records as with superb comic verve short film clips are repeated in rapidly alternating forward and reverse motion. Sergio's contention that people always need someone to think for them is given point by a close-up of a poster of Castro and the Playa Girón. A shot of Pablo at the airport on crutches and behind glass emphasises Sergio's isolation and also reinforces his desire for lucidity—'a disagreeable emptiness'.

Sergio is as alienated by Hemingway's escapism as by the writers' conference on 'Literature and Underdevelopment'. His memories come between him and action in the present. Tangled tree-roots, successive dissolves and slow pans of trees and foliage illustrate his half-remembered, peaceful idyll with Hanna, his first love, and the complex motivation whereby he let her go. Ominous hints of encroaching bureaucracy as his property is ponderously checked are followed in rapid succession by Sergio's despairing reflection—'My life is like a sterile ornamental plant.' Then the farcical court case, in which Sergio's victory is marred by his world-weary comment that he is too educated to be innocent and his accusers are too ignorant to be guilty. With the missile crisis of October 1962, external, political pressures finally impinge on Sergio's situation: tanks and armored convoys urgently threaten his non-alignment and reveal the impossibility of the individual solution in a Communist society.

Cinema 74

Mireille Ameil

The Cuban Revolution was supported by many members of the intelligentsia; that is to say, that part of the bourgeoisie was not radically detached from it. Moreover, there is Fidel Castro's well-known affirmation that "the Revolution must act in such a way that the artists and intellectuals who are not truly revolutionary can function inside the Revolution and be able to express themselves."

In Cuba, there is no split between the revolutionary literature and the literature of the sixties. In cinema there is no effort to push documentaries, apologias, and systematic propaganda, at least for the moment.

Tomás Gutiérrez Alea's film *Memories of Underdevelopment* must be seen in this light. Adapted from a novel by Edmundo Desnoes, the film immediately accepts fiction, contemporaneity, and the classical structure of the Occidental film. That makes it all the more persuasive, sincere and dialectical. . . .

A representation of the bourgeoisie that is both contemporary and dialectical is a fairly rare event (all the more in revolutionary cinema). Ordinarily, "political" cinema celebrates a historical event, traces a society's evolution, extols the virtues of the proletariat. When the bourgeoisie is portrayed, it is often a caricature, at times nostalgic. . . .

The strength of Tomás Gutiérrez Alea's film resides in his art of painting a class through an individual, so dialectically that the criticism of that class is included in the painting.

There is hardly a more truthful model of the bourgeoisie in world cinema. His closest brothers are the characters of Helvio Soto's *The Metamorphosis of a Political Police Chief* (it is even more painful to see the failure of Sergio's lucidity in a revolutionary process he participates in himself) and above all Dalio in *The Rules of the Game,* a sad spectator of his own inability to adapt.

The antidote is in Buñuel. There is no third way. On the one hand lucidity, and the certainty of belonging to a class no longer valued; on the other hand, the politics of the ostrich, the slow and easy death of happy imbeciles.

If this film by Tomás Gutiérrez Alea touches us so profoundly under its tranquil surface (which allows for humor, brilliance, and anecdote), it is because it is an unequivocal condemnation of all temptations to compromise and to adopt a policy of reform; it rigorously censures not only the Batista period, but through it a particular social class, the bourgeois intelligentsia, for its corrupt involvement with a morality and culture based on class.

From *Cinema 74* (Paris) (October 1974).

Undoubtedly Tomás Gutiérrez Alea has given us a most serious warning in building his film dialectically: it is a true portrayal of a revolution in progress, the mistakes and defects of which he takes the opportunity to denounce (the visit to the apartment and especially the trial are examples) and which he counterpoints with Sergio's subjective vision.

In the end, everything is played out between Castro's claim that everyone has a place inside the Revolution, the character of Sergio, incapable of taking this place, and Tomás Gutiérrez Alea, assuming the role the Revolution has assigned him, although he himself is a bourgeois and an intellectual. We are truly involved.

Cinema & Film

Piero Spila

Memories of Underdevelopment, a Cuban film directed by Tomás Gutiérrez Alea, comes at the perfect time for the birth of a genuinely free
cinema, one whose freedom emerges from the very center of its creation,
from the need to express oneself and not the need simply to express. Having
evolved beyond the moment of self-questioning, the need to know and to repre-
sent reality, the didactic necessities and responsibilities of the medium, the creative dialectic between the objective and the subjective—having evolved beyond
all these Alea can finally afford to take the risks of cinema as cinema, cinema as
artistic and personal transference: to engage in a cinematographic conversation
on the subject of the Revolution without the "expressive" imperative of the Revolution itself. The transference from inside the Revolution to outside has the
purpose of observing it not subjectively or didactically, but with an absolute faith
in the objectivity of things rather than in their interpretation.

Memories of Underdevelopment is above all an honest film, the most cou-
rageously honest film of the Pesaro '68 Festival. Alea's honesty lies not only in
his refusal to make a partisan film, but also in his refusal to make an objective
film. This is a contradiction in appearance only: given the way things are in
Cuba, given what the facts demonstrate, it is objectivity itself that would reveal
the intention to make a partisan film.

Alea chooses a dialectical approach at various stylistic and ideological levels:
the subjective and the documentary, memory and reflection, ambiguity and understanding, regret and accusation, past and present, and above all, the point of
view from which the Revolution is examined. . . .

Memories of Underdevelopment marks a moment in cinema in which the pleasure of cinematic risk and freedom is rediscovered—cinema both as an instrument of experience and as an instrument of research, discovery, and adventure.

Alea's purposes might well have remained simply purposes; the results of his
undertaking might have remained ambiguous; Sergio's path to awareness might
have come to an equivocal end; the truth of the Revolution might have failed to
surface from the memory of a past both longed for and denied, from a few
subjective observations on the Third World.

In passing through these dangers, in overcoming them, Alea triumphs with his
cinema, triumphs with means that are exclusively cinematic.

From *Cinema & Film* (Rome), no. 5–6 (Summer 1968):52.

A Dialectical and Partisan Film

Fernando Pérez

The conga drums of Pello burst deafeningly onto the screen and a crowd abandoned to rhythm and music shakes. . . . The dance leaves no room for reflection: only movement, voluptuousness, body language. In an instant, between the drums and the noise, two shots are heard, as if they were another percussion instrument or a new variation of the rhythm. Above the corpse—an unknown, a body without music—the human river forms an almost electric wave and little by little takes on again the form of a surge that drags along in its thrust everything foreign to the immediate exaltation. The feet have not stopped moving, the surroundings have not had time to assimilate the bloody happening. When this moment ends, the camera captures in detail some images of a multitude that unconsciously dilutes itself in the frenetic cadence, surrendered in body and soul to the total dance. In the end, it fixes itself in front of the startled face of a young black woman, sweating, panting, . . . underdeveloped?

Beginning with its first images, *Memories of Underdevelopment* shows itself to be a film that demands active participation from the spectator. This participation imposes, above all, the necessity of a definition from the public: it is not only understanding of the message that inspires interest, but rather the perspective, the engagement that every viewer will feel once the projection is over. The means taken to achieve this end are not reduced to the simple narration of a story, but rather to presenting the elements necessary to render a definitive judgment about the point under analysis. In this sense *Memories* offers a solid structure in which two contrary planes are interwoven and put into play: reality seen through the subjective prism of an individual and reality as it is. This in itself would not have larger significance if it is not kept in mind that the point of departure of the film is the presentation of a problematic from its opposite angle—from the bourgeois point of view, not the revolutionary's. For this, the protagonist (Sergio, an intelligent man, ex-owner of a furniture store, with concerns that raise him above the intellectual poverty of the Cuban bourgeoisie) is the one who sustains, at first, the direct dialogue with the public. The reasons that justify this reversal are found in the double objective of the film: to present clearly the focus of an ideologically limited, determined individual and, at the same time, to offer the premises of its negation. The result is a dynamic relation which enriches the development of the argument and allows the most subtle contradictions of the protagonist to be profoundly analyzed. The chosen path in the production of the film, therefore, makes

From *Pensamiento Crítico* [Havana], no.42 (1970). Translated by Laura Kaplan.

evident the need for a nonstatic approach to the problems it poses (definition of a character through his points of view, contrasted with a second point of view, and commitment of the spectator with regard to what is seen). *Memories of Underdevelopment* unfolds with extraordinary fluidity among these three levels, allowing each one of the independent planes to establish a harmonious interrelation always in motion, always interacting. Stemming from this idea, the film has everything at its disposal to express content: its structure is solid and compact, but is always free, open, clear—like the novels of Pio Baroja: "a bag in which everything fits." The intention takes the form of a collage, but a collage skillfully organized from the cinematographic point of view. On the one hand is the nervous punctuation of Sergio's dialogue with the public; on the other, the vital reality that arrives by the most unexpected means (headlines, documentaries, simple historical fragments).

The freedom of this narrative line continues to follow—without seeming to— an absolutely necessary logic that incorporates into the structure of *Memories* its true meaning: Sergio's history and the revolutionary reality come together, through an internal dialectic, toward the final thesis of the film. The itinerary followed by the protagonist is defined with an objectivity that permits exegesis on the part of each viewer, but at the same time demonstrates the precise intention of the filmmaker. It is worth the trouble to examine this trajectory up close, which is definitely the best achievement of a film whose principal characteristic is that it causes one to reflect.

When Sergio says goodbye to his family as they depart for "el Norte," he understands that between them there is a barrier much more impenetrable than the fragile pane of glass at the airport made grimy by lips and palm prints. His decision to stay behind can be taken as a need to make a break with a way of life he questions, or as an individual's simple desire to observe what could happen. From the beginning, the cards are on the table: the character has arrived at a key moment in his life, in which his most permanent values have begun to topple, have reached a crisis. The first step of the trajectory is given: by staying, Sergio has chosen the path of confrontation with history. The situation enters a much more complex phase, because the protagonist is going to try to assimilate, from his limitations and his decrepit conceptions, a circumstance as essentially new and all-encompassing as the Revolution—and at this point the film gives a glimpse of a new circumstance that would not be risky to emphasize: Sergio is not simply a bourgeois ex-landlord, he is a typical bourgeois intellectual, which enriches the confrontation even more. The way the character approaches reality carries the stamp of his superficial, skin-deep focus. His intent to assimilate is produced at a distance, with a mixture of rejection and objectivity that is somewhat more than mere self-sufficiency: it is a product of his mentality, formed within the ideals of a class. In his exclusive role of observer, never of activist, Sergio continues receiving flashes of a changing reality that confronts him with his own emptiness and throws light upon his past. It is here, on its second level, that the film takes the opportunity to anatomize, in a dynamic analysis and an apt cinematographic montage, the definitive characteristics of the mercenary forces at Playa Girón. As in an unplanned anthology, the invading army passes before the eyes of the spectators—and of Sergio—offering a microcosm of the Republic: in it are "the priest, the businessman, the torturer, the philosopher, the politician, and the innumerable sons of good families." The images show them separated in times of peace, but united by the invisible threads that have woven them into one mercenary enterprise. It does not escape Sergio that "the truth of the group is in the murderer," nor that his own pursuits cannot be channeled into the ideals of an underdeveloped bourgeoisie; but he is incapable of understanding that the passive attitude of the spectator is incompatible with a historical moment that elicits urgent responses. (It is not superfluous to remember Fanon's phrase: "Every spectator is a coward or a traitor.")

The episodes fulfill their double expressive function (breaking the protagonist from his former life—symbolized by his friend Pablo—and development of the second comparative level), while the structure continues balancing its internal dialectic—something that is absent from the novel from which the film is adapted, although in this case it is better not to speak of adaptation, but rather of the magnificent Desnoes-Alea collaboration.

It is then that the character begins the second stage of his trajectory, marked by a critical attitude that will explain his nonparticipation in the revolutionary process. Sergio succeeds in rejecting the uselessness of a life shared until that moment with his class, because the Revolution has made clear the sterility, the emptiness, and the definitive historical conclusion of a period closed in itself. Trapped between the end of a society in which he has been formed—and to which he cannot return—and the beginning of a new possibility, Sergio takes refuge in a static dualism, in the intermediate zone of his contradictions. His original cynicism gives way to a defensive critique that is the reflection of a split—and in this sense one should point out the justification for *Memories* in focusing on the character, who is treated with psychological depth.

What is considered underdevelopment changes necessarily with the point of reference: of all the circumstances that bedevil Sergio, it is this one that accelerates his crisis (by being precisely that which in the revolutionary process demands the greater strain, the most profound practical disposition). Dialogue is constructed within the protagonist's formulations—he meticulously observes the external appearance and the typical reactions of the underdeveloped masses that surround him (on the screen primitive faces will be seen, earthy women, ancestral altars, male chauvinist attitudes: all the violence vital to this part of the world). Sergio's glance, keenly scrutinized by the camera, focuses all its attention on the moral side of underdevelopment, which is certainly what most disturbs him. His power of penetration is almost always accurate (and at times humorous), but lacks historical relevance by not relating superstructural opinions to the economic causes that they produce—another success of the film: ideas never escape the ideological circumstances that distinguish the character. Thus the initial sequence acquires its capacity to shock: isolated from a context that explains the causes, the violence of the happening remains like an abstract act, difficult to understand in the way Sergio perceives it.

The reading of a paragraph from the Second Declaration of Havana acts as a catalyst for the static ideas of the character: underdevelopment is a living reality, changing, in full transformation, and its presence demands more than a sacrifice. The urgency of this truth provokes in Sergio another advance of the spiral: his frustration as a social being is accompanied by escape into frequent erotic adventures, primarily with Elena, one of the best delineated characters of the film and a perfect example of what Oscar Lewis has baptized the "culture of poverty": not knowing how to relate things, not accumulating experiences, living in the present. Here, the second level of the narrative line is subordinated to the first, answering an expressive necessity: *Memories,* more than a film about underdevelopment, is the study of a specific attitude toward the problems which the film itself examines.

The sharpening of the conflict thus moves the psychic springs of the character toward a new refuge, another form of escape. The corrosive look of the past is changed in an evasive memory and makes necessary the sequence with Hanna in which Sergio evokes with nostalgia his only chance at personal realization. But now it is not only the memory of Hanna, but rather all the memories: his friend Francisco, daily escapades at the whorehouses, the places frequented, everything that acquires in his memory the dignity of what is distant. For Sergio, the cycle is totally closed: he is already a man beyond history, a being without possibilities. The moral collapse of the character becomes inevitable: the Revolution has shown him the bankruptcy of his most deep-rooted values, but Sergio is incapable of breaking with his decrepit mentality, and is incapable of acting.

Thus the logical development of the film comes to its exact culmination: the definitive annihilation of the individual who has not known how to live at the height of his era. It occurs in one of the most beautiful moments of the revolutionary process, the October Missile Crisis. Locked in his apartment, foreign in a city that displays without fear maneuvers of the antiaircraft guns or serene faces of the militiamen in an artillery platoon, Sergio attends the failure of his noncommitment. Outside, a dawn of whitish and blinding luminosity (definitely one of the most successful shots of our cinema) announces the activity of a people sure of the dignity with which they have to live.

It is in this sequence that the work's structure reaches the point of convergence of the two levels which the narration has maintained, and furthers the definition of the third (commitment of the viewer). However, the description of the October Crisis is only halfway present, and this is one of the small fissures (together with the somewhat forced episode in the Hemingway Museum, "An Adventure in the Tropics") that occurs in the solid structure of the film. The same logic of the argument culminates in the Crisis as a dramatic necessity and it is at that point that the movie should abandon the subjective level of the character in order to incorporate that which is truly important: the opposite level, the tremendous reality that Sergio has not been able to understand, the tension of those who have understood their historical role.

What remains to be noted evidently becomes detached from what is affirmed in principle: the perfect structure of the work starts from a problematic exposed from the opposite point and concludes with necessary unity: *Memories* is a film about commitment and a committed film, and this definitely continues to be its greatest merit two years after its debut. Its production—one should mention the music, the photography, the skilled acting—achieves an objectivity that, without ceasing to be dialectic, is partisan: the objectivity of the revolutionary artist. In this sense, *Memories* is a clear example of analysis, a lesson in cinematographic craft.

Memories of Underdevelopment in the Land of Overdevelopment

Julianne Burton

Never has a film from Latin America made such an impact in U.S. critical circles as that produced in 1973 by the Cuban feature MEMORIES OF UNDERDEVELOPMENT. *Newsweek*'s Arthur Cooper wrote, "MEMORIES OF UNDERDEVELOPMENT is clearly a masterpiece—a film that is intricate, ironic and extremely intelligent . . . the last word on the ultimate outsider." *New York Times* critic Peter Schjeldahl's praises of the film were even more enthusiastic: "It is a miracle. It is also something of a shock. I'm not sure what I expected of my first exposure to post-revolutionary Cuban cinema; something raw and horatory, probably. MEMORIES, though deeply political, happens to be the reverse: a beautifully understated film, sophisticated and cosmopolitan in style, fascinating in its subtlety and complexity." *New York Times* film critic Vincent Canby included the film in his list of the year's ten best, and the National Society of Film Critics voted a special plaque and a $2,000 award to the film's director, Tomás Gutiérrez Alea.

The Cubans now rejoice in the knowledge that the film was not assimilable in the end. The State Department denied the director's request for an entry visa, and the Treasury Department threatened to prosecute anyone receiving the award in Gutiérrez Alea's stead under the Trading with the Enemy Act, thus proving to the Cubans that their cultural products retain their integrity even, to use José Martí's phrase, "in the belly of the monster." Ultimately impossible to digest, they cannot be co-opted even by the all-consuming North American media industry.[1]

What the Cubans have not asked is why this particular film proved so palatable to so many American critics. They seem to assume that any Cuban film in the same circumstances would have met with a similar response. Perhaps to an extent they are right. Part of the film's acclaim here was no doubt a result of the discrepancy between the narrowness of critical expectations and the breadth and subtlety of the actual film experience. Since the Cuban film industry—barely 15 years old now, with less than a decade behind it when MEMORIES was filmed—is one of the most lively and original in the world (more on its originality later), the viewing of virtually any Cuban film is bound to demolish Cold War expectations of sledgehammer socialist realism.

From *Cinéaste* 8, no. 1 (Summer 1977):16–21.
1. For a Cuban view of the response to MEMORIES OF UNDERDEVELOPMENT in the United States, see Daniel Diaz Torres, "Cine Cubano en EEUU" in *Cine cubano* #86–87, pp. 65–71.

Still, something in this particular film seems to have struck an especially responsive chord among American critics. Andrew Sarris, incoming president of the National Society of Film Critics at the time of the flap, asserted the group's critical purity, implying that professional critics have an uncanny ability to sever any film from its national socio-political context: "I would submit that MEMORIES OF UNDERDEVELOPMENT has no more been honored by us as a product of socialist Cuba than DAY FOR NIGHT has been honored as a product of capitalist France. . . . We vote the works of individuals, not of systems." "Indeed," he continued, "what struck most of us favorably about MEMORIES OF UNDERDEVELOPMENT is its very personal and very courageous confrontation of the artist's doubts and ambivalences regarding the Cuban Revolution."

Here, it seems lies the crux of the enthusiasm generated by the film among sophisticated circles in this country. The theme appears in numerous reviews. Ambivalence, detachment, distance, equivocation: these familiar motifs of political and cultural alienation make Gutiérrez Alea's film accessible to sophisticated North American audiences. Indeed, they virtually ensure its warm reception. The film is viewed as openly critical of the current Cuban regime, but its impassioned denunciation of pre-revolutionary Cuba goes either unperceived or uncommented in this country.

The film engages in the act of criticism on numerous levels: Sergio is critical of what he sees around him, but increasingly rejects his own formation as well; the film often steps back from Sergio and offers a critical perspective on *him;* and in the sequences when the author of the original novel and the director of the film appear in the flesh, the film also becomes self-critical. The subjective experience of the protagonist is constantly complemented and amplified by intercut documentary footage. In a film of such structural intricacy and thematic complexity, the viewer is compelled to exercise certain perceptual priorities. These are culturally conditioned and reinforced, and tend, I believe, to generate a selective and fragmented view of the film among American audiences when the film's most outstanding achievement is its synthesis—the integration of diverse components into a unified whole.

Many of the recent spate of 'political' films (Maximillian Schell's THE PEDESTRIAN and David Miller's EXECUTIVE ACTION, to name two disparate examples) have incorporated documentary footage in order to achieve an aura of historical veracity. In an attempt to incorporate the individual into a broader historical context, emphasis is either placed on the former at the expense of the latter, or vice versa. A film like Bertolucci's THE CONFORMIST, for example, dissects the connections between a character's psycho-sexual development and the formation of his political mentality. Others, best exemplified by Pontecorvo's BATTLE OF ALGIERS, favor the portrayal of historical action and interaction over psychological penetration and richness of personal detail. In the face of contemporary filmmakers' attempt to balance the terms of this disjunction,

Gutiérrez Alea's film offers a strikingly effective solution. It is a 'political' film which makes that very category irrelevant because of its completeness as human experience. MEMORIES OF UNDERDEVELOPMENT is perhaps the most masterful elaboration to date of film's capacity to convey the dialectical interaction between historical circumstance and individual consciousness.

The multilayered irony which pervades the film can be traced back to the genesis of the project. Filmmaker Gutiérrez Alea chose the theme of the role of the bourgeois intellectual in an emerging revolutionary society, and used an early post-revolutionary novel of the same theme as his point of departure. The ironic dimension begins with the fact that novelist Desnoes and filmmaker Gutiérrez Alea are both 'contaminated' by what Che Guevara metaphorically termed 'original sin.' Their sympathetic, multidimensional portrayal of Sergio, as they collaborate to bring him to life on the screen grows out of their personal experience and is itself an expression of their own attempt to overcome the syndrome to which Sergio succumbs in the end.[2]

Desnoes' novel takes the form of a desultory collection of undated diary entries sporadically recorded in a curt, conversational style by an increasingly isolated Cuban intellectual, who begins his diary upon the departure of his wife and parents for Miami and points north. By the end of the novel, the minutiae of the protagonist's pointless existence, contrasted to the enormity of the historical mo-

---

2. Edmundo Desnoes was born in Havana in 1930. Bilingual (his mother was Jamaican), he received some of his schooling in the United States and later lived in New York City for several years writing for and editing the magazine *Visión*. He returned to Cuba after Batista's ouster where he now works at the national publishing house and sits on the board of Casa de las Américas. He continues to publish poetry and essays as well as fiction.

Tomás Gutiérrez Alea, born in Cuba in 1928, received his law degree from the University of Havana and subsequently studied filmmaking at the Centro Sperimentale in Rome from 1951 to 1953. In Cuba in 1954 he collaborated with Julio Garcia Espinosa and Alfredo Guevara (the former now a major filmmaker and theorist, the latter director of the Cuban film institute since its inception) on EL MEGANO (THE CHARCOAL WORKER). This medium-length documentary, though confiscated at the time by the Batista regime, now has the distinction of being the only national antecedent for the development of post-revolutionary Cuban cinema.

During the struggle against Batista, Gutiérrez Alea worked with Cine-Revista, a sort of guerrilla newsreel organization. With the triumph of the revolution, he was one of two Cubans with advanced prior training in the art of filmmaking. His subsequent career is a varied one: from the early documentary works (ESTA TIERRA NUESTRA [THIS IS OUR LAND], 1959; HISTORIAS DE LA REVOLUCION [TALES OF THE REVOLUTION], 1960; ASAMBLEA GENERAL [GENERAL ASSEMBLY], 1960; and MUERTE AL INVASOR [DEATH TO THE INVADER], 1961) he moved on to full-length features (LAS DOCE SILLAS [THE TWELVE CHAIRS], 1962; CUMBITE, 1964; MUERTE DE UN BUROCRATA [DEATH OF A BUREAUCRAT], 1966). Since the filming of MEMORIAS DEL SUBDESARROLLO (released in 1968), he has made two more features (UNA PELEA CUBANA CONTRA LOS DEMONIOS [A CUBAN FIGHT AGAINST THE DEMONS], 1971; and LA ULTIMA CENA [THE LAST SUPPER], 1976), and has collaborated on numerous films by less experienced filmmakers, in keeping with ICAIC's policy of encouraging the development of younger artists.

ment between the Bay of Pigs Invasion and the Cuban Missile crisis, convince him of the futility of his literary attempt to exorcise the void:

> This diary is useless. Underdevelopment and civilization. I don't learn. . . . Everything that I'm saying is something that consumes and sinks me. . . . To scream. Scream for what. Why add a question mark. Periods, let-ters. . . . The head is a trap. I'm tied down. Thought. It separates me from everything. It, it negates me. . . . The crisis of the Caribbean. To name the most enormous things is to kill them. Words are small, petty. . . . I have finished. Man is (I am) sad, but I want to live. . . . To go beyond words.
>
> (Spanish version, p. 94, my
> selection and translation)

Desnoes' novel, in both the original Spanish and subsequent English ver-sions,[3] lacks the density and especially the artistic distance of great fiction. It is, above all, a *document*—an exploration of the mentality of a would-be writer (male) of particular social background and economic circumstances during a given historical moment at a specific point on the globe. Like a mirrored surface which gives only the illusion of distance or depth, the distance in the novel is but the minimal space between the author and his reflection, his alter-ego projected on the page. It is ironic, but nonetheless extremely significant given the different modes and meaning of the 'documentary' approach in each, that the novel's weakness becomes the film's strength. In the novel the documentary technique is the product of a single consciousness projected inward upon another ('imagi-nary') individual consciousness, whereas in the film the documentary technique is a product of many points of view and is directed outward, toward the world at large.

Though Gutiérrez Alea, in Desnoes' view, "betrayed" the original novel, it was a creative, illuminating betrayal. The novelist acknowledges that the film achieved a level of artistic success which the novel missed because Gutiérrez Alea "objectivized a world that was shapeless in my mind and still abstract in the book. He added social density. . . . He has shown me—through documentaries of the torn world of the revolution—the character's background." The unmiti-gated subjectivity of the novel's introspective and (literally) myopic protagonist is juxtaposed in the film to the "objective" reality (a product of collective rather than individual subjectivity) of a society in the throes of revolutionary transfor-

---

3. The original Spanish version, under the title *Memorias del subdesarrollo,* was published in Cuba by Ediciones Unión in 1962. After collaborating on the film, Desnoes rewrote several parts of the novel, added new ones inspired by the film production, and published a second version in English under the title *Inconsolable Memories* (New York: New American Library, 1967). In 1973, no doubt motivated by the success of the film in Europe, Penguin Books of Great Britain issued a paperback edition of the novel under the original title, *Memories of Underdevelopment*. This edition, unfortu-nately, is not available in either the U.S. or Canada.

mation, threatened by reactionary forces from without and within, and preparing to resist the assault with the amassed strength of all its people. Assassination, counterrevolutionary bomb attacks, the Bay of Pigs Invasion, commodity shortages, mass mobilization and arms deployment, all find their way into the film, if not completely into Sergio's consciousness. According to the director's own account, work on the film

> began once we reached agreement about one basic point: we intended to make a sort of documentary about a man who ends up alone. What the film process could contribute to the novel was the 'objective' vision of reality in order to make it clash with the subjective vision of the protagonist. Photography, direct documentation, fragments of newsreels, recorded speeches, filming on the street with a hidden camera on some occasions were resources which we could count on and needed to develop to the fullest. . . . In this way, we were able to develop to a greater degree than in the novel that thread which reveals the 'objective' reality surrounding the character and which little by little tightens its grip until it suffocates him at the end. This thread alternates with the story line of the protagonist himself and is put together basically with documents, that is, with direct testimonies from the period.
>
> ("Apuntes de filmación," *Hablemos de cine* #54, Lima, Peru, p. 19)

The film opens with scenes of a street carnival. Through the credits we view dancing couples—detached, absorbed—gyrating to the insistent beat of Afro-Cuban drums. This 'typical' scene, virtually *de rigeur* in films made in Cuba throughout the country's ignominious pre-revolutionary cinema history, is here filmed in highly atypical style, the handheld camera darting back and forth through the crowd more like a participant than a spectator. Shots ring out. A man lies prostrate. On the pavement a shiny substance catches the light. Anxious onlookers block the view. A man flees, instantly swallowed up in the crowd. The inert body is hoisted high and carried away. The dancing continues, but the camera fixes on the sweat-glistening face of one black woman who stares back— arch, intent, challenging. Freeze frame. End of credits.

In a matter of seconds a stereotypical vision of Cuban life has been revived only to have its illusion of exoticism and obliviousness shattered by unexpected and unidentified violence. Nor is this the prologue of a police thriller. What has been established is the tension between past and present, archetype and reality, daily life and indiscriminate counterrevolutionary violence. The participant-spectators resume their dancing, but the camera intervenes to freeze the action like an exclamation point at the end of a sentence. The film audience, non-participatory spectators at the outset, are challenged to consider their own role *vis-à-vis* the film which is about to unfold. What follows continues to startle, to provoke, to challenge its audience.

A mound of suitcases on a moving dolly and the blare of departure instructions over a loud speaker situate us in an airport. But these are not casual departures. The tears and anguish on the faces of the departing passengers, the definitiveness with which an official in army uniform, a pile of wristwatches beside him on the table, stamps "SALIDA" on the passports indicate that this is no temporary parting. Sergio Correri, the film's protagonist, visibly impatient, bids goodbye to his parents and his wife, shrugs, and nonchalantly mouths the English phrase, "Well, bye-bye." On the bus toward Havana, he thinks back on the farewell scene. In the flashback, the camera reveals his wife's face rather than his own. The pain and anger in her eyes are a jarring contrast to his detachment.

Whistling, he enters and surveys the ample apartment, pretentious and luxurious but not quite elegant, which he now has all to himself. He loosens his tie, stretches out on the broad bed still strewn with his wife's clothes, fixes himself coffee and toast, scratches, burps, and wanders out to the balcony to survey the city and the coastline from his elegant Vedado vantage point, with the aid of a telescope. "Todo sigue igual," he observes: everything remains the same. Havana seems unreal to him, a city of cardboard, changeless and yet somehow fundamentally different. "Has the city changed, or have I?" "This great humanity has said 'Enough!' and has begun to move," he quotes Fidel. And then, ironically, "Like my parents, like Laura, and they won't stop until they reach Miami." Chirping birds in a wire cage call his attention. He removes one, shakes its inert body, and drops it over the side of the balcony, intoning, "It is the hour of parting / Oh abandoned like the wharves at dawn / All in you was a shipwreck." Despite the ironic tone and distancing effect of Sergio's poetic diction, it becomes increasingly clear as the film progresses that the shipwreck he refers to is his own life.

These first four sequences, which alternate subjective and objective camera styles, set up a tension which will continue throughout the film. The aggressive camera and quick cutting of the opening sequence give way to a more restrained *cinéma vérité* style in the airport scene. The flashback on the bus reviews the airport farewells from Sergio's point of view, but they are paradoxically less 'subjective' because of the potential disparity between our response to them and Sergio's. In the apartment sequence, the camera alternates between Sergio's point of view as he surveys his apartment and later the city below and a more 'objective' shot which includes him in the frame. We are distanced from Sergio by his obvious boredom and detachment; his yawns and belches do not exactly stimulate audience identification. But we are also made to identify with him both when the camera dwells on him (though, as in the kitchen scene, we may resist when the camera dwells overlong) and when it conveys his subjective recollections. Humor, with Sergio as agent (the dead bird, his ironic use of Castro's triumphal phrase) or victim (collapsing onto the wooden hanger) again brings us closer; when he switches to poetic diction, he distances us once more. The telescope is a visual metaphor for Sergio's distance from his fellow human beings.

Our view of him is also mediated, however, by a similar if 'invisible' instrument. Thus the first sequences of the film establish a dynamic and many-leveled relationship between the viewer and the protagonist, largely controlled by the camera's careful regulation of point of view.

Ensconced in the womb of his apartment, Sergio indulges his fantasies—wrapping himself in the clothes his wife left behind, fondling her underwear, playing with her lipstick, replaying a recording he had made of an argument between them. At other times he sits at his typewriter, trying to convince himself of his own existence by setting his thoughts down on paper. "All those who loved me and kept fucking me over have now gone," he begins his diary—just as Desnoes began his novel. Listless, he breaks off, scratching his belly, pulling at his earlobe, or futilely running his fingers along the one-dimensional contours of a print of Botticelli's Venus. Though his erotic reach extends to this zenith of female sensuality, the ultimate affirmation of his cultivated 'European' sensibility, his potential grasp extends only as far as the maid, Noemí.

When he ventures forth to the street, he flounders as if in some foreign element. Nostalgic for the old Havana, he attributes his current discomfort to the proletarianization of the city, to its conversion from the "Paris" to the "Tegucigalpa" of the Caribbean. Still, for his survival, he must venture forth. Bookstores, museums, restaurants, his monthly compensation check in return for his expropriated property, and of course the possibility of a pickup to while away his aimless hours, keep him from barricading himself in his apartment.

But Sergio is not oblivious. His active critical intelligence sustains him and sustains the audience's interest in him. The film accompanies him both backward and forward in time, recreating memories from his privileged boyhood—his training at a religious school, his first visit to a brothel, his transition from aspiring writer to furniture store proprietor, his lost European love, his marriage to Laura—and recording the ups and downs of his current existence, including his short-lived love affair with Elena, a working-class Cuban girl whom he meets on the street.

Component and sometimes conflicting elements of Sergio's personality are embodied in the people who share his life. Of the four women, Laura, his wife, represents the Euro-Americanization of the Cuban bourgeoisie. Sergio has transformed her from a "slovenly Cuban girl" into a woman of elegant exterior as artificial and empty as the cosmetics on her dressing table or the gowns she left behind in her closet. Hanna, in contrast to Laura, is a natural blonde who represents the real thing rather than the imitation. Having fled Germany with her family during the war, she finished her schooling in Cuba where she became, for Sergio, "the best thing that ever happened in my life." Though idolizing her still as the ideal woman, Sergio let her slip through his fingers, postponing their marriage and his literary career for the sake of his furniture store. Material aspirations, rather than more appropriately romantic obstacles, are revealed to be responsible for the loss of Sergio's one 'true love.' Elena is of working-class stock, but clearly not a 'new Cuban woman.' She aspires to become an actress so she can "unfold her personality" and longs for elegant goods from the U.S., but she scorns the mold into which Sergio tries to fit her. She has a vitality which Sergio dismisses as hopeless inconsistency, a symptom of underdevelopment. In contrast to Elena, Noemí represents the rural proletariat, exoticized for Sergio by her Protestant religious beliefs, but in the end purely an object of fantasy. Sexual relations with her are as impossible as with Botticelli's Venus, for she is after all the maid, and his class bias, inertia, and *angst* prevent any attempt on his part to realize his fantasies. Besides, the disparity between the reality and his elaboration of it is always too great, as indicated by the contrast between her baptism ceremony as he eroticizes it in his imagination and the documented reality of the photographs she brings him.

Pablo, his one male friend, represents everything in his past life which Sergio now actively rejects. He is small-minded, crude, self-deluding, and self-righteously 'apolitical.' Sergio, on his second trip to the airport, watches Pablo and his wife leave with relief, "as if I had thrown them up." "Although it may destroy me," Sergio thinks in voice-over, "this revolution is my revenge against the stupid Cuban bourgeoisie. Against idiots like Pablo." Pablo signals to Sergio through a glass partition, gesticulating dramatically and mouthing words which Sergio cannot or will not comprehend. Looking at Pablo, Sergio sees himself in the glass, but it is a self which he now consciously rejects. They now belong to different worlds; there can be no communication between them.

Each of these personal relationships sheds light on Sergio's concept of underdevelopment. For him, 'culture' and 'civilization' are synonymous with economic and technological development. He rejects Cuban cultural forms in favor of the more 'cosmopolitan' tradition of Europe and the U.S. Hanna is the woman of his dreams because she belongs to this world, but he settles for Laura, whom he successfully molds into a third world imitation of first world elegance. Laura, however, abandons him for the very comforts of the developed world which he has taught her to appreciate. Sergio, unlike his parents, wife, and friend, does not opt for permanent residence in the U.S. when the opportunity arises, but stays behind in Cuba. Despite his class and cultural bias, he feels a certain bond (he describes it as "curiosity") to the fate of his small but determined island homeland. The decision to stay notwithstanding, he retains his former assumptions and continues trying to live "like a European," shepherding Elena around to museums and bookstores and eventually ditching her when she fails to let herself be 'developed' according to his formula.

This, then, is Sergio's subjective world as the film presents it—part of which he rejects, part of which he cannot escape. It is, basically, the world which Desnoes presents in both versions of the novel. But the film adds a new dimension, placing Sergio in his historical context by making extensive use of documentary footage of both contemporary and historical events. There is a remarkable variety to these documentary sequences. Montages of still photos in the style of the Cuban documentarist Santiago Alvarez are inserted at several points: when Sergio reflects on hunger in pre-revolutionary Cuba and in all of Latin America; when he recalls the humble origins of the late Ernest Hemingway's faithful Afro-Cuban servant; when the Russian tourists at the Hemingway residence, now a museum, thumb through Papa's photographic momentoes of the Spanish Civil War. There is television footage of Marilyn Monroe, of American soldiers at Guantánamo Naval Base, of blacks being beaten in the heyday of the U.S. Civil Rights movement (actually televised footage from Santiago Alvarez' film NOW!) and finally, of Fidel's speech reaffirming Cuba's autonomy and resistance in the face of Kennedy's nuclear innuendos. At one point the camera peruses a newspaper from headline to comic strip. Sequences at the José Martí Airport, at the swimming pool, along Havana's streets, in the Hemingway museum are recognizably 'real' rather than reconstructed for the filming. The actors insert themselves into these situations in such a way as to interact with and against a natural background.

The longest documentary section comes relatively early in the film. Sergio, angered by Pablo's political obtuseness, equates his mentality with that of the Cuban *gusanos* who returned as part of the Bay of Pigs Invasion. "Listen to this," he tells Pablo as he begins to read from a book (Leon Rozitchner's *Moral burguesa y revolución*) which we saw him purchase earlier. There follows an elaborate reconstruction composed of both still photographs and moving footage, with extensive use of voice-over, of the aftermath of Playa Girón—the defense of the prisoners, the accusations by the populace at the public trials, and an analysis of the division of labor and self-exculpating rationale of the invaders. Newsreel footage from the Batista period, including scenes of the leisured class at a full-dress ball, is strikingly intercut in this sequence.

The transition from fictional to documentary line, which seems so brusque and arbitrary to American audiences who are further distanced by the very Hispanic analytical abstraction of the prose, is actually a very smooth and subtle one. Pablo is washing his hands (of automobile grime or of Cuba and its problems?) when he tells Sergio that he is finally prepared to take a political stand—in Miami. Sergio's revulsion at Pablo's hypocrisy and obtuseness impel him toward the opposite position. He counters Pablo's vacuous rhetoric with what is perhaps an equally rhetorical but substantive psychological analysis of others who acted on political assumptions parallel to Pablo's. Finally, the fact that it is Sergio who narrates in voice-over firmly ties this long documentary sequence to the 'primary' plot line.

Another documentary sequence adds a special note of self-reflectiveness and self-criticism to the film. Sergio attends a round-table discussion on "Literature and Underdevelopment" (an event which actually took place in 1964). Among the participants, as representative of Cuban letters, is none other than Edmundo Desnoes. As he pontificates on the Negro-like status of all Latin Americans when in the U.S., the camera, first in medium and then in long shot, underlines the fact that Desnoes and the rest of the panel are being served by a black attendant who fills their water glasses—completely unacknowledged by them. Desnoes, together with the rest of the panelists, exposes himself to further criticism or even ridicule when a member of the audience (Jack Gelber, a New York playwright) interrupts the proceedings to criticize—in English—the "sterile and impotent form of the discussion" as inappropriate to a revolutionary society. The planes of 'reality' and 'fiction' are mixed when Sergio, whom the editing identifies with Desnoes, leaves the event profoundly troubled. "I don't understand," he says, slowly advancing toward the camera. "The American was right. Words devour words and they leave you in the clouds." The graininess and increasing close-up nature of the shot causes Sergio to disintegrate before our eyes as he muses, "Now it begins, Sergio, your final destruction."

Such critical self-reflectiveness is not confined to the appearance of Desnoes. When Sergio brings Elena to ICAIC (the Cuban film institute), the 'friend' whom he has promised to introduce her to turns out to be Gutiérrez Alea himself. The transition from the restaurant where Sergio has picked up Elena to the film studio is nothing short of brilliant. Elena says she wants to be an actress so that she can be someone else without people thinking that she's crazy. Sergio answers that actresses, like broken records, only repeat the same movements and the same lines over and over again. The ensuing shots—cyclically repeated scenes of female nudity and not quite culminated sexual contact—are revealed to be, when the lights come on, film fragments within the film: a collection of erotic clips which Batista's censors, always obsessed with keeping up appearances, found "offensive to morals and good breeding." As the three of them walk out of the screening room, Sergio asks Gutiérrez Alea what he plans to do with the film clips. The director replies that he intends to use them in "a sort of collage, a film that will have a bit of everything." The viewer discovers that Sergio's doubts about whether or not 'they' will release such a film are ultimately unfounded, since the film described in this conversation is none other than the one we are viewing.

The same self-conscious and self-reflective technique used in Desnoes' novel is employed by Gutiérrez Alea with more subtle skill and much greater success. This sequence is a kind of crossroads in the film, a high point of humor and virtuousity which also reveals false attitudes toward sexuality. (What has been shown, after all, is the same kind of hypocritical sexual elusiveness and game-playing that Elena herself is about to engage in with Sergio.) Simultaneously, the sequence takes brilliant advantage of the camera's ability to reduplicate action, transcend space and ignore time, totally confuses the planes of 'fiction' and 'documentary truth' which remain more clearly separate in the rest of the film, undermines the entire question of censorship, and, most important, allows the film's director in person to present his audience with a major key to understanding the film. For MEMORIES OF UNDERDEVELOPMENT is indeed a cinematographic collage, not only in its variety, scope, eclectic technique and juxtaposition of evidence from real life on the film canvas, but also in its effect, in the way the combination of the fictional and the documentary, the 'artifice' and the 'reality' exceeds and transcends the sum of both parts.[4] Finally, as a key to the self-reflectiveness of the film as a whole, and the purpose behind it, this sequence postulates an alternative to Sergio—that of Gutiérrez Alea himself, a bourgeois artist who has turned his energies, and the skills which are a product of his former privilege, toward creating a complex and uncompromising work of art from a perspective of political commitment.

The resonances between the documentary and fictional segments, their complex and multifaceted interaction, are what make this such a thought-provoking and fertile film. Through this interaction, and often as a function of dramatic irony, the vision of the film not only exceeds that of its protagonist but often undermines or contradicts it. Sergio reads aloud a Marxist analysis of the fallacies of bourgeois morality as evidenced by the Bay of Pigs invaders, and as he does so the film offers a visual rendering of this analysis. Its impact is to demonstrate that actions, not intentions or rationales, are the final arbiter of an individual's social role and ideological stance. Though intellectually grasping the point, Sergio fails to make any connection with his own life. He fails to realize that he too is an accomplice of reactionary forces precisely because he won't desert his position of critical superiority to participate, to act, to engage himself in the world around him. His only field of action is the women whom he objectifies and tries to transform according to borrowed criteria. He condemns Hemingway for the way he molded his servant to his needs: "The faithful servant and the great lord. The colonialist and Gunga Din. Hemingway must have been unbearable"; but he fails to realize how the same criterion should be applied to himself for his persistent cultural and sexual colonization of the women in his life.

Sergio is, in fact, at his most sympathetic in his analysis of Hemingway. The idea of this great writer, perhaps a model for Sergio's own literary aspirations, as a colonialist would never have occurred to him before. Yet this discovery, ironically, is made on one of the compulsory museum trips intended to 'develop' Elena. Sergio dumps her here. Perhaps his new insight prompts him to let go of his 'prey,' but his increased understanding of the cultural mechanisms of under-

4. In his brilliant analysis of camera style in Godard's WEEKEND ("Towards a Non-Bourgeois Camera Style," *Film Quarterly*, Winter 1970–71), Brian Henderson asserts that "the difference between montage and collage is a complex question." The distinction he proceeds to develop is highly relevant to procedures used by Tomás Gutiérrez Alea in MEMORIES:

> Montage fragments reality in order to reconstitute it in highly organized, synthetic emotional and intellectual patterns. Collage does not do this, it collectes or sticks its fragments together in a way that does not entirely overcome their fragmentation. It seeks to recover its fragments as fragments. In regard to overall form, it seeks to bring out the internal relations of its pieces, whereas montage imposes a set of relations upon them and indeed collects or creates its pieces to fill out a preexistent plan.

development apparently does nothing to increase his sympathy toward other victims of the process. Elena, for her part, finds her release more of an affront than a liberation, and in due time takes her revenge.

In form and technique as well as narrative content, the film constitutes a relentless critique of false consciousness. Sergio is the main target, but the working class is not exempted. The scenes with Elena's family who, after Sergio dumps her, accuse him of rape and bring him to trial, severely criticize the assimilation by the proletariat of moral values borrowed from the bourgeoisie. "Girls must go to the altar as virgins," Elena's mother cries. "That is the greatest treasure a woman can give in marriage!" This confrontation is shot in front of the most elegantly stocked store window seen in the film. Half a dozen mannequins display bridesmaids' dresses and wedding gowns, just in case someone might be missing the point about the ultimate fetishized commodity—the female body. The trial sequence and its outcome reveal Sergio's misjudgment of revolutionary justice. "Now everything is 'the people,' " Sergio observed in voice-over during the courtroom scene. "Before, I would have been the respected one and they the ones condemned to guilt." But to his surprise and discomfort, he is absolved of the charges. "It was a happy ending, as they say. For once, justice triumphed." Despite his acquittal, however he realizes the extent of his implication. "I've seen too much to be innocent. They have too much darkness inside their heads to be guilty."

The film makes ample and varied use, on a thematic and artistic level, of another technique which produces results similar to the interpolation of documentary footage. Four times in the course of the film, the camera returns to a past sequence in an apparent repetition which instead lends new meaning to the scene. An obvious example is Noemí's baptism sequence; the photographs of the ceremony point up the absurdity and self-aggrandizement of Sergio's earlier fantasies (without negating the lyric beauty of the imaginary sequence). In another sequence repetition, we return in the middle of the film to the carnival scene with which the film opened. This time Sergio is among the crowd, and the Afro-Cuban rhythms are replaced by more abstract, distancing strains which identify the viewer with Sergio's consciousness rather than with the world of the dancers. The editing suggests that Sergio sees the assassin, but once again he remains the passive spectator who sees and comprehends but does not act.

The repetition of the airport sequence, mentioned earlier, provided the first visual evidence of the discrepancy between Sergio's responses and those of the people around him. In contrast to Sergio's detachment, Laura's pained expression, however fleeting, prepares us to understand better than Sergio the rift between them. It is in the tape recorder sequence that the history of the separation is revealed, though not until the second segment of that sequence do we realize that this was the argument which led to Laura's departure and their permanent separation. In the first segment, listening intently to the recording of their increasingly heated exchange, Sergio drapes one of Laura's gowns over his shoulders, and rifles through the drawers and dressing table. At the height of the argument, we hear him informing her that the entire exchange is being recorded, that it will be great fun to listen to later on. When she screams "You are a monster!" the camera shows Sergio with one of her stockings over his head— monstrous, brutal, deformed. How thin and transparent is the veneer of 'civiliza-tion' on which he prides himself. It is both ironic and paradoxical that the dis-carded components of Laura's artificial beauty here reverse their function and make Sergio's inner monstrosity externally apparent.

After Elena's tumultuous 'seduction,' Sergio again relives the sequence with Laura. Much of what we heard earlier is repeated, but this time we go beyond the tape-recorded data to witness the result of the confrontation. Vertiginously fol-lowing Sergio's movements as he tries to defend the tape recorder from Laura's enraged assault, the camera brusquely cuts to Laura falling backwards, then sprawled on the floor. Hysterical, she gets up and backs away from Sergio in fear and rising rage. "I never want to see you again!" she screams at fever pitch. "I'm leaving! I'm going alone. I don't want you to come with me. . . . I won't be a guinea pig for your whims and little games. I'm going to live my own life!" This scene, though difficult because of its perhaps exaggerated intensity, gives Laura a suggestion of autonomy denied to the other women in the film, mediated as they are by Sergio's view of them. It also provides a key to Sergio's rela-tionships with women, for in fact, they *are* his 'guinea pigs,' amusing creatures to be shaped and experimented on.

This 'double-take' technique requires the viewer's intellectual collaboration and provides a means of increased comprehension within the scope of the film. Point of view is shown to be a crucial determinant of any version of reality. Where the purely subjective novelistic technique only elicits vague suspicions about the narrator's unreliability, impossible to verify within the context of the work, the camera provides an alternate perspective and an external vantage point, whether juxtaposing one person's subjective view to another's or juxtapos-ing the social and historical context to the individual one.

Not unrelated to this is the richness of detail which the camera encompasses, its voracity in 'objectively' recording, for instance, the artifacts in Sergio's apart-ment—just as diverse and 'un-Cuban' as the trophies and souvenirs which Ser-gio criticizes in the Hemingway house—from the magazine cover with Brigitte Bardot to the bizarre collage of a photograph of Pope John framed in a toilet seat above a chalk outline of a naked female body. This wealth of accumulated detail, the alternative points of view provided by the subjective and non-subjective cam-era, as well as the dialectical relationship between Sergio's personal life and his historical context, combine to create artistic complexity through distance. Des-noes, in his appraisal of the film, observed that the use of filmic techniques to create this distancing effect "lets us see what is ours as if it were someone else's." Gutiérrez Alea provides a more penetrating assessment of the film's quantum enrichment of the original literary rendering:

We are not interested in simply mirroring reality; we want to enrich it, to excite and develop the sensibilities, to ferret out problems. We are not interested in smoothing out the dialectical process by means of formulas or idealized representations of reality. Instead, we want aggressively to give it life, to become a component in that dialectical process, cognizant of all this signifies in terms of disturbing tranquility.

Sergio observes the popular mobilization in preparation for an imminent attack from the United States and, uncomprehending, accuses his countrymen of not taking the crisis seriously, of playing some sort of children's game. But the expressions on the faces of the citizenry in militia uniforms—their quiet deliberation and confidence as they stand, armed yet relaxed, beside rows of tanks and machine guns—contrast sharply with Sergio's isolated desperation as, sleepless, he paces about his apartment, terrified at the prospect of imminent annihilation. Fast-paced parallel cutting and alternation of sound bands heighten the contrast between Sergio's state of suspended animation and the determined activity of the world outside his hiding place. Finally—in a pathetic substitution for the real activity which surrounds him but which he cannot join—he strikes out in calculated but futile fury and decapitates a glass rooster.

The final shot of the film leaves Sergio literally up in the air. From the balcony of his apartment, as in one of the opening scenes, he surveys the city below. The sun is rising over the horizon; we have come full circle. As Sergio observed in the earlier sequence, everything remains the same and yet everything has definitively changed. Where earlier there were lovers on the hotel terraza, now anti-aircraft guns are being hoisted into position. Sergio, behind his telescope, remains a spectator. He cannot go forward, and there is no going back—as the film's examination of the circumstances of his past and present life reveals. His memories of underdevelopment provide no refuge. By now it is abundantly clear that, although the realities of economic underdevelopment and political dependency are a fact of life on this struggling tropical island, the title of the film refers more pointedly to Sergio's own moral and political underdevelopment. For overcoming underdevelopment in its many forms is not a matter of individual divestiture but of collective endeavor. The segment of Fidel's speech is incorporated near the end of the film not as a naked propaganda device but as a moving affirmation of this principle:

We will never renounce the sovereign prerogative that within our borders we will make all the decisions. . . . Anyone intending to inspect our country should come in battle array. . . . They threaten us by saying we'll be nuclear targets. We are part of humanity and we run the necessary risks, yet we are not afraid. We have to know how to live during the age we happen to live in, with the dignity to know how to survive. Every man and woman, young person and old, we are all one in this hour of danger, and it is the same for all of us, revolutionaries and patriots, and the victory shall be for us all. *Patria o muerte! Venceremos!*

Sergio tries to transform consciousness with consciousness, failing to realize that even psychological change is only achieved through action and activity. The film asserts that the Revolution will survive and advance without Sergio; it asserts with equal conviction that, without the Revolution, Sergio can neither survive nor advance.

There is a certain open-endedness here which is common to post-revolutionary cinema, because Cuban filmmakers have been consistently more interested in the process of the search than in prescribing pat solutions. Interpretations of Sergio's prospects vary according to the context and assumptions of the audience. If Cuban audiences see Sergio as defeated and dead-ended at the close of the film, North American audiences feel a greater stake in optimism regarding his eventual fate. The fact that many North American viewers tend to 'edit out' the documentary sequences in the film explains why they can cling to a more romanticized view of the protagonist's future prospects. The converse of this is also true.

I referred earlier to the originality of post-revolutionary Cuban filmmaking, though in fact the industry has on occasion been accused of the opposite. A film like MEMORIES (or—to take another Cuban film most familiar to American audiences—Humberto Solás' LUCIA), whose visual style and technique are so clearly indebted to a long evolution of film language which took place primarily in the United States and Europe, is occasionally criticized as bourgeois in form and consequently non-revolutionary in content. It is too mechanical and arbitrary to dismiss these films as essentially derivative because one detects a touch of Fellini here, of Godard there, of Jean Vigo somewhere else. Cuban cinema makes no claim to be *sui generis*. In fact, all the arts in Cuba build openly upon an internationalist but particularly Western cultural tradition which necessarily passed through an historical phase of bourgeois dominance. We run too great a risk, particularly in our own alienated and fragmented society, of failing to grasp the whole for petty concentration on the parts. Viewed in a North American, or to spell it out, a capitalist cultural context, MEMORIES OF UNDERDEVELOPMENT works to break down viewer dependency on narrative structures which artificially isolate the individual in their concentration on him or her; it works to break down our resistance to the 'intrusive' elements of historical and social reality. The challenge to the viewer is to perceive the completeness of the film.

The meaning of what *Playboy* magazine referred to as the film's "turn-off title" evolves as the film unfolds. Sergio sees the evidence of underdevelopment all around him, but fails to perceive it within. He never realizes that his sophisticated cultural perspective and Elena's more vulgar taste are but opposite sides of the same coin. On the broadest level, however, the entire filmmaking process was also a 'memory of underdevelopment': "We filmed with very limited resources," Gutiérrez Alea recalls. "At each step we felt the touch of underdevelopment. It limited us, it prevented us from dreaming like the protagonist. It also conditioned the language with which we expressed ourselves. To a greater extent than ever before, we used a kind of spontaneous shooting whereby we would provoke an occurrence . . . and would film it as a newsreel cameraman would."

"I have to say," he concludes, "that this is the film in which I have felt most free . . . in spite of the everpresent limitations imposed by underdevelopment. Perhaps, I felt free precisely *because* of those limitations."

"Witnesses Always Everywhere": The Rhetorical Strategies of *Memories of Underdevelopment*

Enrique Fernández

Any discussion of film and ideology must deal sooner or later with the complex issue of cinematic point of view. This seems particularly true if we keep in mind: (1) that "point of view" in everyday speech can mean an opinion, i.e., an ideological reading of phenomena; (2) the importance that criticism has placed on the study of point of view in written narrative (studies by James, Lubbock, Booth) invites us to apply these approaches to filmic narrative; (3) that the issue of "authority" implicit in narrative point of view has obvious political implications, thus Nathalie Sarraute's rebellious "Who said that?";[1] (4) the optical qualities or attributes of the cinema seem to indicate that film is, in some ways, a point of view. Fittingly enough, it was the politically motivated and informed post-May '68 French critical project that began the most penetrating study of cinematic point of view in a series of now famous polemical articles on the subject. I take as my own point of departure an American contribution to this debate, Nick Browne's rhetorical model for the structure of filmic narration. His model focuses on what he calls the "construction and significance of narrative space by the mutually implicating 'positions' of camera, character, [and] 'spectator.' "[2] Browne concludes that the position of the "spectator-in-the-text"[3] corresponds to the moral position of the narrator rather than to a literal point of view.

Even the most casual viewing of the film *Memories of Underdevelopment* (1962) brings to mind the issue of narrative point of view. First, Sergio, the protagonist, is obviously the voice-over narrator; the visual text orbits around and often within his consciousness. Second, the viewer who knows that the film is an adaptation of Desnoes' novel may assume a priori that the director has found cinematic equivalents for Desnoes' first-person narration. In addition, the pro-

From *Wide Angle* 4, no. 2 (Winter 1980): 52–55.
1. Nathalie Sarraute, "The Age of Suspicion," in *Approaches to the Novel*, ed. Robert Scholes (San Francisco: Chandler Publishing Co., 1966), p. 213.
2. Nick Browne, "Narrative Point of View: The Rhetoric of *Au Hasard, Balthazar*," *Film Quarterly* 31 (Fall 1977):19.
3. Brown, "The Spectator-in-the-Text: The Rhetoric of *Stagecoach*," *Film Quarterly* 29 (Winter 1975–76):35.

tagonist, in both novel and film, positions himself as spectator: his project is to stay in Cuba just to see what happens. The famous shot of Sergio behind the telescope underscores the role of the protagonist as spectator in the filmic text. The conflict in the film's plot results from Sergio's move from spectator to participant in his pursuit, seduction and rejection of Elena, that is, his transformation from narrator to protagonist. As I have pointed out elsewhere, Sergio's failure at erotic commitment corresponds to his failure at political commitment and underscores the intractability of his alienated posture.[4] My project in this article is to articulate the rhetorical strategies the film utilizes to produce its meaning. To do this I will first outline the ways in which Sergio serves as narrative authority in both diegesis and discourse. I will then go on to discuss Sergio's move from narrator to protagonist as a moral repositioning of the spectator. Finally, I will look at the text's double function as historical witness and inscription.

Sergio as Narrative Authority

1. DIEGESIS
1.1. Sound track
1.1.1. Dialogue and/or sound spoken or heard by Sergio, e.g., Sergio and Pablo talking.
1.1.2. Sergio's voice in readings or tape recordings originating in diegetic space, e.g., Sergio's reading of Rozitchner's *Moral burguesa y revolución*.
1.2. Visual track
1.2.1. Point-of-view shots, often moving and hand-held camera, e.g., the first shot of Elena, in which the camera moves around and up and down her body in representation of Sergio's erotic glance.
1.2.2. Over-the-shoulder shots or other visual strategies which show the spectator and the spectacle, e.g., the shot of Pablo and Sergio riding in Pablo's car, shot from Sergio's side but including him in the frame.
1.2.3. Intertexts, e.g., the porno collage Sergio views at ICAIC.
2. DISCOURSE
2.1. Sound track
2.1.1. Sergio's voice-over narration: corresponding to the text Sergio is writing.
2.1.2. Music accompanying Sergio's reveries: Leo Brower's score.
2.2. Visual track
2.2.1. Fantasy sequences, e.g., Sergio and Noemí making love.
2.2.2. Memory sequences, e.g., Sergio and Hannah making love.
2.2.3. Intertexts, e.g., the mini-documentary "The truth of the group is in the murderer" accompanying Sergio's reading of Rozitchner.

---

4. Enrique Fernández, "Three on Two: Gutiérrez Alea and Edmundo Desnoes," *Diacritics* 4 (Winter 1974):55-60.

As we watch the film, it becomes obvious that what Sergio says, reads, hears, sees, imagines or remembers constitutes most of the film and that in these instances Sergio's authority for the enunciation of the text corresponds to his self-appointed position as a spectator of the Cuban revolutionary phenomenon. However, even though Sergio seems to show and/or tell most of the film, in certain moments Sergio is himself shown and told. Before going any further, we should remember that filmic rhetoric traditionally allows for the showing of the narrator in the frame (e.g., the over-the-shoulder shot of classical Hollywood films) and that the narrator need not be a literal point of view, but is instead a moral position that can shift according to the rhetorical strategies of the text. What are, then, the cinema-specific signifiers of the shifting moral position of the narrator/spectator in *Memories of Underdevelopment?*

In order to find these, I wish to call attention to the most accessible structuring mechanism of the narrative text: the plot. In it I discern four movements:

Movement 1: *Letting Go.* Sergio, the alienated bourgeois intellectual, bids farewell to family and friends who are leaving Cuba. He beings writing his *Memories.*
Movement 2: *Getting It On.* Sergio seduces Elena and begins a futile relationship with her.
Movement 3: *Getting It Off.* Sergio tries to get rid of Elena but is finally confronted by her family which presses legal charges against him. Sergio is arrested, tried and acquitted.
Movement 4: *Epilogue: The Missile Crisis.* Sergio watches his country prepare for war during the Missile Crisis.

Movement 1 is exposition. Movements 2 and 3 constitute the actual intrigue with its emphasis on individual romance, adventure and psychology and its classic resolution in a trial. Movement 4 has little relation to the intrigue but serves as an epilogue, underscoring the final state (loneliness, alienation) of the protagonist after the experiences of the plot. The protagonist moves from passivity (Sergio is not going away) to action (he is going after Elena), from detachment (Sergio is alone) to engagement (he is with Elena). In Movement 3 he begins a process of detachment (Sergio avoids Elena), precipitating a crisis that will leave him detached and passive in Movement 4 (Sergio is alone and does nothing).

The first movement identifies Sergio as spectator-of-and-in-the-text and the source of narrative authority. In the telescope/balcony sequence we see Sergio seeing, and then we see what he sees in the masked shots of the Havana cityscape. We also hear his narrative voice which has been identified with the *Memories* he is writing. This filmic/novelistic narrator who from the outset assumes the role of detached spectator and ironic commentator of Cuban social reality probes into his environment through written/spoken discourse, i.e., the *Memories*/voice-over narration, or through sight. This aggressive sight—probing—is encoded in two particular moves: (1) Sergio's use of lenses (eyeglasses, telescope), and (2) the first-person camera: shots from Sergio's point of view with his voice off-screen. Sergio at the telescope is an example of (1); the camera's erotic exploration of Elena at La Rampa is an example of (2).

The first movement also includes sequences in which we see Sergio alone in his apartment. Here the absence of the Other is structured by the camera's identification with the character. The candid shots of Sergio alone, e.g., burping his breakfast, are part of the narrator's strategies for self-knowledge, the confessional aspect of the *Memories* he is writing. In these sequences Sergio can be read as the authority for the shots of Sergio.

The intrigue of the second movement begins with the traveling shot of Elena, identified with Sergio's erotic glance. Sergio's voice off-screen accentuates the position of Sergio and Elena as subject and object: Sergio is approaching Elena, looking at her and asking her questions; Elena is the object of his movement, his glance, and his interrogation. The film cuts to Sergio, in place inside the restaurant, ready to be the object of Elena's glance, in classic shot-reverse shot *découpage,* as he smoothly orders a dry martini. The camera's position and movement in the shot of Elena signify desire in Sergio's glance, as they did in similar previous shots of women Sergio sees and follows in the streets. Sergio's off-screen voice in this syntagm will rhyme with the flashback sequence in which Sergio's wife is tormented by him, and in both instances the presence of his absence in the frame, signified by his voice, suggests his intellectual and emotional domination of the woman.

As the plot progresses to its climax in the third movement, Sergio is visited by an Urban Reform Committee composed of a working-class man and woman. This sequence begins with a lengthy one-shot of Sergio in medium closeup with the off-screen Committee's uncomfortably probing questions about Sergio's property. The spectator's position has shifted: now Sergio himself becomes the spectacle, structured by the glance of the Absent One, the glance of the spectator, a function Sergio has imbued with power and desire. When Sergio is finally brought to trial by Elena's family, he is questioned off-screen by the prosecutor, who instructs him to face the judge, a position that corresponds to the camera. The specifics of the Urban Reform Committee sequence have taken names: off-screen voice = prosecutor, camera = judge. The spectator's powerful function has shifted from Sergio to the Law.

Sergio is acquitted but as he admits: "I have seen too much to be innocent."[5] Back in his apartment he looks at photographs of Noemí's baptism, the thought of which had earlier provoked an erotic fantasy, and he notices that other people were present: "The witnesses who are always everywhere."[6] Sergio is guilty of being the spectator; so his punishment is to become the spectacle himself, to be in turn, witnessed.

5. Tomás Gutiérrez Alea and Edmundo Desnoes, *Memories of Underdevelopment,* ed. Michael Myerson (New York: Grossman, 1973), p. 103
6. Ibid., p. 104

In the last movement or epilogue Sergio regards the spectacle of war preparations in the streets and appears to retreat to his apartment. This sequence of parallel syntagma shows footage of Sergio and of Havana streets; neither series of shots authorizes the other. The spectator's position reclaimed by the Law now moves to the spectator-outside-the-text who, as the Law, must judge Sergio and must judge the Cuban people for the historical role they are (or are not) playing. The spectator must judge the text: in other words, the text's last rhetorical move is to engage my moral function and to ask me to consider the spectacle I have just seen.

And what has this spectacle been? First, it has been an historical witness. *Memories of Underdevelopment* is a collage of film texts which document a certain period of Cuban history. As such, it serves as a reminder of the power of the cinema as historical recording and of the political work of cinematic recording of history (much, if not most, political filmmaking is documentary). But a spectacle always implies a spectator, a point of view, an opinion, an ideologically informed version of history, a moral position. *Memories* chooses the point of view of a self-appointed witness and writes the text as his memoirs, a strategy that identifies the witness-in-history with the spectator-in-the-text. At the points of greatest narrative tension, the text shifts its point of view from Sergio to the Law and finally to the spectator-outside-the-text, the film viewer, whose other scene is history.

The final sequence ends with a shot of Sergio's telescope in the balcony followed by telephoto shots of the Havana cityscape. This syntagm retraces the montage that inscribed Sergio's position as spectator-in-the-text early in the film, with one salient difference: the shot of the telescope leaves the viewing end out of the frame. The viewer, Sergio, has been deleted by the camera position, his diegetic presence or absence is irrelevant, he is out of the game. The shots of the city are authorized by the text itself, by the narrator, not as a character but as a moral position or set of rhetorical strategies. As I see the last shot, autonomous and authoritative, zoom in on the street from the perspective of the telescope in the balcony, I don't want to ask Nathalie Sarraute's "Who said that?" The question of film enunciation strikes me as naive. I know who said that, the film said that, although it pretended to say it as Sergio most of the time. The steps of the narrator have left a trace, the filmic text *Memories of Underdevelopment*. Viewing it I have retraced the steps so faithfully that I, the spectator, have experienced the text from a position inside of it; such is the power of filmic rhetoric. But before the film ends, Sergio and I part company. He is the spectator-in-the-text, I the spectator-of-the-text, the witnesses-who-are-always-everywhere. Outside is the street and history.

Filmography and
Bibliography

Alea Filmography, 1950–1988

1950   *Una confusion cotidiana (An Everyday Confusion)* (short) in collaboration with Nestor Almendros, based on Kafka's story of the same title.

1953   *El sueño de Juan Bassin (The Dream of Juan Bassin)* (short)

1955   *El Megano (The Charcoal Worker)* in collaboration with Julio García Espinosa.

1958   *Havana 1762* (D)

1959   *Esta tierra nuestra (This Land of Ours)* (D)

1960   *Historias de la Revolución (Stories of the Revolution)* Script by Alea and José Hernandez.

1961   *Muerte al invasor (Death to the Invader)* (D) in collaboration with Santiago Alvarez.

   Asamblea General (General Assembly) (D)

1962   *Las doce sillas (The Twelve Chairs)* Script by Alea and Ugo Ulive, based upon the Russian novel by Ilya Ilf and Eugene Petrov.

1964   *Cumbite (Work Party)* Script by Alea, based on *Les Gouverneurs de la Rosée* by Haitian novelist Jacques Romain.

1966   *La muerte de un burocrata (Death of a Bureaucrat)* Script by Alea.

1968   *Memorias del subdesarrollo (Memories of Underdevelopment)* Script by Alea and Edmundo Desnoes, based upon the novel *Inconsolable Memories* by Desnoes.

1971   *Una pela cubana contra los demonios (A Cuban Struggle against the Demons)* Script by Alea and others, based upon a work by Fernando Ortiz, a leading Cuban ethnographer.

1974   *El arte del tabaco (The Art of the Cigar)* (D)

1976   *La ultima cena (The Last Supper)* Script by Alea, Tomás González, and Maria Eugenia Haya.

1978   *Los sobrevivientes (The Survivors)*
Script by Alea.

1984   *Hasta cierto punto (Up to a Point)*
Script by Alea.

1988   *Cartas del parque (Letters from the Park)*
Script by Gabriel García Marquez.

Selected Bibliography

Armes, Roy. *Third World Film Making and the West*. Berkeley and Los Angeles: University of California Press, 1987.

Burton, Julianne. "Film and Revolution in Cuba: The First Twenty-Five Years." In *Cuba: Twenty-Five Years of Revolution,* ed. John Kirk and Sandor Halebsky. New York: Praeger, 1985.

———— "The Intellectual in Anguish: Modernist Form and Ideology in *Land In Anguish* and *Memories of Underdevelopment.*" Commentary by Edmundo Desnoes. Latin American Working Program Paper #132, ed. Sara Castro Klaren. Washington, D.C.: Woodrow Wilson International Center for Scholars, 1984. Reprinted in abbreviated form in *Post Script: Essays in Film and the Humanities* 3, no. 3 (Winter 1984): 65–84 and, complete, in *Ideologies and Literature/Nueva Epoca* 1, no. 1–2 (Winter–Spring 1985): 81–119.

Chanan, Michael. *The Cuban Image.* Bloomington: Indiana University Press, 1985.

Downing, John D. H. "Four Films of Tomás Gutiérrez Alea." In *Film and Politics in the Third World,* ed. Downing, pp. 279–303. Brooklyn, N.Y.: Autonomedia/Praeger, 1987.

Engel, Andi. "Solidarity and Violence." *Sight & Sound* 38, no. 4 (Autumn 1969): 196–200.

Fornet, Ambrosio, ed. *Alea: Una retrospectiva critica.* Havana: Editorial Letras Cubanas, 1987.

Fernandez, Henry, David I. Grossvogel, and Emir Rodriguez Monegal. "Three on Two: Henry Fernandez, David I. Grossvogel, and Emir Rodriguez Monegal on Desnoes and Alea." *Diacritics: A Review of Contemporary Criticism* 4, no. 4 (Winter 1974): 51–55, 55–60, 60–64.

Gutiérrez Alea, Tomás. *Dialectica del espectador*. Havana: Ediciones Union, 1982. Trans. Julia Lesage. *The Viewer's Dialectic*. Havana: José Martí Publishing House, 1988.

The same translation appeared in the journal *Jump Cut: A Review of Contemporary Media,* #29 (Feb. 1984): 18–21; #30 (Mar. 1985): 48–53.

Kavanagh, Thomas M. "Dialectics and the Textuality of Class Conflict." *Journal of Latin American Lore (UCLA)* 4, no. 1 (1978): 135–143.

Kernan, Margot. "Cuban Cinema: Tomás Gutiérrez Alea." *Film Quarterly* 29, no. 2 (Winter 1976): 45–52.

Kovacs, Katherine. "Revolutionary Consciousness and Imperfect Cinematic Forms." *Humanities in Society* 4, no. 1 (Winter 1981): 101–112.

Michaels, Albert L. "Revolutionary Cinema and the Self-Reflections of a Disappearing Class." *Journal of Latin American Lore* 4, no. 1 (1978): 129–134.

Myerson, Michael, ed. *Memories of Underdevelopment: The Revolutionary Films of Cuba.* New York: Grossman Publishers, 1973.

Santi, Enrico Mario. "Edmundo Desnoes: La sub-novela." *Cuban Studies/Estudios Cubanos* 11, no. 1 (January 1981): 49–64. (In English, with a Spanish summary).